Sept 2020

MAKING SCHOOL INTEGRATION WORK

To Joel and Diane,
with love and
admiration

Dierdre

MAKING SCHOOL INTEGRATION WORK
LESSONS FROM MORRIS

PAUL TRACTENBERG
ALLISON RODA
RYAN COUGHLAN
DEIRDRE DOUGHERTY

TEACHERS COLLEGE PRESS

TEACHERS COLLEGE | COLUMBIA UNIVERSITY

NEW YORK AND LONDON

Published by Teachers College Press,® 1234 Amsterdam Avenue, New York, NY 10027

Cover design by Jeremy Fink.

Library of Congress Cataloging-in-Publication Data

Names: Tractenberg, Paul L., 1938– author. | Roda, Allison, author. |
    Coughlan, Ryan, author. | Dougherty, Deirdre, author.
Title: Making school integration work : lessons from Morris / Paul
    Tractenberg, Allison Roda, Ryan Coughlan, Deirdre Dougherty.
Description: New York, NY : Teachers College Press, 2020. | Includes
    bibliographical references and index.
Identifiers: LCCN 2020000697 (print) | LCCN 2020000698 (ebook) | ISBN
    9780807763629 (paperback) | ISBN 9780807763636 (hardback) | ISBN
    9780807778449 (ebook)
Subjects: LCSH: School integration—New Jersey—Morris (Township)—History.
    | Public schools—New Jersey—Morris (Township)—History. | Morris
    School District (N.J.)—History.
Classification: LCC LC214.23.M67 T73 2020 (print) | LCC LC214.23.M67
    (ebook) | DDC 379.2/630974974—dc23
LC record available at https://lccn.loc.gov/2020000697
LC ebook record available at https://lccn.loc.gov/2020000698

ISBN 978-0-8077-6362-9 (paper)
ISBN 978-0-8077-6363-6 (hardcover)
ISBN 978-0-8077-7844-9 (ebook)

Contents

Acknowledgments

During our 3-year case study of the Morris School District that led to this book, we have been fortunate to receive invaluable support from many people and organizations.

We are indebted to Thomas Ficarra, former superintendent of the Morris School District, who gave us the green light to study the district, and to Mackey Pendergrast, the current superintendent, whose door has always been open to us.

We thank the Morris Educational Foundation for its financial and other support of this project. In that connection, we owe special thanks to the foundation's executive director, Debbie Sontupe. She not only brought our project to her board's attention and encouraged the members to support it, but she also provided her unique personal insights as the daughter of a longtime teacher and school board member, a graduate of Morristown High School herself, and the mother of two children who are recent graduates.

We appreciate the generous financial support of our major donors:

- The Ford Foundation, whose funding enabled us, among other things, to hire two Spanish-speaking researchers—Mellie Torres and a co-author of this book, Deirdre Dougherty—who interviewed, interacted with, and observed the Latinx community in Morristown;
- Rutgers University in Newark's chancellor and law school for providing two different seed grants to help support our writing of a school integration action plan that we drew upon in the concluding chapter of this book;
- The Fund for New Jersey; and
- The private foundation of David Mills, a distinguished graduate of Rutgers Law School in Newark and philanthropist.

A longtime resident of the Morristown community, Dr. Felicia Jamison, has also earned our special appreciation for her contributions to this book. She not only was one of our interviewees, but she also shared her voluminous and invaluable 1976 doctoral dissertation about the history of the Morristown–Morris Township merger. The title demonstrates how prescient and ahead of her time Dr. Jamison's study was: "An Examination of Six Indices of True Integration in the Ten Year Period 1965–1975 in the Morris School District, Morris County, New Jersey." Dr. Jamison's civil rights work continues to be celebrated in the Morristown community in which she has lived since the mid-1950s.

We are indebted to our advisory group members, who assisted us during the initial phase of the study: Elise Boddie, Michelle Fine, Erica Frankenberg, Richard Kahlenberg, Ariana Mangual Figueroa, Patrick McGuinn, Pedro Noguera, Halley Potter, and Amy Stuart Wells. Their insights and constructive criticism throughout the planning stages helped us immensely.

Our special thanks go to *The Century Foundation* for publishing in December 2016 our interim report, "Remedying School Segregation: How New Jersey's Morris School District Chose to Make Diversity Work."

Our research and manuscript preparation efforts were assisted by numerous Rutgers University students, including Nicole Auffant, Alana Miles, Nijla Mingo, and Jason Moreira, who provided research and writing assistance; by Colleen McCauley and Clare Gutwein, who served as interview transcribers; and by Nicki Gonias, who was our final copyeditor.

This book literally would not have emerged under the imprint of Teachers College Press without the support and encouragement of Brian Ellerbeck, the Press's executive acquisitions editor. From negotiating the book contract through reviewing the manuscript, Brian has been the Press's go-to person and someone to whom we could always turn for sage counsel. We can well understand how challenging an endeavor it must have been for him to work on a project with four co-authors who come from different academic and professional disciplines. We appreciate his patience and guidance throughout the entire process.

Perhaps most importantly, we would like to thank the more than 100 school administrators, staff, parents, students, and community members who took the time to share their perspectives on the creation and long-term successes and challenges of the Morris School District. We would especially like to thank those who agreed to be profiled in this book: George Jenkins, Mackey Pendergrast, Linda Murphy, and Manuela Villanueva (pseudonym). One of those profiled, Steve Wiley, was too ill to do more than submit a few written answers to questions and, unfortunately, died long before this project resulted in the manuscript for this book. Nonetheless, his presence is palpable. This book would be incomplete without their insightful and thoughtful stories.

CHAPTER 1

Introducing the Morris Story

The 65th anniversary of *Brown v. Board of Education* on May 17, 2019, stimulated renewed discussion, research, writing, and analysis about where school integration stands, and how much primacy should be given to integration as a reform strategy by those committed to educational equity. Indeed, during the past 65 years many other education reforms have been featured, tending to push school integration into a back corner from which it has had to struggle to emerge despite the constitutional imperative of *Brown*. Some notable reforms that have ignored school integration include school funding equalization, school choice, and standards and accountability mandates mainly through dramatically increased use of standardized tests. Indeed, to some extent these reform strategies have accepted and even used school segregation as a justification. For example, the longest-running, and by many measures most successful, of the school funding equalization cases, New Jersey's *Abbott v. Burke*, has used the extreme isolation of Black and Latinx students in the state's low-income urban school districts as a reason to give primacy to funding equalization. Over the years, education policymakers, researchers, and advocates have argued about the benefits, limitations, and drawbacks of those reforms, as most have conceded that none has fully solved the problems of separate and unequal education.

At the same time, evidence of the positive social and educational effects of school integration, whenever it has managed to emerge, has continued to accumulate. Research has shown that a racially and socioeconomically integrated educational environment can help all students become better equipped to navigate a global, multicultural world, and can help to measurably improve the achievement levels and life prospects of all students, and this applies to White, Asian, Black, and Latinx students.[1]

Research has also shown that students who attend diverse schools experience both short- and long-term academic and social-emotional gains.[2] Students who are educated in diverse learning environments acquire important critical thinking and problem-solving skills, as well as develop positive inter-group relations. Diverse schools also often equate with a highly educated workforce, high property values, a strong economy, and ample jobs. By contrast, a recent randomized experiment found that

individuals living and working in segregated environments form exclusionary attitudes when they are exposed to diverse individuals.[3]

Yet, here we are more than 65 years after the *Brown v. Board of Education* decision condemned de jure segregated schools, and most of the
country's schools still labor under the vise of de facto segregation. Indeed,
the situation seems to be worsening even in the South, where *Brown* had
its greatest impact. One of the latest examples of re-segregation involves
wealthy White communities seceding from larger more diverse school districts to create new segregated districts.

On the other hand, there is a new sense of opportunity for integration, given growing evidence that demographic forces have created more
diversity across the United States, including New Jersey, the site of this
book. This changing demography provides an opportunity for large-scale
school integration that has not previously existed. Yet, paradoxically, it
also seems to incline people toward a state of confusion and denial about
how "diverse" their school system actually is, and even about the ex-
istence of school segregation. This denial was evidenced in a report of
a recent New Jersey poll that found: "More than 80 percent of New
Jerseyans say their local school districts include a good mix of races and
ethnicities, and just 14 percent say their local schools are segregated, despite research that has found high levels of segregation of black and Lat-
in-American students in the Garden State."[4]

Even as demographic trends have increased racial diversity and offered new opportunities for integration, school segregation for many
Black and Latinx students has become deeper[5] and their educational
plight has deteriorated. Indeed, most American schools still struggle with
the specter of segregation, and the situation is worsening. The problem
is more severe in the Northeast and Midwest than in the South where
formal legal segregation was barred by *Brown*. Yet, in 1971, a distinctive
road to school integration was created in an unlikely terrain—suburban
Morris County, New Jersey. This book is dedicated to recounting the
Morris School District story, providing readers with one community's
journey toward true school integration.

A NOTE ABOUT TERMINOLOGY

In a subject as complex as the one addressed by this book, terminology
is important. Ideally, key words would have clear and distinct meanings,
but that often does not accord with common usage. It seemed important,
therefore, to deal explicitly with this quandary early on.

Throughout this book a variety of terms are used to describe the
racial, ethnic, linguistic, and socioeconomic (SES) composition of educational systems at the state and local levels. The starting point for the

discussion, historically and conceptually, is captured by the term "segregation." In its most extreme form, the kind addressed by *Brown v. Board of Education*,[6] segregation refers to the legally dictated separation of students by race. During the pre-*Brown* era, certain states and school districts formally and informally segregated African American, Mexican, Asian, and Native American students in inferior schools. That gave rise to extended legal and policy debates about the distinction between de jure and de facto segregation and the extent to which the latter should be deemed unlawful. Indeed, even more recently, serious questions have been raised about whether there should be a meaningful distinction drawn between the two—that is to say, whether a situation characterized as de facto segregation because there was no explicit statute requiring the separation of the races was necessarily "innocent" and free of government-inspired discrimination.[7]

When the focus shifts to addressing or remedying unlawful segregation, of whatever kind, the terminology issues may get even more complicated. Terms such as "desegregation," "integration," "racial balance," "diversity," "proportionality," "inclusion," and "true integration" find their way into the discussion. Distinguishing among them as a descriptive matter is difficult enough, but the challenges grow when the term is used to define a legal remedy. For example, one of the hottest debates about *Brown* in its early years was whether its objective was to desegregate or integrate unlawfully segregated school systems since desegregation seemed to be focused on ending the de jure segregated status of southern schools whether or not that resulted in students learning together in an integrated setting. As *Brown* proceeded, however, the federal courts clearly opted for integration.

More recently, john powell and other scholars have noted that desegregation and integration, while often used interchangeably, are not the same.[8] These scholars have tended, however, to subtly redefine those terms by suggesting that school desegregation involves the creation of schools with diverse racial/ethnic compositions while educational integration goes deeper and "connotes diversity of the student body's composition, its cultural climate, and the educational processes and contents employed in it."[9]

School integration has further been defined as "the pedagogical, curricular, and cultural mechanism(s) inside of schools that support racially integrated student bodies. Integration is about decentering whiteness—creating educational opportunities and spaces that are affirming and empowering to all students."[10] This definition effectively invokes the more contemporary notion of "true integration." Truly integrated schools are racially/ethnically and socioeconomically balanced at every level—district, school, and classroom. Such schools would not separate students by perceived ability reflecting race/ethnicity and SES backgrounds; instead they strive for inclusion and equity for all. Truly integrated schools also would utilize nonpunitive forms of discipline, like restorative justice, to avoid disproportionate rates of detention and suspension by race and class. Truly integrated schools would strive for sports and music programs, clubs, and afterschool activities that are representative of the overall student population. They would train teachers to use culturally responsive teaching practices, and also employ hiring practices that diversify the teaching staff.

However, the goal of this book is also to show where racially diverse districts might still have work to do. One challenge for diverse districts has been to avoid the tendency to respond to the threat of White flight by prioritizing the demands of White parents and students in the name of preserving diversity. This perceived threat, along with the larger U.S. educational reform context through the years that has relied on standards, accountability, and testing, has contributed to inequities in access, opportunities, and outcomes by race and SES.

In New Jersey's current state court litigation[11] for school desegregation, one remedial theme looks toward "racial balance wherever feasible," a state constitutional standard that emerged in the *Jenkins* case almost 50 years ago.[12] *Jenkins* was the case that gave rise to the creation of the Morris School District, the focus of this book. By contrast, at the federal level, "racial balance" has been a politically charged topic since at least the Civil Rights Act of 1964, which explicitly barred any federal official or federal court from taking action to achieve racial balance in the schools.[13] In addition, a series of U.S. Supreme Court decisions, culminating in the 2007 *Parents Involved* decision,[14] has ruled that racial balancing "for its own sake" is impermissible. *Parents Involved* went so far as to strike down plans voluntarily adopted by two school districts with the approval and support of their communities.

To make these definitional matters more complicated, over the years the demographic realities have changed dramatically. What was once commonly thought of as a Black-White segregation issue at the time of both *Brown* and *Jenkins* has morphed into a far more variegated challenge as the percentage of White and Black students has declined, and the percentage of Latinx and Asian students has increased rapidly to the point where the Latinx student population is virtually double the Black student population both nationally and in states such as New Jersey. As Nancy Denton reminds us, "we are no longer in a two-group world . . . the segregation of Asians, Hispanics, and the various subgroups of each has been measured, analyzed, and generally found to be lower than that of African Americans."[15] Thus, to talk about "racial balance" as a key descriptor or as a remedial objective seems decidedly dated. To complicate matters even more, English language proficiency is an important variable that should be taken into account in determining how "nonsegregated" school districts are.

The use of "diverse" or "diversity" has become the most generic way to refer to school districts that are not segregated, and we have often deferred to that usage in our book. But diversity does not have a fixed meaning, and it does not look the same across schools or districts. One view advanced is that a school or district that is relatively proportional to the county or state levels would be considered diverse. Another view suggests that a district with at least 15% of two or more groups can be considered diverse because it means no group is totally isolated. By either of these definitions, the Morris School District that is profiled in this book would be considered diverse. It also has two racial subgroups, White and Latinx, that make up more than 15% each of the student population, a smaller percentage of Black and Asian students, as well as a significant group of English Language Learners and more than a third of students who are eligible for free or reduced-price lunch.

We agree with the view that defining school diversity is complicated.[16] For example, to conclude that a school district with 90% or more Black and Latinx low-income students, or 90% or more White and Asian advantaged students is "diverse," as has been done with other scholarship, seems incompatible with the thrust of this book. The definition of what makes a school diverse is dependent on many school-specific and contextual variables. In the case of the Morris School District, diversity could be defined by a wide range of measures, including geographic location (e.g., as compared to the mostly White, affluent Morris County), academic achievement (e.g., higher test score averages and students who are more likely to attend college than similar districts), and increased opportunities (e.g., access to high-level courses for all) leading to lower chances of dropping out—not to mention all of the social-emotional skills that students gain by attending diverse schools.[17]

THE MORRIS SCHOOL DISTRICT IN NEW JERSEY AS AN IMPORTANT CASE STUDY

This book tells the story of how one predominantly White and wealthy suburban community and its more diverse and urbanized adjoining community committed themselves to solving the confounding problem of school segregation. These communities—Morris Township and Morristown—aided and abetted by New Jersey's State Supreme Court and Commissioner of Education, almost 50 years ago defied the state's unusually strong commitment to localism and local control of schools to combine their districts into a single racially and socioeconomically diverse and unified K–12 district, the Morris School District (MSD). These communities, however, did not stop at the district borders; they sought to bring meaningful integration to the school building level and, hardest of all, to the classroom and program level.

At the heart of this book is an in-depth historical and contemporary case study of MSD. We look broadly at the legal and educational policy implications of its almost 50-year history, but we also use a mixed methods research approach to delve deeply into a series of questions about how MSD has sought to successfully implement the legal and administrative action that led to its creation and development. Broadly speaking, we explore what makes for successful educational leadership in diverse settings. We found evidence of effective school leadership, culturally responsive administration and teaching, strong community-school relationships, and progressive and multicultural curricula and pedagogy.

Our abiding belief—and one of our greatest incentives for conducting this study and writing this book—is that, in the current climate of racially divisive and fear-driven politics, there is an especially great need for stories like that of MSD. We need more multiracial and socioeconomically diverse schools, the communities that give rise to them, and the students who benefit from them to combat ethnocentrism, racism, and discrimination in our society.

An In-Depth Look at Morris

Nestled 25 miles west of New York City in a predominantly White, upper-income and politically conservative county, MSD has been quietly pursuing its decades-long effort to cultivate and maintain a diverse, integrated, and equitable school system. In this unlikely place, a critical mass of community residents has been dogged in building and nurturing a just educational system. They have fully recognized that their effort is a marathon not a sprint, capable of succeeding only if it continues in perpetuity.

The story began in earnest in the 1960s when a group of Morris residents committed to integration cohered around the vision of a fully integrated school system. Students, teachers, parents, school administrators, and other leaders today continue this important work. Indeed, strikingly, some of them have been involved virtually from the start of the effort.

MSD was formed in 1971 in a distinctive manner. It was an outgrowth of a major constitutional lawsuit designed to prevent predominantly White and wealthy suburban Morris Township from withdrawing its students from the more diverse and more urban Morristown High School to attend a proposed new high school in the township. A unanimous decision by the New Jersey Supreme Court in that case found that the state Commissioner of Education had whatever power was necessary to assure that students of both districts were educated in a racially balanced setting, including the power to order a merger of those districts. Shortly thereafter the commissioner ordered the two legally separate but long affiliated K–12 school districts to be consolidated to serve children

Figure 1.1. Morris School District

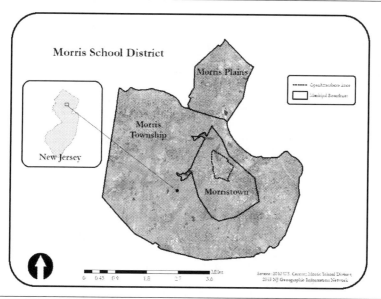

Source: 2010 U.S. Census, Morris School District, 2015 NJ Geographic Information Network

of all grade levels living in both communities. A third adjacent, relatively suburban, and predominantly White district—Morris Plains—continued to send its high school students to Morristown High School but remained an independent elementary school district (see Figure 1.1).

Like many areas of the United States, these northern New Jersey municipalities were—and continue to be—racially segregated by neighborhood if not by entire community. The passion and perseverance of concerned members of the Morristown and Morris Township communities, however, ensured that MSD came to fruition and that the ongoing efforts to achieve true integration, equity, and justice endure. The people who brought the Morris School District to life and who continue to serve it earned the spotlight in the story we share in this book.

No one individual can take full credit for the monumental endeavor of shaping MSD into a diverse and integrated system focused on ensuring equity, but the stories of those involved in this ongoing work illuminate how it came to be and why it persists. Early in each chapter of this book is the story of one individual or group whose efforts have been essential to the school integration process.

Steve Wiley

It is fitting to begin the Morris story with Steve Wiley. Among his many notable accomplishments, Steve was the main architect of the *Jenkins* case that ultimately led to the creation of the racially and socioeconomically diverse Morris School District. Born in Morristown in 1929, Steve grew up as the son of the Morristown school district's longtime superintendent, Burton Wiley. Steve attended the Morris public schools, graduating from Morristown High School in 1947. He made Morristown and Morris Township his home after graduating from Princeton University and Columbia Law School and serving in the U.S. Army from 1954 to 1956.

Over the course of his life, Wiley embodied many of the roles essential to creating and sustaining a vibrant and racially and socioeconomically integrated Morristown and Morris School District. He was a lawyer, a businessperson, a state senator who chaired the Senate Education Committee, a gubernatorial candidate, a nominee for the New Jersey Supreme Court, and a devoted husband and father. In his spare time, he also was a devoted outdoorsman and nature lover, and, starting at age 70, a published poet. He spearheaded community drives to rehabilitate the Community Theater (now the very successful Mayo Performing Arts Center, which regularly features performances by world-class entertainers and musicians), the joint Morristown and Morris Township public library, and the historic Morristown Green.

One of the leading historians writing about New Jersey, John Cunningham, also a Morristown High School graduate, said of Steve Wiley that he was "the heart and soul of Morristown" and simply "Mr. Morristown." In the same vein, other Morristown and Morris Township friends and admirers said of him in local newspaper articles[18] that:

- "You can't walk a block in Morristown without seeing something he made better."
- "Today we live and work and go to school in one of the only truly diverse communities in New Jersey. Look at the football team, the cheerleaders, the band, the kids in the stand, the supervisors and coaches on the field, and you will see something really beautiful, and I think, unique. We all play together and celebrate together and solve our problems together. We like each other. Steve Wiley did that. And I am so grateful."
- "Anything that's great in Morristown, Stephen B. Wiley had something to do with it."

Throughout his life, Steve Wiley maintained especially deep and strong ties to the Morris schools and to the Morris Educational Foundation, whose creation and operation he spearheaded. When we interviewed

Debbie Sontupe, the current executive director and herself a Morristown High School graduate and mother of two recent graduates, she said of Wiley that "we would not be who we are today without his leadership. His memory will live on in our work each day."

In the late 1960s, Wiley felt compelled to step up and advocate for continued diversity in the district and its high school when his then hometown of Morris Township threatened to create a separate high school for its mostly White[19] and upper-income students. Until then, as they had for the better part of a century, Morris Township students attended the more racially and socioeconomically diverse, and more urban, Morristown High School following their elementary schooling in the township. The proposal to create a separate high school in the township deeply troubled Wiley. Simply put, he did not want upper-income Whites in Morris Township, Morris Plains, and even Morristown itself, to isolate themselves in a suburban high school, just as they had in so many other parts of New Jersey during that period. Wiley had the foresight to know that if you gave White, wealthy families a choice between a Morristown High School or a new high school in Morris Township and township schools, the result would likely be de facto school segregation followed by educational inequality.

What accounted for Steve Wiley's success at winning people over to the integration cause? Not only was he an accomplished and successful lawyer, legislator, and businessman, but he also had formidable interpersonal skills. One current Morristown resident likened him to a Pied Piper who "had a way of talking to everyone as if you were doing the most amazing job. . . . It wasn't just the money he raised. It was the spirit he infused in the community."[20]

Another, a teammate of Steve's on Morristown High School's unbeaten 1947 football team, said that Steve was "not going to make a lot of noise. But he could sit down with you and others, and he would find the right way, and when you're done, you would be convinced we're doing the right thing. He would answer the questions that need to be answered."[21] Still another resident, a former chairman of the Community Theater in Morristown, amplified on that skill of Steve Wiley to engage people when he commented that "he's really good at engaging people in conversation," and that he had a "warm personality, strong organizational skills, relentless follow-through and a penchant for surrounding himself with good people and sharing the glory."[22]

Notwithstanding the supportive people who joined Steve Wiley in pressing for an integrated Morris School District, it was a tough and sometimes brutally ugly fight, especially in the early years. In 2008, almost 4 decades after the merged district was created by the commissioner of education, Steve said of the time, "That was a bloody fierce battle . . . and I was not a popular person."[23] A former Morristown Councilwoman put a fine point on it when she said, "By the time the court-ordered hearings were held, bitterness was all that most can remember. Wiley bore the brunt of many of the attacks because as a graduate of Morristown High School in 1947 and the son of J. Burton Wiley, the former longtime superintendent of schools for the district, [Steve's] friends and neighbors felt he should have been protecting their interests rather than the minorities he represented."[24]

Yet Steve Wiley was sustained by a much broader view of the situation. He reportedly believed that White flight from Morristown and from Morristown High School would be a disaster for everyone:

> Having a minority center and a white ring around it is nothing but a guarantee of an explosion and you're going to lose everyone. So anyway, to me the key to the success and stability and prosperity of this area, economically and otherwise, is the school. . . . If you don't have a good Morris School District, a school system that is attractive to parents who . . . have a choice, you're gonna have trouble. You are gonna have trouble.[25]

He said this as he listed other New Jersey cities that had sharply declined in the 1970s.

Steve's special role in making the creation of the Morris district viable and giving it a foundation for long-term success is a good example of a more recent research finding—that having prominent "policy entrepreneurs"[26] as the face of a movement is a strategy that has proven to be important to the success of other grassroots desegregation movements. Other examples include Minnie Liddell, leader of Concerned Parents of North St. Louis; civil rights lawyer William Russel; Margaret Tinsley in East Palo Alto; and Elizabeth Horton Sheff in Hartford, Connecticut.

In Morris, Steve Wiley eventually teamed up with Beatrice Jenkins and seven other residents of the town and township who had been the original petitioners in the *Jenkins* lawsuit. Another local lawyer, Frank Harding, had been the petitioners' attorney, and both the Morristown and Morris Township boards of education were originally named as respondents. However, with Steve Wiley as its attorney, the Morristown board in effect changed sides, joining the petitioners. The petitioners, new and old, worked closely throughout the litigation with the local arms of such venerable civil rights organizations as the Urban League and the NAACP.

The core of the petitioners' claim was that the new high school proposed to be built by the township would segregate the two adjoining districts and lead to separate and unequal education for all their students. Their main legal goal was a K–12 merger of the districts for racial balance purposes. The Commissioner of Education agreed that merger would be preferable, but stated that he lacked the power to order it. Ultimately, the New Jersey Supreme Court sided with the petitioners and assured the commissioner that he had the power. The order of merger followed. During our 2015 interview with former Commissioner of Education, Carl Marburger, he reflected on his decision to consolidate the two districts: "I figured that I've got the power if the courts say so. I took advantage of it. . . . I felt that it was the most significant decision I made while I was with the state."

People we interviewed who were around during the time of the merger remembered how significant the decision was to them. When we asked a man who had been vice principal of Morristown High School in 1972 how, with the benefit of 20-20 hindsight, he would rate the success of the Morris School District on a 1–10 scale, he responded "a 12 because it was an epiphany that we are part of something great." Others with whom we spoke said they were opponents of merger at the time but have since changed their minds because they have come to appreciate the positive benefits of diversity in the schools.

Steve Wiley's core view that a successful school district is the bedrock of a healthy community was also a prevalent theme in many of the more than 100 interviews that we conducted as part of our 3-year study of the Morris School District—showing that Wiley's legacy about the benefits of integration lives on in the hearts and minds of current members of the community, district, and school. Even today, the superintendent of schools, Mackey Pendergrast, works to fulfill Wiley's vision of school integration. He notes, "We feel the goal is to have a healthy community. If you have a healthy community, community members, students, parents, and teachers are working hard to understand and partner with each other for the success of the child. The healthy community has to come first, and then the other things are possible."[27]

THE MERGER PROCESS AND ITS AFTERMATH

The legal battle for school district consolidation was neither easy nor trouble-free. Beyond Steve Wiley's personal travails, already described, the community could have been torn apart. The wonder is that it was not. A 1973 *New York Times* article described the "painful" and "agonizing" process of the forced merger.[28] A year later, only a few years after the merger, Morristown High had what some called a "race riot." The state commissioner of education lost his job after ordering the merger. Two additional New Jersey communities, Plainfield and New Brunswick, who sought the "Morris remedy," were turned down by a successor commissioner. His stated justification was that Morris was a "unique" situation in the state.

It was not until 1992 that the New Jersey courts corrected that legal and policy misunderstanding, but it was too late for Plainfield and New

Brunswick to embrace the Morris remedy. Today their student populations continue to be virtually 100% Black and Latinx, and about 90% low-income. By comparison, the Morris district currently has 47% White students, only recently and perhaps temporarily down from 50% the year before, a higher percentage than the statewide demographic profile of just over 43% White students.[29] Yet, even as Plainfield, New Brunswick, and many of New Jersey's other urban and suburban school districts have remained segregated by race and class, Morristown's diversity has persisted.

THE MORRIS SCHOOL DISTRICT OF TODAY—
ALMOST 50 YEARS AFTER MERGER

Today, the Morris School District and its constituent municipalities are considered a great place to raise a family. New and diverse middle-class residents are attracted to the community because it provides them with a mix of urban and suburban living. The community has a walkable downtown, trendy nightlife and restaurants, combined with tree-lined streets and green space in which to play and relax. The historic Morristown Green hosts farmers' markets and other community events on a regular basis. The Mayo Performing Arts Center offers world-class entertainment, as well as serving as a venue for local attractions, such as the Morris Educational Foundation's annual *Morristown Onstage*—its premier fundraiser showcasing a wide variety of amateur acts with performers of all ages. The impressive Morristown and Morris Township Public Library is an important gathering place for residents.

Morristown is also attractive because of the easy train commute to Newark and New York City. A recent *New York Times* article included a quote from a Morristown realtor who described recent buyers in Morristown as: "young families who have run out of space in Jersey City, Hoboken and Manhattan—but also empty-nesters who decide to downsize from large houses in the nearby suburbs."[30]

Located in conservative and mostly White Morris County, in the northeast part of New Jersey, MSD serves three municipalities—Morristown and Morris Township for K–12 and Morris Plains for grades 9–12. MSD contains eight elementary schools, one middle school (6–8) and one high school (9–12). MSD uses geography to achieve racial diversity in the primary (K–2) and intermediate (3–5) schools by designating the center of town as an open assignment area because it continues to be where many of the low-income Black and Latinx residents live (see Figures 1.2 and 1.3). Students living in this area are bused to various schools across the district to desegregate those schools and to achieve racial and SES balance. Students in every other assignment area attend a "neighborhood school," but, because of high levels of residential segregation, the

Figure 1.2. Morris School District Elementary School Zones

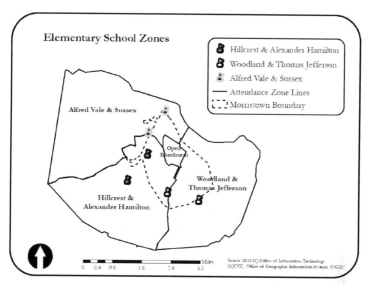

Source: 2014 NJ Office of Information Technology (NJOIT), Office of Geographic Information Systems (OGIS)

so-called "neighborhood schools" are strategically located outside of the immediate neighborhood and most students are bused to school.

The Morris School District has an operating budget of approximately $117,000,000 and employs 440 teachers, 112 other certificated staff, and 286 noncertificated staff.[31] Overall, the district spent $23,834 per pupil, which outpaces the average per-pupil spending across New Jersey. The fact that it has generous educational resources available no doubt lessens the burdens of accommodating to its highly diverse student population. The teaching staff is overwhelmingly White (80.8%) and female (76.5%), while 6.3% of teachers are black, 10.5% are Hispanic, and 2.5% are Asian.[32]

Demographic trends in MSD show that the White student enrollment has decreased slowly over time—from 67% in 1987 to 47% in 2019.[33] There has been a steady influx of Latinx students and a steady decline of Black students since the 1970s. The 5,100–student Morris School District 2018–19 student demographic profile was 47% White, 9% Black, 39% Latinx, and 4% Asian. Approximately 34% of MSD's students received free or reduced-price lunches and 13% were English Language Learners.

Recent demographic trends should give district leaders pause because of the influx of Hispanic students and the sharp decline of the Black student population. Figure 1.4 shows striking demographic changes in the student population over the past 20 years. Over this period of time,

Figure 1.3. Populations Across Morris School District Elementary School Zones (Clockwise from Top: White, Black, Asian, and Hispanic)

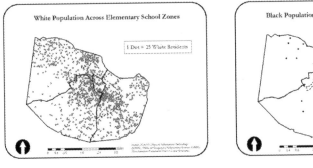
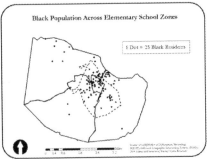
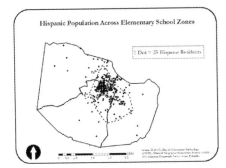
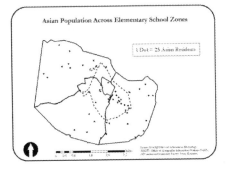

Source: 2014 NJ Office of Information Technology (NJOIT), Office of Geographic Information Systems (OGIS), 2014 American Community Survey, 5-year Estimates.

the Asian student population has decreased by 5% and the White student population has decreased by 7%. What is most notable is that the Hispanic population has grown by 140% and the Black population has decreased by 50%.

Beyond the districtwide data trends, MSD stands out for its school-by-school integration at the elementary level. Using the proportionality/dissimilarity benchmark, there are extremely low levels of racial and SES dissimilarity among MSD schools serving children in kindergarten through grade 5 despite persistent residential segregation within the district's neighborhoods as delineated by census tracts. For example, while only 5% of Black or White students would need to move schools to create perfectly proportional populations of Black and White students at the K–5 schools in the MSD, 40.1% of Black or White residents would need to move neighborhoods (as delineated by census tracts) in order to create perfectly proportional populations of Black and White people across

Figure 1.4. Population Change 1999–2019, Morris School District

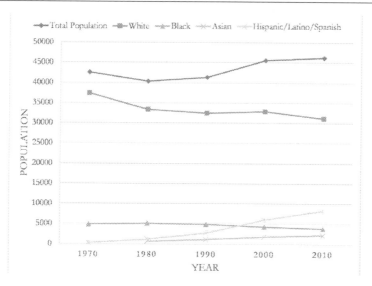

neighborhoods. Dissimilarity indices between White and Black students, White and Hispanic[34] students, Black and Hispanic students, and students who qualify for free or reduced-price lunch and students who do not are all less than 15.0. In other words, less than 15% of these populations would need to move schools to create student populations that are perfectly proportional by these demographic groups.[35]

It is important to note that because of the 2007 federal *Parents Involved in Community Schools v. Seattle School District #1* decision, districts cannot rely solely on the use of race in their student assignment plans. However, there are currently over 80 districts that use SES integration plans to diversify student populations.[36] Other districts, like Berkeley, California, use geography to balance students by race and class across schools.

At the middle and high school level, Frelinghuysen Middle School and Morristown High School (MHS) offer their students a wide array of courses, programs, afterschool activities, and sports. For example, the high school provides 28 Advanced Placement classes, five world languages, a Humanities Academy, a STEM Academy, more than 40 extracurricular programs, and nearly 30 varsity sports. Graduates are regularly accepted into Ivy League and other highly selective universities, as well as major public universities, and notable alumni include the Atlanta Falcons head football coach and the founder of craigslist.

Families living within the Morris School District have many schooling options, since there are numerous private schools in the area and one themed charter school as well as the public schools. While private school enrollment rates among Morris Township students are nearly double the state average, with 19.5% attending private K–8 schools and 27.3% private high schools, as compared to 10.8 and 11.6%, respectively, in the state, they are relatively reflective of those found in surrounding upper-income communities.[37]

MSD'S CURRENT LEVEL OF INTEGRATION
AS COMPARED TO THE STATE AND NATIONAL PICTURE

In addition to all of this, or perhaps because of it, the Morris School District remains one of the most diverse and integrated school districts in the state and nation and it lives out every day a credo articulated by Steve Wiley:

> Our schools teach the ABC's with distinction, but young people in Morristown High and the grade schools also learn the D's, E's, and F's. By association and experience they learn about democracy and diversity, about equal opportunity and ethnic strengths, about freedom and fraternity, about the whole alphabet of America.

MSD stands out as a diverse by choice public school system when compared to the vast majority of segregated schools across the nation. It defies the status quo because, even as the United States becomes increasingly diverse, the number of racially and socioeconomically isolated schools is on the rise.[38] A U.S. government report showed that the number of segregated public schools in which 75 to 100% of students are Black or Latinx and low-income doubled from 7,009 in 2000 to 15,089 in 2016.[39] Perhaps surprisingly, White students are the most isolated group given the fact that they attend schools where, on average, 82% of their classmates are White.[40] Meanwhile, Asian and Pacific Islander students are the most integrated groups in U.S. schools.

The Morris district's long-established diversity also stands in contrast to the larger picture of school segregation in New Jersey. The state is the sixth most segregated for Black students, and seventh most segregated for Latinx students in the United States, with these student subgroups mostly concentrated in poor urban areas.[41] In addition, the level of racial/ethnic and SES imbalance and inequality *among* New Jersey school districts is ranked second highest in the country (after Long Island).[42] This is the case because New Jersey "epitomizes a fragmented political system" with 674 school districts for 8.9 million residents.[43] "With the exception of Asian students, the typical student from all other racial groups in New Jersey attends schools where the same racial group of students makes up the largest proportion of the school's student body."[44] Reflecting national

Figure 1.5. Morris County Unified and Elementary School Districts

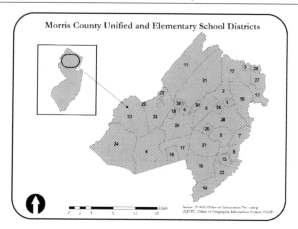

Source: 2014 NJ Office of Information Technology (NJOIT), Office of Geographic Information Systems (OGIS)

trends, in the last 2 decades, White students in New Jersey are the most isolated group in schools, and an increasing number of English Language Learners are being triple-segregated by race, class, and language ability.

Figure 1.5 shows the elementary and unified school district boundaries for Morris County. These educational boundaries do more than provide differential access to opportunities and resources—they also divide schools and communities by rich and poor and Black, Latinx, Asian, and White, which has a negative effect on equal educational opportunity. In Morris County, the school boundary lines sharply divide most students by race and economic status. As Table 1.1, which pairs with Figure 1.5, highlights, three-quarters of the Morris County School Districts are over 60% White; three school districts are predominantly Hispanic; one district has a combined Asian and White population that exceeds 80%; and only four districts in addition to the Morris School District have student populations that reflect the diversity of New Jersey's student population. Table 1.1 also provides data about students who qualify for free or reduced-price lunch, demonstrating the ways in which these school boundaries separate students by economic status as well. [45]

Looked at broadly, school segregation matters because district boundary lines shape children's opportunities to learn in profound ways. Children living in urban, high-poverty school districts, as opposed to suburban, affluent districts, generally have less access to highly trained teachers, have fewer advanced courses, have lower per pupil funding, and are educated alongside mostly low-income peers.[46] Low-income students of color living in segregated neighborhoods are more likely to be victims of

Table 1.1. Morris County School Elementary and Unified School District Demographics, 2018–2019

District	Asian	Black	Hispanic	Other	White	Free/Reduced Lunch	Total Students
1 Boonton Town School District	13.9%	6.0%	18.7%	2.2%	59.2%	31.2%	1388
2 Boonton Township School District	5.9%	2.0%	3.4%	2.2%	86.6%	1.5%	410
3 Butler Public School District	2.4%	1.7%	20.7%	1.7%	73.5%	23.1%	1164
4 Chester School District	6.4%	1.3%	11.6%	1.8%	78.8%	5.7%	1086
5 Denville Township K–8 School District	8.1%	2.8%	10.4%	4.5%	74.2%	4.3%	1618
6 Dover Public School District	2.1%	3.6%	89.2%	0.3%	4.9%	75.7%	3171
7 East Hanover Township School District	16.0%	1.2%	10.0%	1.7%	71.1%	1.0%	900
8 Florham Park Public Schools	10.2%	6.7%	7.2%	5.1%	70.9%	0.0%	990
9 Hanover Township School District	13.9%	2.5%	10.9%	5.7%	67.1%	1.2%	1371
10 Harding Township School District	4.7%	1.4%	4.0%	9.0%	80.9%	1.1%	277
11 Jefferson Township Public School District	4.5%	1.4%	9.8%	2.7%	81.5%	10.4%	2876
12 Kinnelon School District	7.4%	0.9%	6.2%	2.2%	83.3%	2.8%	1805
13 Lincoln Park School District	6.4%	2.0%	20.1%	2.0%	69.5%	17.5%	909
14 Long Hill Township School District	7.5%	0.8%	14.1%	2.4%	75.2%	3.5%	851
15 Madison Public School District	8.6%	2.4%	12.1%	1.9%	75.0%	7.1%	2619
16 Mendham Borough School District	2.5%	0.4%	5.1%	3.3%	88.7%	2.1%	512
17 Mendham Township School District	6.7%	3.2%	3.8%	2.9%	83.5%	0.0%	690

District							
18 Mine Hill Township School District	8.1%	3.8%	47.7%	8.1%	32.3%	28.5%	344
19 Montville Township School District	24.3%	1.7%	7.1%	3.2%	63.7%	2.8%	3594
20 Morris Plains School District	10.4%	5.1%	9.0%	0.7%	74.9%	8.4%	569
21 Morris School District	4.0%	8.5%	38.8%	1.6%	47.1%	34.0%	5113
22 Mount Arlington Public School District	7.8%	6.9%	23.9%	3.1%	58.3%	17.2%	360
23 Mount Olive Township School District	12.9%	6.6%	16.1%	3.3%	61.2%	12.8%	4618
24 Mountain Lakes Public School District	13.5%	1.2%	7.9%	2.6%	74.7%	1.7%	1487
25 Netcong School District	2.1%	5.6%	37.5%	1.8%	53.0%	37.5%	285
26 Parsippany-Troy Hills Township School District	44.0%	3.0%	13.4%	3.3%	36.2%	14.0%	7146
27 Pequannock Township School District	2.7%	0.8%	9.6%	1.0%	86.0%	4.0%	2086
28 Randolph Township School District	12.9%	2.9%	14.9%	1.9%	67.4%	8.1%	4614
29 Riverdale School District	6.3%	5.1%	18.6%	4.8%	65.3%	17.1%	334
30 Rockaway Borough School District	9.7%	3.8%	28.8%	1.8%	55.9%	23.6%	555
31 Rockaway Township School District	8.6%	2.7%	20.2%	3.9%	64.4%	10.4%	2267
32 Roxbury Township School District	4.9%	3.0%	18.7%	3.4%	69.9%	14.7%	3512
33 The School District Of The Chathams	11.5%	0.5%	5.5%	4.4%	78.0%	1.5%	4119
34 Washington Township School District	5.5%	1.7%	7.9%	2.0%	83.1%	3.6%	2000
35 Wharton Borough School District	5.3%	4.9%	66.6%	1.0%	22.2%	51.3%	733

crime, attend lower-performing schools, and be exposed to water and air pollution; an issue frequently labeled "environmental racism."[47]

As we stated at the beginning of this chapter, the American effort to advance the goals of school integration and educational equity since *Brown* has been an uneven and incomplete one. Even in the southern states where integration got some traction for a time, remedies such as busing, magnet schools, and interdistrict transfer programs tended to disproportionately burden Black and Brown students; White students were less likely to be bused for the purposes of integration, White schools were not closed, and White teachers were not fired. As it turned out, the pre-*Brown* days were, by some measures, better for Black communities.

Since the 1896 U.S. Supreme Court decision in *Plessy v. Ferguson* decision had been construed to permit "separate but equal" educational facilities, Black communities engaged in various efforts to make their schools as equal as possible. Black community members founded and supported the growth of their own schools, staffed them with highly qualified Black teachers, and endeavored to provide Black students with a quality education despite their having limited access to resources and, in many cases, limited control over school policy decisions. Desegregation, for many Black families, seemed to be a necessary tactic that could help ensure quality education for Black children in public schools. But, decades after the *Brown* decision, scholars and citizens have begun to question the impact of desegregation on Black schooling and have interrogated the assumptions made about Black educational spaces and Black communities themselves. In writing this book about a community's journey toward true integration, we have become aware that to fully create equitable educational opportunities for Black and Latinx students, integration must not only be realized down to the classroom and program level, but also be accompanied by sufficient fiscal and human resources in the schools and a commitment to valuing the needs, experiences, and voices of historically marginalized families.

WHY A BOOK ABOUT THE MORRIS SCHOOL DISTRICT?

We chose the Morris School District as an instrumental case study because it represents an intriguing and potentially important counter-story to the state and national pattern of persistent or even worsening segregation in many schools. The intervention of the state courts and the commissioner of education's consolidation order were galvanized by the leadership of eight residents of Morris Township and Morristown, and came to be supported by a critical mass of residents of both communities, by their civic and religious organizations, and by the merged school district's leadership and staff. Indeed, we define this school-community leadership as culturally responsive and use this concept as an analytical tool to investigate the ways in which the district has moved toward the goal of integration or been challenged by it in its organizational and cultural practices.

The Morristown community exemplifies a *multicultural island* and its story highlights the benefits and challenges of school integration. Sheryll Cashin defines multicultural islands in the United States as diverse by both race and class, and formed over time because of their "multicultural character, established diverse identity, diverse housing . . . [and] an abundance of community organizations that build community."[48] Yet, it must be stressed that even multicultural islands have to work hard and persistently to move beyond "diversity" to "true integration" and the systematic creation of culturally responsive systems of education. We draw upon Django Paris's definition of culturally sustaining pedagogies (CSP) as a lens through which we analyzed the interview data for this study:

> Culturally sustaining pedagogy seeks to perpetuate and foster—to sustain— linguistic, literate, and cultural pluralism as part of the democratic project of schooling. In the face of current policies and practices that have the explicit goal of creating a monocultural and monolingual society, research and practice need equally explicit resistances that embrace cultural pluralism and cultural equality.[49]

Although the Morris story of true integration is not yet finished, it is a hopeful story about how integration *can* happen, rather than how it has failed. It is a tale of how the Morris district achieved merger, how it was able to avoid White and middle-class flight afterward, and how the district maintains intradistrict diversity over time because the structures are in place to accomodate demographic changes. While other books on the topic of desegregation focus on resegregation of schools or other forms of persistent inequality,[50] this book is focused on the positive and long-lasting commitment to diversity at the district, school, and curricular levels. The lessons that can be drawn from its creation and continuing progress toward school integration are highly relevant to other districts across the country, which we explain in later chapters of this book.

This book should appeal to education professionals, researchers, public-policy makers, education and civil rights advocates, lawyers and law professors, and members of the public interested in education law and policy, in school desegregation, and in social justice—those who consider education and the equalization of educational opportunities and outcomes to be a major challenge for the United States. It highlights a long-term solution to interdistrict segregation and inequality—namely school district regionalization for racial and SES balance and related educational purposes.

The Morris story recounted in this book will address in detail:

- how the merger and the resulting diversity came about;
- how diversity once achieved was maintained, not only at the district level but also at each of the schools, in the face of predictions that merger would result in massive White exodus and, ultimately, a segregated district; and
- what the district must do to ensure diversity is being used to the educational advantage of all students as the district moves toward "true integration."

We acknowledge that it may be tempting to write off the Morris district as a unique outlier. The case study that is at the heart of our book will identify those elements of the Morris experience that account for its persistence and will consider their applicability to other districts in New Jersey and beyond. It may well be the case that the Morris district is not a perfect model capable of being transferred intact to other districts. However, that is not the point; the district offers important and broadly applicable lessons for the school integration process—such as the importance of stable and committed leadership, strong community-school partnerships, buy-in from a diverse group of families, and a strong sense of pride, trust, and hope for a truly integrated school system.

OVERVIEW OF THE BOOK

Each of the chapters contained in this book will highlight a distinct aspect of the MSD integration story from the legal strategy that led to the formation of the district to the culturally sustaining leadership work that has helped sustain school integration for almost 50 years. Like this opening chapter, each of the succeeding chapters will feature a vignette of a key player in the Morris story and will conclude with a "Lessons Learned" section that other school districts can use to inform their own unique contexts, and to move them forward on the path from diversity to the ultimate goal of true integration.

In Chapter 2, we will describe in greater depth the historical context, the social and educational goals, and the grassroots efforts that led to the litigation and, ultimately, the merger ordered by the state commissioner of education. This chapter will include an analysis of the legal strategy, the court's doctrinal approach and the role of the state commissioner of education in ordering the merger remedy. We will describe how the New Jersey courts' construction of the state constitution differed in important respects from the federal courts' construction of the U.S. Constitution. We will explain how and why Morris remained committed to diversity while other New Jersey communities abandoned the fight (e.g., the Plain-field and New Brunswick school districts that initially sought a regional-ization remedy). The chapter will conclude with current efforts in New Jersey, building in part on the Morris district's history, to pursue state-wide school integration through litigation and other means.

Chapter 3 will paint a picture of the postmerger history of the Morris district to today. It chronicles the ongoing culturally responsive school leadership work that promotes and advances the critical mass of com-munity support for diversity today. We will illustrate that when school leaders consider themselves to be community partners and take on com-munity-centered leadership behaviors, student success is positively affect-ed. Without those policies and structures in place, the school integration process, as we have seen in other districts, can falter or be completely abandoned. We also will include interview findings about what draws families to the Morris School District and keeps them there, and the role of realtors in steering potential home buyers to or away from Mor-ris. This chapter's main theme will be how the district has continued to walk the delicate line between aiding lower-income Black and Latinx stu-dents and diversifying all school programs on the one hand and retaining upper-income, advantaged, mostly White students on the other. Overall, we provide evidence that a racially diverse school district flourishes when it supports and is supported by its community.

Chapter 4 will describe the Black student and family experience in the district over time. It shows how Black parents and students have felt that, at times, the district has seemed to "cater" to White families, and even to Latinx families because of the additional resources needed for English-language services. We also illustrate how the district has too of-ten been reactive instead of proactive when issues regarding racial op-portunity gaps were brought up and questioned. We start with laying the groundwork of the Black student population changes over time, showing who's staying, who's leaving, and why. Then, for the Black parents who stay, we discuss their advocacy efforts to break down inequitable struc-tures and policies, and provide a picture of Black students' experiences in the high school in support of the parent's claims.

In Chapter 5, we will describe the large influx of Latinx students who often arrive without the benefits of a solid education in their home coun-tries, and the challenges of integrating them into the schools educational-ly and socially. Using the culturally sustaining leadership framework, we will explore what the school district and community organizations are doing to meet those challenges, how well it is working, and what more can be done. This chapter also will discuss the broader issues of educating Black and Latinx low-income students to their fullest potentials. We will discuss technical and policy-related efforts to create more equity in terms of race and class, such as by avoiding the double or triple segregation many Latinx students often encounter, addressing parent tensions that have emerged because of decisions about where resources are being targeted (e.g., resources for ELLs), and closing gaps in broad educational outcomes. We also will describe the social support services provided by the district, such as resources to assist Latinx families with legal help, food security, and mental health counseling (e.g., for conditions such as posttraumatic stress disorder).

The concluding chapter will tackle the questions of: (1) what can be done in MSD to complete the job of achieving "true integration," diversity not only at the district and school level, but also in every aspect of the students' school-level educational and social experience; and (2) what can we learn from the Morris district that can contribute to progress in addressing the larger issue of school segregation and inequality in other contexts? Ultimately, we consider whether there is something about the Morris district and its community that makes it "unique" or whether "fertile ground" for the Morris remedy or other remedial steps can be found or cultivated elsewhere.

CHAPTER 2

Using Law and Litigation to Advance School Integration

The focus of Chapter 2 is the role law and litigation played in the creation of MSD. Yet that story hardly captures the extent of the efforts and sacrifices made by individual residents of the community to bring about the merger and keep it going for years to come. We start the chapter with a profile of one of those people—George Jenkins—and his recollections of his mother, Beatrice. Mr. Jenkins was one of the first people we interviewed for the Morris project because his life and professional experiences have intersected in so many important ways with our work. Perhaps most dramatically, the seminal 1971 court decision that paved the way for the creation of MSD was *Jenkins v. Morris Township Board of Education*, and the named plaintiff was George's mother, Beatrice, who at the time was deeply involved with the Morris County Urban League.

When we broached the subject of the merger and his mother's involvement in the *Jenkins* case, George, a Black man, stopped us immediately to clarify. His perception was that it was not a "merger," but a preservation of what they had before the township threatened to withdraw its students from Morristown High by building a separate high school. He explained that what his mother wanted to do with the lawsuit was to maintain what they had at the high school level—diversity. What they achieved as a result of the commissioner of education's order to create a unified K–12 school district was racial integration at the elementary level as well.

We asked George how his mother got involved in the litigation that wound up bearing her name. His recollection is that she started out as president of the PTA at Thomas Jefferson elementary school in Morristown and, because of her "feisty" and "forward-thinking" attitude, she was asked to join the Urban League. That was where she met Steve Wiley—the lawyer who was instrumental in the *Jenkins* case. Together they decided the only way to stop the township from building a separate high school was via litigation.

We met with George in his Morristown real estate office. At the time, he was 68 years old and still actively engaged in the real estate business. The fact that George and his mother, until her death, were African

American residents of Morristown is a central part of their story. At the time the *Jenkins* case was filed, George was a recent, 1966 graduate of Morristown High School.

His deep engagement with the town and its schools was still evident when we talked with him. This pride in Morristown was central to his role as a local realtor, which he stressed was to singlehandedly "sell" the area and the school district to newcomers, especially those who had pre-conceived and often negative ideas about the impact of diversity. It was immediately clear to us that this was a labor of love for George and not just a way to try to sell houses. Perhaps it was even a kind of homage to his mother, Beatrice, and her commitment to an integration lawsuit bearing the family name.

Our first question to George was, "How would you describe the Morristown community and schools to someone who isn't familiar with the area?" He didn't skip a beat when he answered, "I have to do that almost every day." As a realtor, George receives daily phone calls from prospective buyers about MSD, as well as the surrounding predominantly White and visibly upscale school districts, such as Mendham, Harding, and Mountain Lakes. George told us that many of these callers assumed those school districts were "more desirable" because of test score averages and that an important part of his job is to balance those perceptions with a more holistic view of he district's strengths. As Table 2.1 demonstrates, when parents only look at test score data and rankings, English Language Arts and Math proficiency rates in the Morris School District are comparable to some of the surrounding school districts, particulary districts with substantial percentages of Black and Latinx students (see Table 1.1).

George believes he can give an insider perspective about Morris, as opposed to other realtors, because he is a Morristown native and an alumnus of the Morris school system. He also stays up-to-date on what the high school has to offer by taking advantage of the open house tours that the Morris district regularly hosts for the real estate community (described in more detail in Chapter 3). As he described during the interview, he feels that he has to "sell prospective buyers on the value of living in the Morristown community and the MSD" because what he often hears on the phone is, "We want to be anywhere but Morristown High School." When he asks people on the phone, who do not know he is Black, why they want to steer away from Morris, they say because it's "cosmopolitan." George takes this to be a code word for too many "minorities." People also say their relocation companies or corporations told them to "stay away from the Morris School District." Therefore, he feels that part of his job is to dispel any myths or prejudices about the "bad reputation" of Morris that is really tied to race, and to inform clients about the benefits of living and going to school in Morristown.

Table 2.1. Morris County School Districts ELA and Math Proficiency Rates, 2018

	GRADE 3		GRADE 8		GRADE 10	
	ELA	Math	ELA	Math	Algebra 1*	ELA
Boonton Town	64.5%	72.4%	65.6%	30.0%	53.7%	59.4%
Boonton Twp	86.7%	86.7%	94.7%	NA	68.4%	NA
Butler Boro	60.3%	70.8%	66.7%	46.8%	42.6%	48.0%
Chester Twp	63.5%	67.6%	82.3%	42.9%	100%	NA
Denville Twp	82.6%	79.0%	85.6%	35.9%	87.9%	NA
Dover Town	40.7%	47.2%	69.1%	30.1%	33.8%	49.8%
East Hanover Twp	70.1%	70.1%	76.1%	40.0%	100%	NA
Florham Park Boro	81.3%	79.2%	90.1%	55.6%	98.0%	NA
Hanover Park Regional	NA	NA	NA	NA	48.6%	71.9%
Hanover Twp	62.7%	67.5%	81.1%	64.6%	100%	NA
Harding Twp	75.0%	85.0%	90.0%	41.2%	NA	NA
Jefferson Twp	55.8%	50.0%	62.5%	17.3%	43.3%	64.9%
Kinnelon Boro	72.2%	85.9%	78.7%	41.2%	71.8%	88.5%
Lincoln Park Boro	61.5%	59.3%	74.5%	60.0%	96.7%	NA
Long Hill Twp	70.3%	76.7%	85.7%	23.5%	100%	NA
Madison Boro	67.2%	67.0%	82.0%	58.8%	80.3%	76.7%
Mendham Boro	66.2%	63.1%	84.2%	NA	86.2%	NA
Mendham Twp	91.1%	91.8%	100%	93.6%	100%	NA
Mine Hill Twp	69.8%	79.1%	NA	NA	NA	NA
Montville Twp	75.7%	77.9%	78.8%	52.0%	81.5%	69.0%
Morris County Vocational	NA	NA	NA	NA	78.5%	91.6%
Morris Hills Regional	NA	NA	NA	NA	42.8%	62.0%
Morris Plains Boro	61.7%	65.0%	87.3%	74.3%	95.5%	NA
Morris School District	54.8%	53.4%	75.5%	25.2%	48.7%	47.8%
Mount Arlington Boro	64.0%	68.0%	83.7%	28.6%	93.3%	NA
Mount Olive Twp	73.1%	68.7%	82.6%	19.8%	56.4%	87.1%
Mountain Lakes Boro	92.4%	92.4%	93.2%	NA	73.6%	81.3%
Netcong Boro	32.4%	40.5%	68.6%	65.0%	100%	NA
Parsippany-Troy Hills Twp	69.4%	76.1%	79.8%	50.3%	66.3%	69.9%
Pequannock Twp	83.0%	79.9%	78.8%	46.7%	79.6%	67.1%

(continued)

Table 2.1. Morris County School Districts ELA and Math Proficiency Rates, 2018
(continued)

| | GRADE 3 | | GRADE 8 | | Algebra 1* | ELA |
	ELA	Math	ELA	Math		
Randolph Twp.	60.3%	53.3%	80.3%	13.8%	59.8%	75.1%
Riverdale Boro	66.7%	80.6%	76.9%	22.7%	100%	NA
Rockaway Boro	46.7%	45.7%	65.3%	26.9%	95.7%	NA
Rockaway Twp.	50.0%	52.7%	68.7%	29.0%	98.8%	NA
Roxbury Twp.	52.9%	49.8%	70.6%	34.5%	56.6%	43.5%
Sch. Dist. of the Chathams	73.1%	83.1%	82.4%	5.7%	79.4%	58.1%
Washington Twp.	57.3%	58.7%	87.8%	56.3%	97.9%	NA
West Morris Regional	NA	NA	NA	NA	55.5%	85.5%
Wharton Boro	47.6%	50.8%	44.6%	27.4%	60.6%	NA

*Algebra I administered in multiple grades.

George told us the following:

My experience was an excellent one, but you have to remember that I graduated in '66. The school system has changed a lot since I graduated; for the better, I think. . . . I think it's an excellent school system and the reasons for that are (1) it's a very diverse community; and (2) I mean, it's got an indoor pool. Show me another community in the area that has an indoor pool or show me another high school in the area that has a radio station. They are just far advanced, unlike when I was in school. It was either . . . General, Business, or College Prep. That shows how far I go back. You either fell into one of those three categories. If you had any interest outside of what they offered, you probably got bored with school and dropped out. But now these kids, no matter what their interest is, they can find something at Morristown High to keep them focused.

As this quote shows, George's sales pitch for the Morris district is really designed to distinguish perception from reality. George's approach is to play up why school diversity matters for future college and career readiness. He said that, even if prospective buyers are not looking for diversity, which some certainly are, he tells them that most likely their children eventually will work in a diverse environment and Morris will prepare them for that reality.

George said that, after they hear about all the benefits of Morris, some of his clients are in "awe" because "nobody told us that." While other realtors might not correct some of the misconceptions people have about the Morris schools, George wants to give his clients all the facts so they can make an educated decision. George explained that he goes one step further to "sell the intentionally diverse community" that his mother Beatrice fought for and won in 1971.

The Morris district story is a special and especially compelling one because the nation is still wrestling with how to desegregate our schools. Indeed, recent evidence indicates the problem has been worsening.[1] School districts in some southern states that had made impressive progress under federal court oversight have seen their schools re-segregate as the courts have pulled back and even called into question the legality of voluntary desegregation plans. School districts in northern and western states never were substantially affected by *Brown*'s desegregation mandate because of the Supreme Court's unwillingness to make *Brown* a truly national requirement. In fact, schools in northern and midwestern states such as New York, Illinois, Michigan, and New Jersey have consistently been the most severely segregated.[2]

Demographic changes in the nation and in many states have made the picture more complicated, but no less bleak. As the White and Black student population percentages have declined, and the Latinx and Asian percentages have increased, the concept of diversity and the meaning of school integration have shifted. Still, the reality on the ground is that the rapidly increasing Latinx student population has joined Black and White students in their educational isolation, which has negative consequences on students' opportunities to learn.[3]

The question remains, how can districts capitalize on these demographic shifts and create intentionally desegregated and integrated school spaces using the law? First, we will explain the historical context of how school segregation came to be the status quo in the northern states regardless of *Brown*'s federal desegregation mandate. Then, we will discuss and analyze the *Jenkins* case and New Jersey's constitutional context.

WHY LITIGATE TO ACHIEVE
SCHOOL DESEGREGATION AND INTEGRATION?

It has often been the case, not just in New Jersey, but also throughout the United States, that desegregation and integration advocates wind up in court. Perhaps that is because requiring young people of different races, ethnicities, and socioeconomic classes to attend school together has such powerful emotional resonance for many Americans. The truth almost certainly is, to the discredit of our nation, that historically many people preferred for their children to be educated and to socialize with children like them. An allure of "school choice" for some parents may be that it enhances the prospects that their children can avoid attending school with "the other." Research has shown that White families tend to choose where to live and send their children to school based on what Jennifer Jellison Holme called "status ideologies"—using the race and class of the student body and recommendations from social networks as proxies for school district quality.[4] Therefore, if left to their own devices, like many of George Jenkins's clients, White parents often opt for homogeneity in their neighbors and in their children's classmates and friends. High levels of neighborhood and school segregation are also key factors in pushing families to make these decisions that become a self-fulfilling prophecy of segregated and unequal education. Yet, as we will show in later chapters, there is reportedly a growing acceptance among White families to actively seek out and choose racial diversity over White-isolated schooling environments for their children's education.

Unfortunately, only occasionally have legislative bodies, at the federal or state levels, taken the initiative to require heterogeneity of housing or schooling, and even broadly framed statutory requirements often have not been vigorously enforced by the executive branch. Thus, proponents of integration or diversity in schools and in housing, such as Beatrice Jenkins, often have to seek support in the courts. Independent federal judges in years gone by, or appointed judges in states such as New Jersey, may be more amenable to desegregation than elected officials, whether they be federal or state legislators or executive branch officials, or even elected state court judges, to require that the necessary steps be taken.

A threshold issue for school integration advocates has been whether to seek relief in the federal courts or state courts. Conceptually, federal courts have some important advantages. They tend to be better known and to have higher status than state courts. In theory at least, their appointed judges have the independence, attached to lifetime tenure, that should enable them to render decisions not yet reflective of a popular majority. Their decisions, if ultimately endorsed by the Supreme Court, have broad, even nationwide, application, making it unnecessary to litigate state by state. Their remedial power is extensive and can override state and local limitations. Federal courts also have constitutional underpinnings, such as the 14th Amendment's Equal Protection clause anchoring *Brown v. Board of Education,* which have become familiar to the public and to governmental officials, if not universally accepted.

But the federal courts also have some significant potential disadvantages for school integration advocates. Because of the federal courts' hierarchical structure, a pro-integration decision by the Supreme Court, such as *Brown,* can set in motion a powerful national movement, but an anti-integration decision, such as *Parents Involved,* can be the death knell to pursuing school integration in the federal courts or to a school district acting voluntarily to promote integration.[5] Even in the case of a favorable decision, though, the nationwide application of such a decision may have several constraining effects. First, the Supreme Court may be loath to render a decision with true nationwide application because of the extent to which circumstances on the ground may differ from state to state or region to region.[6] Second, the Court may be better at announcing broad constitutional principles than at assuring they are effectively implemented. Both of these constraints may be an important part of the *Brown* story.[7]

Prior to the *Brown* decision in 1954, New Jersey had a decidedly mixed history regarding school segregation and broader issues of equality. Unlike the southern states, it never had a formal and generally applicable state law requiring school segregation; nonetheless, the state had segregated schools into the 1950s. They resulted from formal policy or less formal action of local school districts. Ironically, though, in 1850, the state legislature had adopted "permissive legislation," on petition of Morris Township, to enable it to establish a separate school district for the exclusive use of "colored children," and the result was the opening of the segregated Spring Street school in Morristown (at the time and until 1865, Morristown was part of Morris Township).[8]

To demonstrate that it was not "small-minded," however, in 1881 New Jersey became one of the first states to enact a statute barring segregation in the schools,[9] and the state courts strongly enforced that statute. In 1945, the legislature acted again to adopt the comprehensive Law against Discrimination.[10] Two years later, in 1947, New Jersey became the only state to adopt an explicit constitutional amendment barring segregation in the schools.[11] Still, at the time of the *Brown* decision in 1954, some New Jersey schools, especially in the southern part of the state, were formally segregated and many others were de facto segregated. This dichotomy has continued to characterize New Jersey's record regarding school segregation—strong laws on the books and feeble action on the ground. Indeed, thanks to several landmark state court decisions in the 1960s and early 1970s, New Jersey is in the distinctive position of having the strongest state law in the nation barring school segregation and affirmatively requiring racial balance in the schools while it regularly is listed as having one of the country's worst records of school segregation.

As indicated above, New Jersey's state court decisions in the 17 years following *Brown*—culminating in the 1971 state supreme court decision paving the way to the MSD merger, *Jenkins v. Township of MSD*[12]—made those courts far more hospitable to school integration litigation than the federal courts. These decisions came during a period when federal court enforcement of *Brown* was best characterized by the oxymoronic phrase used by the U.S. Supreme Court in its 1955 follow-up decision to *Brown*— "all deliberate speed." The enforcement was slow and limited, with the federal courts seeming to erect more obstacles to meaningful nationwide enforcement than to clear away obstacles imposed by the states.[13,14]

THE *JENKINS* DECISION

Given the willingness of the New Jersey Supreme Court and the state commissioner of education to choose roads less traveled in addressing school segregation, their actions in 1971 might have been predictable. What might be less predictable is that the Morris remedy has not been replicated in New Jersey or in the rest of the nation, even after the substantial success of the Morris district in the intervening years.

The governmental and educational relationship among the three towns involved in the *Jenkins* case, Morristown, Morris Township, and Morris Plains, goes back many years. Morristown is one of New Jersey's and the nation's most historic communities. It was founded as New Hanover in 1715, and, shortly after Morris County was created in 1739, Morristown became the county seat because of its central location and its emerging status as a transportation hub. Both Morris County and Morristown, and for that matter Morris Township and Morris Plains, derived their names from the popular governor of the New Jersey colony, Lewis Morris.

The Enduring Relationship Between Morristown and Morris Township

Morristown and Morris Township were effectively a single municipality and school system for the better part of the 19th century. Public schooling began on a limited basis in the township, including Morristown, during the 1830s. It was not until 1865 that Morristown was formally incorporated as a town within Morris Township by the state legislature. Four years later, in 1869, Morristown High School was established as the first secondary school in Morris County and one of the first in New Jersey. This was at the time when New Jersey, in common with a number of other states, was establishing a true statewide system of public education. Indeed, the establishment of Morristown High School predated by 6 years the adoption of the "thorough and efficient" education clause of the New Jersey state constitution.

In 1895, Morristown became a separate municipality from Morris Township, but Township students continued to attend Morristown High School. Indeed, through formal and informal sending-receiving agreements, that relationship continued until the 1971 merger of the districts (except for a brief hiatus in 1958–59). Morris Plains, an adjoining community with its own K–8 school district, also sent its high school students to Morristown High School and continues to do so. Harding Township, another small adjacent community with predominantly affluent and White students, sent its high school students to Morristown High School until the 1971 merger. Shortly thereafter, it entered into a sending-receiving relationship with the Madison School District and Harding's 9–12 students began to attend Madison's predominantly White high school.

Even before Morristown's incorporation and the establishment of Morristown High School, two events with cross-cutting significance for this book occurred. First, in 1843, the Bethel African Methodist Episcopal (AME) Church was established at 13 Spring Street in Morristown. It was the first congregation established in Morris County by and for Black residents. Its Spring Street site, 7 years later in 1850, played a different and more malign role in Morristown's and New Jersey's educational history. At the petition of Morris Township, the state legislature established within the township "the Coloured School District of Morristown,"[15] which was housed at Bethel AME Church's original Spring Street site. As the name suggested, it was a segregated school for Black students.

The second event occurred in 1881 when State Senator Youngblood of Morris County introduced, and the state legislature adopted, one of the nation's first statutes to bar school segregation and to make it a misdemeanor punishable by fine or imprisonment for a school board member to vote in favor of excluding any child from a school based on "race, creed, color, national origin or ancestry."[16] That law is still part of New Jersey's education code and it has been augmented by a broad-based Law Against Discrimination added in 1945[17] and by a state constitutional provision added in 1947 that explicitly bars segregation in the public schools, the only such provision in the nation.[18]

Despite these constitutional and statutory provisions, as well as path-breaking decisions of the New Jersey Supreme Court in *Booker* and *Jenkins,* among others, New Jersey's overall record at desegregating its public schools has been woeful. In recent years, it has regularly been listed among the nation's most segregated public school systems for both Black and Latinx students.[19] Yet, this recognition has also brought about growing public understanding of the extreme disconnect between New Jersey having the strongest state laws in the nation, not only barring educational segregation, but also affirmatively requiring racial balance in the schools wherever feasible, and also one of the worst records of school segregation on the ground. This phenomenon has led to the filing of a statewide school desegregation case in the state courts on May 17, 2018, the 64th anniversary of the U.S. Supreme Court's first decision in *Brown v. Board of Education.*[20]

The Early Years (1956–1962)

Despite Morristown's and Morris Township's longstanding educational relationship, it has not always been a smooth one. That was true, even before the complications that led to the filing of the *Jenkins* case. The problems sometimes were mutual and often resulted from the overcrowding of Morristown High School. For example, in 1956, reportedly because of such overcrowding, Morristown notified the township board that it would no longer accept the township's 10th-grade pupils at Morristown

High School after September 1958. That may have occasioned both a Morris Township board vote in February 1958 to send its 10th-graders to Madison High School that fall as well as the brief hiatus in the township students' attendance at Morristown High School during 1958 and 1959.

Morristown High School's overcrowding also presumably led to a 1959 referendum in both communities on whether to have the township build its own high school or to have the Morristown and Morris Township school districts consolidate. That core question kept recirculating for at least 15 years with shifting alignments of residents, school board members and educational professionals. Even though there was strong support in the township for a separate high school, there also was consistently strong support for merger from a substantial group of White township residents. It was not until 1971 that the state supreme court's decision in *Jenkins* and the state commissioner of education's subsequent order of merger created the MSD and set it on its current path.

Predictably, the 1959 referendum reflected a closely divided township community, which rejected by 27 votes the proposal to build a new high school, as well as a plan to consolidate the Morristown and Morris Township schools. By contrast, Morristown voters approved consolidation overwhelmingly by a vote of almost 66%. Nonetheless, as part of considering educational severance from Morristown, the township had contacted 18 other districts about becoming "receiving" districts to replace Morristown and had decided upon Madison.

In another referendum, held just a few months later in January 1960, Morris Township voters again turned down a proposal for a separate high school. By 1961, however, the township reversed course and proposed school district consolidation to Morristown, but the latter also reversed course and rejected the proposal. In 1962, the persistent overcrowding of Morristown High School was alleviated by the construction of a 10-classroom addition and, as part of that project, Morristown and the township entered into a new 10-year sending-receiving relationship, which remained intact until the districts were merged in 1971.

The Tumultuous Times (1963–1973)

Despite the new sending-receiving agreement, however, the districts experienced tumultuous times between 1963 and 1973. This may well have reflected shifting public opinions about the value of desegregation, the burgeoning civil rights movement in the United States, and racial protests and unrest in a number of New Jersey cities including Newark and Plainfield. During this time period in the Morris community there were referenda, as well as public and private meetings, about the issue of merger versus a separate high school in Morris Township. All these activities were very much linked to politics and race.

Morristown community members and school officials tended to strongly favor merger, while Morris Township was closely divided on the issue. As was common in other desegregation settings, opponents of merger wanted neighborhood schools and lower taxes. Ultimately, the MSD's timeline for merger demonstrated that the road to desegregated education hardly ever follows a clear and consistent trajectory, and that persistence and staying power are crucial ingredients to success.

For example, in 1963, student "troubles" at Morristown High School reportedly led to the postponement of a student dance, and there was a dispute about whether the "troubles" were racially inspired. The following year, the township board adopted a resolution to build its own high school and notified the State that it planned to terminate its sending-receiving relationship with Morristown at the expiration of the 10-year agreement in 1972. Commissioner Carl Marburger indicated that he found the township notification reasonable notice of its intent to terminate the sending-receiving relationship and that there was "nothing which would prohibit the termination . . . at the end of the current contract."

By 1965, Morristown High School was overcrowded again and the Morristown board sent a letter to the township board indicating that Morris Township students would have to leave Morristown High in 1972 at the end of the 10-year sending-receiving agreement. In the 1966–67 school year, the township board received the Risotto Report it had commissioned in 1965 about a new high school, and the boards of Morristown, Morris Township, and Morris Plains received the Pittsburgh Report addressing the racial, educational and fiscal implications of township students leaving Morristown High. The Morristown superintendent suggested four K–12 merger possibilities and the three boards identified two main possibilities: (1) a new independent township high school or (2) a K–12 merger of Morristown and township schools.

In 1967, the three boards of education authorized a study of a 9–12 regional high school. The township board also held a public hearing and scheduled a January 12, 1968 referendum, not legally binding but "decisive," on whether the township should build its own high school and become a separate K–12 district or should merge with Morristown as a K–12 regional district. That public hearing and the scheduled referendum played a substantial role in crystallizing public opinion and galvanizing civic engagement around the separation/merger issue.

According to court documents, some of the strongest support for merger arose among township residents; a pro-merger group formed with a membership that was primarily White and substantially overlapped with the Morris County Fair Housing Council, another pro-merger organization. A third local group supported merger because they supported "Efficient Education," and saw a single district with a larger student enrollment as more efficient.

Local educational professionals were split on the issue—the township superintendent strongly opposed merger and the Morristown superintendent equally strongly supported it. Some other township administrators and teachers opposed merger because they favored neighborhood schools. The Morristown board unanimously voted in support of merger and, although a majority of the Morris Township board initially voted for merger, the board tilted against it as antimerger candidates prevailed in the 1969 and 1970 school board elections. A township antimerger group expressed its preference in the following terms: "The racial balance of our schools, while very important, is not the decisive factor in making what is primarily an educational decision."[21]

The January 12th nonbinding referendum in 1968 resulted in a relatively narrow decision in favor of a separate township K–12 district with a new high school (2,164 to 1,899). In a letter to the Morris Township board and the state commissioner of education, the Morris County Urban League formally protested the proposed withdrawal of township students from Morristown High School and requested further study of the issue. The Morristown school board commissioned a study by the Engelhardt firm of the effect of withdrawing township students from Morristown High School. In June of that year, Morris Plains requested that the county superintendent conduct a feasibility study of a 9–12 regional high school. In September, the Morris Township board scheduled a March 27, 1969 referendum on whether to authorize capital expenditures for a new high school.

The Merger Effort Embraces a Legal Approach (1968–1971)

Perhaps because the efforts to resolve the educational relationship among Morristown, Morris Township, and Morris Plains, and the fight over school integration, were proving so elusive, complicated, and inconsistent, five residents of the township, including Beatrice Jenkins, and three of Morristown joined together to seek a legal solution.

On October 26, 1968, a petition was filed with the Commissioner of Education by their lawyer Frank Harding, who was a board member of the local Urban League. The caption of the case was *Jenkins et al., v. The Township of Morris School District and Board of Education and The Town of Morristown School District and Board of Education and The Borough of Morris Plains Board of Education* (the Harding Township schools were also served with the petition because its students were attending Morristown High School at the time). The petitioners sought as alternatives to the proposed Morris Township High School: (1) a K–12 regional district merging Morristown and Morris Township and precluding the township from creating its own separate high school (with the strongest support allegedly coming from White township residents); (2) a 7–12 regionalization; or (3) maintenance of the current sending-receiving arrangements.

In November 1968, answers to the petition were filed by all four school boards; the Morristown board, represented by its lawyer Steve Wiley, also filed a cross-petition supporting the request of the eight individual resident petitioners[22] for a complete K–12 merger of the Morristown and Morris Township school districts, as well as a prohibition against the township withdrawing its students from Morristown High School. The Morris Plains board also filed a cross-petition seeking consideration of a 9–12 merger. On December 12th, the Morristown school board filed a motion with the Commissioner for preliminary relief, namely, to restrain the township board from proceeding with its plan to build a new high school or to hold any referenda in that connection, and the individual petitioners joined in that request. The township board moved for judgment on December 23rd in favor of the pleadings contending that neither the original petitioners nor the cross-petitioners had stated any basis upon which the Commissioner could grant relief.

In February 1969, the township board moved ahead with its effort to build a new high school by formally setting March 27 as the date for a referendum. Also in February, the county superintendent released a report requested by the Morris Plains board of all possible high school configurations. As a result of this cross-petition, Wiley wound up working with Frank Harding to represent the petitioners, as well as on behalf of the Morristown board mergers involving 3-, 4-, or 6- year configurations.

On March 21, Commissioner Marburger denied the township's motion to dismiss the petition without a full hearing and enjoined the township from holding its scheduled March 27th referendum because it would impair the Commissioner's upcoming hearing in the case. Marburger also recommended that the Morristown and Morris Township school boards immediately begin to study an all-purpose regional school district comprising the two municipalities, and any other appropriate alternatives. The Appellate Division of the New Jersey Superior Court upheld the Commissioner's action, and the March 27th referendum was not held. On April 11th, the Morris County Superintendent of Schools launched a study of district merger, but the township board declined to participate, reportedly because building a new high school was a higher priority.

In July, Congressman Peter Frelinghuysen announced that the township had been awarded a $100,000 U.S. Department of Housing and Urban Development (HUD) grant for advanced planning of a new high school. After protests to HUD from the Morris County NAACP, as well as many other organizations and individuals, HUD agreed not to make the grant available until after the commissioner's hearing was held. The hearing was postponed twice, first due to the death of the township's attorney and then due to the illness of the head of New Jersey Department of Education's Controversies and Disputes office, who was to have conducted the hearing.

The commissioner's hearing finally was held before hearing officer Robert Greenwood, a deputy attorney general, between October 6 and December 19, 1969. The Greenwood report was submitted to the commissioner on June 17, 1970, and the hearing officer found that the withdrawal of township students would have negative effects on Morristown High School. Although the commissioner agreed with that finding, on November 11, 1970, he ruled that he had no authority regarding either the withdrawal of township students from Morristown High School or the merger of the districts and, therefore, he dismissed the petition and cross-petition pending before him and lifted the restraint against the township's referendum. The township thereupon scheduled it for March 4, 1971.

In February 1971, however, the New Jersey Supreme Court granted a stay of the referendum. That spring, the parties presented arguments to the New Jersey Supreme Court in the *Jenkins* case. On June 25, the Court unanimously ruled that the commissioner had the authority to take suitable steps toward preventing the township from withdrawing its students from Morristown High School and toward effectuating a merger of the Morristown and Morris Township school districts.[23] The court ruled that the commissioner must have the power to allow students to cross district lines to avoid "segregation in fact," which we detail in the next section of this chapter.

The township board decided not to appeal the New Jersey Supreme Court decision. On July 30, the commissioner signed an order merging the two school districts into a single, all-purpose (K–12) regional district. An interim board of education was established for the merged district, with an election of the first regular board scheduled for February 1, 1972. On that date, the new MSD board was elected with five members from the township and four from Morristown. The May newsletter of the Morris district included a President's Message from Michael J. Barry, the last president of the township board and the recently elected first president of the new MSD. Barry said:

> As spokesman for our Board of Education, and as a parent, let me affirm that our primary concern at all times is our most important product, our children . . . .With you, I look forward to this initial exciting year, which will be the beginning of an educational system limited in scope and quality only by your own ambition.

On July 1, the merger formally took effect after a last-minute legal attempt by township residents to block it because they had been denied an opportunity to vote on the question. On September 7, 1972, the schools of the newly formed MSD were opened.

In sum, the Morris district resulted from a forced merger of two school districts in largely suburban and predominantly White Morris County. The merger was ordered by the state commissioner of education explicitly for racial balance reasons after the New Jersey Supreme Court ruled that he had the power to take such action if he deemed it educationally appropriate and necessary to satisfy the state constitutional requirements for education. To this point, the Morris district is the only one in New Jersey, indeed in the United States, to have been born in that manner. Its success at achieving and maintaining a remarkable degree of student diversity in a world where homogeneity is the norm makes one wonder why. By one benchmark of diversity—how a school district's student population compares to statewide averages—the Morris district is one of the most diverse school districts in New Jersey. As noted in Chapter 1, its 2018–19 demographic profile was 47% White students, 9% Black, 39% Latinx, 4% Asian, and 34 % receiving free or reduced-price lunch (FRPL; that is, low-income) against a state profile of 43% White, 15% Black, 29% Latinx, 10% Asian, and 38% FRPL.[24]

Beyond the districtwide numbers, the Morris district has achieved and maintained remarkable diversity at the building level in its elementary schools. These schools are where the desegregation rubber begins to meet the road since the Morris district has only one middle school and one high school, and it is there that the Morris district shines. Despite the fact that students live in relatively homogeneous, segregated neighborhoods, the elementary schools they attend defy that pattern. For example, to achieve perfect racial balance between Black and White students at the elementary school level, only about 11% would have to change their school assignments. Similarly, to achieve perfect racial balance between Latinx and White students at the elementary school level, only about 6% would have to change their school assignments.

The two main mechanisms for accomplishing that impressive degree of school level diversity involved: (1) the adoption of the so-called "Princeton Plan," which paired a primary (K–2) school with an intermediate (3–5) school—with one of the paired schools located in the town and the other in the township; and (2) the designation of a centrally located residential area of Morristown, where many Black—and now Latinx—residents live as an "open attendance zone" whose students were dispersed to different elementary schools to assure diversity in each. The Morris district's version of the Princeton Plan also reassigned teachers among former Morristown and Morris Township schools. Chapter 3 provides more detail about how the Morris district achieves this level of diversity across schools, from the time of the merger until today.

ANALYZING *JENKINS*

Since the New Jersey Supreme Court's decision in the *Jenkins* case was the main impetus for the creation of the Morris district, it deserves detailed attention here. The case took an unusual, but expedited, route from the commissioner of education to the Supreme Court. The statutorily specified process at the time[25] was for a decision of the commissioner of education to be appealable to the State Board of Education, whose decision could in turn be appealed to the Appellate Division of the New Jersey Superior Court, the intermediate appellate court. In cases of special urgency or importance, the case could be certified for hearing directly by the state supreme court.

Although the *Jenkins* petitioners did appeal to the State Board from the commissioner's dismissal of their petition, the appeal was never decided there. Apparently, when the State Board advised the petitioners "it had not found time to hear the appeal," the petitioners chose to seek an immediate review of the commissioner's decision in the supreme court, and five of the seven justices agreed to hear the case directly, over the sharp dissent of a sixth justice.[26] In his dissent, Justice John J. Francis suggested how controversial the *Jenkins* case was when he wrote that "I cannot escape the feeling that [the State Board's] failure [to render a decision on appeal] was motivated by a desire to escape the performance of a duty (which no matter how onerous or tension-charged) it had the obligation to perform."[27]

Another introductory point about *Jenkins* worthy of reference is that the opinion for a unanimous New Jersey Supreme Court was authored by Justice Nathan Jacobs. Six years earlier, Justice Jacobs had written the majority opinion for the court in the *Booker* case. As indicated earlier in this chapter, taken together *Booker* and *Jenkins* charted a course for the New Jersey courts in school integration that placed them far ahead of the federal courts. In *Booker*, the supreme court had rejected the distinction between de jure and de facto segregation; in *Jenkins*, the court had recognized the state commissioner of education's power, and quite possibly duty, to racially balance the schools across district lines. Despite Justice Jacobs's prominent role in those decisions, however, when he retired from the court and later died, neither of those opinions was highlighted.[28]

The *Jenkins* case itself involved a factually simple and straightforward context for the court to announce an important extension of its school integration jurisprudence. The case was factually simple because Morristown and Morris Township—the urban hole in a suburban doughnut—had a close and longstanding municipal, educational, social, and commercial relationship that extended from at least the early 1800s to the present time.

As the court indicated at the beginning of its opinion:

Prior to 1865 Morristown and Morris Township were a single municipal unit. In that year Morristown received permission to incorporate as a separate entity and arbitrary boundary lines were drawn between the Township . . . and the Town . . . . Despite their official separation, the Town and Township have remained so interrelated that they may realistically be viewed as a single community, probably a unique one in our State.[29]

Of particular relevance, the town and township had a close and longstanding educational relationship. In fact, for more than 100 years "the Town and Township have had a sending-receiving relationship under which the Township sends Township students to Morristown High School."[30] However, the *Jenkins* case arose because the Township, a K–8 elementary district, was seeking to build its own high school, thereby becoming an all-purpose K–12 district and withdrawing its students from Morristown High School.

The petitioners, both the eight residents of the town and township who had initiated the case and the Morristown Board of Education that had joined them as a cross-petitioner, opposed the Morris Township's proposed action. Their concern was both educational and about avoiding racial isolation.

Justice Jacobs's opinion in *Jenkins* stressed that Morristown High School, with its student population drawn from Morristown, Morris Township, Morris Plains, and Harding Township, "is an excellent educational institution[31] and offers diversified and comprehensive courses of instruction" for all its students. But, if Morris Township were to withdraw its students, and even more so if Morris Plains and Harding students followed the township students' exodus, it would leave only Morristown students at Morristown High School. If that happened, the hearing examiner found that nine enumerated disadvantages would occur.

These would include: a reduction in the scope and variety of courses offered because of the reduced enrollment; the loss of highly motivated and capable students who could serve as role models for the rest of the students; a decline "in the scale of excellence in terms of breadth and quality of program;"[32] greater difficulty in attracting and keeping high quality faculty; and, as a result of changes in program and reputation and loss in tuition revenue, a possible decline in the ability or willingness of Morristown to support the school system financially.

The hearing examiner also wrote that the students remaining at Morristown High School would be from "lower socioeconomic backgrounds" and, therefore, "less oriented toward academic achievement, with the result that the program structure will have to be drastically reoriented."[33] He predicted that in a few years there would be an increasing percentage of Black students at Morristown High School, especially if Morris Plains and Harding students left, which would result in the Morristown and

Morris Township students being "denied the privilege of an integrated education."[34] Lastly, the hearing officer found that the "sudden alteration in the racial composition of the high school might aggravate the tendency of potential White buyers to avoid purchasing houses in Morristown."[35] This last finding presaged George Jenkins's interview statements to us more than 45 years later.

By contrast to the negatives the hearing examiner found would result from the township students' departure from Morristown High School, he reported that most of the considerable testimony he had heard about a total K–12 merger of Morristown and Morris Township "persuasively supported the high educational desirability and economic feasibility of such a merger."[36] In his view, "if there is a failure to merge 'the Black student population of Morristown—particularly at the elementary school level—will suffer the same harmful effects that the commissioner of education has worked so hard to eliminate within single school districts throughout the State.'"[37]

Justice Jacobs' opinion also seemed influenced by the Engelhardt educational consulting firm report commissioned by the Morristown Board of Education and introduced into evidence at the hearing in this case. It identified many advantages of a K–12 merger for both the Morristown and Morris Township districts. Like the hearing examiner's conclusions, the Engelhardt report included both educational and social benefits including:

1. Establishment of a racial balance which represents the racial composition of the community. Biracial experience will be available in the early grades where it has important benefits for both White and Negro students in terms of interracial attitudes and preferences[38] and at the later years where it will have important benefits to members of minority groups.
2. Representation of the socioeconomic spectrum of the community at all levels of schooling.
3. Equal educational opportunity available to all students without regard to background, race, or residence.
4. Avoidance of invidious comparison between the Morristown High School and a Township school, a comparison ultimately based on race. . . .
10. Reduction in the number of school districts in the area from four to three.
11. Development of greater vertical coordination of program and greater flexibility in facilities, curriculum and organization.

Commissioner of Education Marburger shared many of the hearing examiner's concerns about the withdrawal of township students from

Morristown High School, but concluded, nonetheless, that he had lacked the legal power either to prohibit the withdrawal or "direct any steps on the part of the respective Boards towards merger of their systems, or to grant any other relief towards avoidance of the baneful effect he so soundly envisions."[39]

The Supreme Court immediately jumped on the commissioner's "flat disavowal of power despite the compelling circumstances," and proceeded to lecture the commissioner on his broad powers to supervise the State's public education system and to guarantee its "thoroughness and efficiency."[40] The Court also explicitly linked the State's constitutional commitment to assure a thorough and efficient system of free public schools with "its policy against racial discrimination and segregation in the public schools," and characterized the "history and vigor" of those policies as "matched."[41]

After citing a series of decisions over the years that had established the reach of the commissioner's powers and duty to assure the thoroughness and efficiency of the New Jersey schools, the court shifted its attention to the state's and the court's parallel and equally important efforts since 1881 to prevent racial discrimination and segregation in the schools. Not surprisingly, Justice Jacobs emphasized his opinion for the court in *Booker* 6 years earlier and his focus on the commissioner's "proper goal" being "a reasonable plan for the entire school system achieving the greatest dispersal [of students] consistent with sound educational values and procedures."[42] That was at sharp variance with the commissioner's view that a plan, which eliminated only schools that were "completely or almost entirely Negro," was sufficient.

After underscoring the importance of *Booker*'s decision that state school authorities acting under state law and state education policies could compel the elimination or reduction of de facto segregation even if the federal courts had not quite reached that result under federal law,[43] Justice Jacobs went on to deal with a cross-district remedy. He pointed out that:

> It is true that Booker dealt with a community which was wholly contained within a single district fixed by municipal lines whereas here the community involves two districts. When dealing with de jure segregation the crossing of district lines has of course presented no barrier whatsoever.[44]

More broadly, in a prominent 1964 voting rights case, *Reynolds v. Sims*,[45] the U.S. Supreme Court pointed out, according to Justice Jacobs, that political subdivisions of a state are not "sovereign entities" and "may readily be bridged when necessary to vindicate federal constitutional rights and policies."[46]

Justice Jacobs extrapolated from that U.S. Supreme Court pronouncement the core of the *Jenkins* decision:

It seems clear to us that, similarly, governmental subdivisions of the state may readily be bridged when necessary to vindicate state constitutional rights and policies. This does not entail any general departure from the historic home rule principles and practices in our State in the field of education or elsewhere; but it does entail suitable measures of power in our State authorities for fulfillment of the educational and racial policies embodied in our State Constitution and in its implementing legislation. Surely if those policies and the views firmly expressed by this Court in *Booker* (45 N.J. 161, 212 A.2d 1) and now reaffirmed are to be at all meaningful, the State Commissioner must have power to cross district lines to avoid "segregation in fact" (*Booker*, 45 N.J. at 168, 212 A.2d 1), at least where, as here, there are no impracticalities and the concern is not with multiple communities but with a single community without visible or factually significant internal boundary separations.[47]

On the basis of that strong view, the New Jersey Supreme Court concluded in *Jenkins* that the commissioner had erred by dismissing the petition and cross-petition regarding both the withdrawal of township students from Morristown High School and the merger of the Morris Township and Morristown school systems.

The Court's final words on the subject were:

The Commissioner is adequately empowered to entertain such further proceedings pursuant to the petition and cross-petition as he finds appropriate and to grant such prayers therein as he considers warranted including (1) direction for continuance of the sending-receiving relationship after the expiration of the present contract and (2) direction that the Boards of the Township and Town proceed with suitable steps towards regionalization, reserving, however, supervisory jurisdiction to the Commissioner with full power to direct a merger on his own if he finds such course ultimately necessary for fulfillment of the State's educational and desegregation policies in the public schools.[48]

This last point is precisely what the commissioner did on July 30, 1971, when he ordered that the Morris Township and Morristown school systems be merged into a single K–12 all-purpose school district, the MSD. In an interview for this book, Marburger told us that the merger order was his proudest moment as New Jersey's commissioner of education and that he deeply believed it was the right thing to do.

THE IMPACT OF THE *JENKINS* DECISION

The creation of a merged MSD grew out of unlikely soil since it was in the midst of largely White and largely conservative Morris County. On the other hand, as the New Jersey Supreme Court recognized in *Jenkins*, for more than 100 years Morristown and Morris Township had formed a single community geographically, commercially, socially, and even governmentally. For most of those 100 years township students attended Morristown High School based on voluntary consensual arrangements between the two districts.

Nonetheless, the merger was accompanied in some quarters by strong opposition and dire predictions that its likeliest outcome would be massive White flight of township students. Even when the merger became a fait accompli, there was ongoing turbulence in the local community,[49] but the merged district did move forward with students from Morristown and Morris Township sharing the elementary schools and middle school, as well as Morristown High School, where they were joined by students from Morris Plains. The next chapter describes in detail the educational and social consequences of the merger. For now, suffice it to say that the massive White flight of township students predicted by merger opponents never materialized and that the Morris district continues today as one of New Jersey's most integrated districts.

Unfortunately, the positive impact on other New Jersey school districts seeking the Morris merger remedy was blunted by two interrelated factors. First, Marburger wound up failing to be confirmed for another term as commissioner. At the end of his 5-year term, he was nominated for another term by Republican governor William Cahill, but his confirmation failed to be confirmed by one vote in the State Senate. Most commentators attributed that result to his still controversial decision to merge the Morristown and Morris Township school districts.

The second factor was a combination of the consequent unwillingness of Marburger's successors as commissioner to follow his path and some language in the *Jenkins* opinion, which gave them a plausible justification for parting company with him. In explaining why the commissioner had the power to order merger of the Morristown and Township districts, the court's justification included reference to the special character of those districts where "the concern is not with multiple communities but with a single community without visible or factually significant internal boundary separations."[50]

Those words became the "single community doctrine" of successor commissioners of education, which they believed justified their decisions to reject the claims of both the Plainfield and New Brunswick districts to the Morris merger remedy. Today, both those districts have fewer than 1% White students as nearby predominantly White sending school districts were permitted to withdraw their students from their more urban and diverse neighbors and keep their segregated district boundaries intact. It is quite possible that Morris Township and perhaps Morris Plains similarly might have left the Morristown schools but for the merger.

It was not until 1992 and the Englewood–Englewood Cliffs school segregation case that the New Jersey courts laid the "single community doctrine" to rest. Judge Virginia Long, who later was named to the state supreme court, wrote the opinion for the three-judge Appellate Division panel. She addressed head-on the argument made by Englewood Cliffs and Tenafly that "the single community principle is a part of the fundamental holding of *Jenkins* and that the State Board erred in dispensing with it."[51] Judge Long wrote:

> A fair reading of *Jenkins* evidences no intention to restrict its remedial scope to such circumstances. The expansive general principle enunciated in *Jenkins* was that cross-district regionalization is an available arrow in the Commissioner's desegregation quiver. The Court took pains to explain the importance of this remedy in vindicating our State's Constitutional and statutory policies. It described the municipalities under review (Morristown and Morris Township), as a single municipality because they were physically, socially, commercially and governmentally interdependent (58 N.J. at 485-86, 270 A.2d 619). Most importantly, the Court declared the configuration before it as "probably a unique one in our state" (Id. at 485, 279 A.2d 619). It is inconceivable to us that the Court intended its far-reaching statement of policy to be limited to a fact pattern which, it recognized, was unlikely to reoccur. That is the interpretation urged by Cliffs and Tenafly. Its effect would be to eviscerate *Jenkins*, a result we will not allow.[52]

Despite Justice Long's resounding affirmation of *Jenkins*, it did not lead to the embrace of regionalization as a weapon against school segregation either in Englewood or elsewhere. Indeed, New Jersey's record of segregation on the ground continued largely unabated for 26 more years until May 17, 2018, the 64th anniversary of the U.S. Supreme Court's first decision in *Brown v. Board of Education*. On that date, New Jersey's second statewide school integration case was filed in the state courts. Styled as *Latino Action Network et al. v. State of New Jersey*, the case sought wide-ranging remedies, including regionalization.

As of the publication of this book, the case is still in the preliminary stages. After the plaintiffs filed their voluminous and detailed complaint alleging that New Jersey's educational system was in violation of multiple state constitutional provisions including the education clause and the antisegregation provision, the State moved to dismiss the case or, at least, have it referred to the Office of Administrative Law (OAL) for a hearing there instead of in the courts. Those motions were denied, at least for the moment in the case of the referral to OAL, and the parties spent months in discussion about a possible settlement of the case. That possibility seems at an end, at least for now, and the parties are moving forward with the litigation process. Most recently, the State sought again unsuccessfully to have the case dismissed because the plaintiffs had failed to join all the almost 600 school districts in New Jersey and to have the case transferred to the commissioner of education and OAL for the creation of a record.

The two primary issues in that case are: (1) whether the substantial and long-standing racial and socioeconomic segregation of the state's public education system, especially in its larger urban districts, is unconstitutional; and (2) if it is, what remedies should be ordered by the court. Since one of the focal points of the plaintiffs' challenge is the New Jersey school attendance statute, which established the principle that students are entitled to receive a free public education in the district where they reside,[53] a remedial focus of the complaint is to devise ways for enabling students to cross existing district lines, either by some form of cross-district attendance programs or by changing district lines. In both those respects, the Morris district's experience is highly relevant.

Although immediately after the LAN complaint was filed, Governor Murphy issued a statement supporting school integration, more recent signs are that the State will contest the case strongly. That would be consistent with the position it has taken in several recent education cases on behalf of low-income students of color, where the State has seemed intent on maintaining the status quo of segregation and inequality.[54]

How the LAN case is finally resolved will say a great deal about how influential the *Jenkins* case and the Morris district experience prove to be legally. Of course, it is quite another matter if the other branches of state government were to decide that school integration is a high priority for state action and they were to act accordingly. In that case, too, the Morris model could, and should, loom large.

LESSONS LEARNED

What lessons can be learned from the Morris remedy of school desegregation via regionalization? Although the Morris experience opens the door to individual mergers imposed upon school districts by a court or by state education authorities, it would be far preferable for the rearrangement of school district lines to proceed pursuant to a statewide school integration plan embraced by the legislative and executive branches. During the past dozen years, New Jersey has taken some steps in that direction. In 2007, when the position of county education superintendent was upgraded, one of the charges to the "executive county superintendents" was that each should develop a plan to consolidate school districts within their respective counties so that all were full-purpose K–12 districts. Although the driving force behind that requirement seemed to be cost-saving rather than integration, and although little came of that requirement, that would not preclude future legislative action from giving primacy to integration.

A more recent legislative initiative, pressed by Senate President Sweeney, would go even further by exploring the benefits of countywide school districts, again seemingly to serve fiscal and educational, rather than desegregation, purposes.

Another lesson from the Morris district experience is that law and litigation can be used strategically, in combination with other techniques, to press for school integration in individual districts where districtwide diversity has not been extended to the school building level, or where building level diversity has not been extended to the classroom and program level. It also can be deployed to press for statewide legislative or executive action to restructure school district lines to enhance the prospects of integration. There must be serious buy-in by enlightened school leaders who are committed not only to seek student diversity, but also to use it to enhance the educational and social experience of all students. Local leaders are crucial to a successful school integration effort, but so are state leaders, including prominently the state commissioner of education.

One possible avenue already in place is the pending LAN case, which has begun to press the State to take far-ranging action, including by school district mergers, to integrate New Jersey's schools. Another legal strategy grows out of the state constitution's education clause by emphasizing its mandate of an "efficient system of free public schools for the instruction of all the children between the ages of five and eighteen." Proving that the State's current system is inefficient in fiscal and educational terms should not be difficult, and that could open the door to a fundamental restructuring to enhance educational quality and equality, cost effectiveness, and integration.

As the Morris experience and this chapter's discussion of legal strategies make clear, state constitutions and state statutes, at least in states with court systems amenable to forceful constructions of their requirements, are much preferable vehicles now for seeking school integration than federal law and courts. An issue still unresolved, though, is whether, in the interplay between federal and state law, federal antidiscrimination precedents, such as *Parents Involved*, might conflict with, and even prevail over, state constitutional school integration requirements, such as *Booker* and *Jenkins* in New Jersey.

Although the "single community" doctrine was ultimately rejected by the New Jersey courts, mergers are more likely to be successful, both legally and educationally, if the individual districts have a pre-existing relationship with one another, educationally and otherwise, and if a critical mass of local support for integration exists or can be generated. However, for school district restructuring, by merger or otherwise, to be more than a relatively rare and isolated remedy for school segregation, the State and integration advocates must think comprehensively about how to accomplish it. That means creative solutions have to be developed to overcome the almost complete segregation of New Jersey's large urban districts.

Any fiscal complexities or disincentives associated with district merger should be eliminated or at least minimized. This is likely to require legislative action. Indeed, in this and other ways, thoughtful legislative and executive action can enhance the prospect of voluntary district mergers for integration, as well as for fiscal and educational, purposes.

If litigation seems to be necessary, it can be an end in itself, but preferably it can work in tandem with other mechanisms. In that connection, a lesson from the Morris experience is that a critical mass of community residents and organizations must be mobilized to "do the right thing" regarding school integration, including supporting litigation if need be. In Morris, the critical mass included longtime and influential residents, many of them White residents of both constituent districts, as well as civic, social service, religious, and advocacy organizations.

There must also be efforts among local realtors, such as George Jenkins, encouraged and supported by municipal and school district officials, to sell the Morris district as a destination of choice. The success of such an effort will swell the ranks of residents committed to diversity. One of our interviewees, James, a Black parent who moved to Morristown from the Midwest, offered an important insight into how that might be accomplished. Because Morris County has one of the nation's highest levels of average income, many people considering it as a destination can choose where in the county they will live. To get people to choose the Morris district, you have to emphasize how much the district has to offer. Said James, "We offer a lot of programs, options, including our advanced placement programs, and we have a radio station in our district."

All those who support integration and diversity must commit themselves to be engaged intensively and for the long haul. As we explain in the next chapter, school and community leadership, as well as the broader public, parents, students and school staff, must plant and constantly nurture the seeds of true integration if it is to bloom and flourish. To that end, they must use the tools, such as the Princeton Plan, that have proven successful in the Morris district. And they must be vigilant to ensure that the fruits of their effort are not soured by the forces of re-segregation as has happened in so many instances.

CHAPTER 3

The Role of Educational Leadership

Mackey Pendergrast is a White administrator who is currently serving as the MSD superintendent. One of the first things Pendergrast did when he started the job in 2014 was to visit the NAACP, the local churches, and other community organizations to spread his message and vision of integration and inclusion and to hear what others had to say about the district's challenges. Mackey told us during the interview that he was attracted to the Morris superintendency by the fact that a third of the students were economically disadvantaged. He was coming to Morris after being the superintendent of a wealthier and Whiter school district in New Jersey, and, while he was up for the challenge of Morris, he wanted to be supported by the community: "I don't want to go into a situation if I can't do anything about it, so the community and the resources that are here and the intellectual commitment I discovered was here in the interview process, I thought we could do something with this. . . . How many public schools are actually overcoming poverty gaps? How many? Not many."

Stability in the community and board of education was a key factor that attracted him to the position. "When I interviewed, the board of ed here was so impressive and dedicated to each of the kids. . . .You've gotta have [support] from the board of ed all the way straight down through everybody, everybody really rooting and trying hard."

This can-do attitude was a strong theme throughout all of the interviews, as a Morris Educational Foundation (MEF) staff member described, "I think the school system is kind of a microcosm of what's happening in our larger community and I think a strong school system especially—at MEF we're always saying this all of the time. A strong school system is at the root of a strong community so people should invest and care about their public schools."

Superintendent Pendergrast said that when he spoke at a recent MEF event, he told them:

The community succeeds. It's the community that succeeds. . . .
For a long time I went, 'Ah, everywhere is the same. Morristown,

some town in Wyoming, some town in Texas. They're all the same. Towns are towns. People are people.' I don't believe that anymore. . . . I think if we all took a little more ownership of our towns and the values that we express and act on, I think it's important. That's where I think there's a unique advantage to the Morris school community, the Morris School District and this community. I just think there's a lot here, tradition, the churches, the community.

He also pointed out that the people in Morris are important because they "stick around, and feel like they've got skin in the game."

From the community organizations to the churches to the board of education, they all come together to support the work of the school district. For example, the local churches and the Neighborhood House (a community organization founded in 1898 to serve new immigrant families) partner with the district to offer tutoring services and afterschool activities, such as sports, dance, and music. Another example is the annual bus tour of the community that the district requires of new teachers to help with multicultural understanding. To that point, the superintendent said that they did a listening tour last spring by visiting community organizations and meeting with parents at each of the schools. They went around to the Home School Associations (HSAs), where, Pendergrast said, the mothers spoke about the community and how important it is to build relationships with all of the parents.

Pendergrast told us that it is inspirational to him to find this different kind of community that really values diversity. He commented, "White parents challenge me to make sure that immigrants are included. You don't have that in every community." For all these reasons, Pendergrast said, the school district has been able to maintain such a high level of racial balance and high quality education when so many other districts have failed.

It is also very important for Mackey Pendergrast to live by the school district's mission *to come together to learn from and with each other.* He said, "We don't want to use the word diversity unless we're using the word inclusion along with it. We want to make sure all students are included in all the different types of learning that take place in a school system." Therefore, one of his priorities has been to recruit and hire a diverse teaching staff. For example, the district is responding to the influx of Latinx students by recruiting and hiring more Spanish-speaking staff. The superintendent reported that, since June 2015, the district has hired 10 bilingual teachers, and 31% of all new hires (counselors, administrators, and teachers) speak Spanish. When asked about the challenges the district has faced with students coming from Central American countries, Pendergrast replied, "We feel the goal is to have a healthy community. If you have a healthy community, community members, students, parents, and teachers are working hard to understand and partner with each other for the success of the child. The healthy community comes first, and then the other things are possible."

THE LINK BETWEEN MACKEY PENDERGRAST AND STEVE WILEY

We began this chapter with a vignette about Mackey Pendergrast because there are important linkages between him and Steve Wiley, whose role, as described in Chapter 1, was so instrumental in creating the merged district in the late 1960s and early 1970s. Mackey's tenure at MSD holds the promise of being the culmination of Steve's vision.

Both leaders present a concept of true integration—students learning together side-by-side in the same classrooms, not just in the same school district and school buildings. MSD has made great strides in providing its students with an integrated education, especially in the elementary grades and when compared to most other New Jersey and U.S. school districts, even those with similar demographics to MSD. However, it has not yet fully achieved the district's and Steve's vision. Doing so is at the top of Mackey's agenda, and it is the main thrust of the Equity and Inclusion Plan he and his administration have proposed recently and are beginning to implement, which we will describe and analyze later in this chapter.

To really understand the Morris story, indeed the story of American public education over the past half century, one must appreciate how much the linked concepts of diversity and integration have changed over the period since the merged MSD was created. What propelled Steve Wiley and his colleagues to act in the late 1960s was the specter of a predominantly Black Morristown High School resulting from the departure of White students who lived in Morris Township, Harding Township, and possibly Morris Plains. The situation then was literally Black and White, with few Latinx or Asian students. Media reports showed that Steve was fearful that Morristown would join the list of New Jersey urban school districts where Black students were educated in isolation from nearby White suburban students.[1] In Steve's view, that would be disastrous for the students and for the broader communities. He believed profoundly, as does Mackey, that you cannot have healthy communities without healthy schools because they are in a symbiotic relationship.

We found this general premise—that a school district does not exist in isolation from the community—to be a major part of MSD's culture. Indeed, the story and continued legacy of MSD is rooted firmly in its mission, stated below, which is to educate a racially and socioeconomically diverse community of learners:

> Since 1854, the Morris School District has been a unifying social force and a source of tremendous pride in our community. In our classrooms and on our playgrounds children of every race, religion, and economic background come together to learn with and from each other.

We saw this mission statement prominently framed on the wall of the district's main office and reiterated on each of the district's school websites. It firmly sends the message that the district's diversity is a source of pride and strength for the community. Even the Morristown municipal website states that, "diversity is one of Morristown's greatest strengths."[2]

On the surface, this credo sounds promising—particularly in a New Jersey and U.S. education context that is mostly characterized by segregated and unequal education. However, the heart of this book lies in uncovering the nature of this community's commitment to the essential goal of diversity. What lessons can be learned from the creation, and ongoing successes and challenges of the MSD? How far and deep does diversity actually go in MSD? Does having district- and school-wide desegregation as a priority necessarily mean that all students are being educated to their fullest potentials in integrated classrooms and programs? Do students from all backgrounds, as the mission statement reads, *"come together to learn with and from each other"*?

This chapter attempts to answer these questions by taking a closer look at the role that educational leadership—at the district, school, and community levels—has played in sustaining a commitment to racial/ethnic and socioeconomic integration over the years. Two themes emerged from our data that highlight the importance of both the philosophies of school leaders on the one hand and the cultivation of school-community relations on the other. The first helps to explain how the Morris district has flourished for so long, while most other district desegregation efforts in New Jersey have not. It is exemplified in the perceptions and actions taken by school administrators to further the idea that a successfully integrated district needs buy-in and support from the community *and* culturally responsive school leadership in the schools. A key ingredient of this ongoing support is a focus on creating their own unique culture and community.

Another strong theme that emerged was the belief that a healthy community is possible only if the public schools are of a high quality. While school quality is typically measured by aggregate test score averages, in Morris, the reality is that they cannot do that like homogeneous districts can. Instead, their image of success is when student subgroups (by race and SES) show gains in achievement. Substantial evidence emerged from our interviews that such conditions were essential to the Morris schools maintaining their racial diversity for as long as they have.

In so many ways MSD has made enormous strides toward true integration, especially when compared to districts that have similar demographics. However, the goal of this book is also to show where the district still has work to do. One challenge for the district, from the time of the merger implementation in 1972 to today, has been to avoid the tendency to respond to the threat of White flight by prioritizing the needs of White parents and students in the name of preserving diversity. One of the principal themes we will address throughout this book is the extent to which the district's ongoing and successful efforts to discourage White flight and maintain a high level of White student enrollment have taken a toll on the district's efforts to provide the highest possible level of access of Black and Latinx students to a high-quality education that recognizes and honors who they are and what they bring to the classroom.

Leadership has had to walk a fine line between catering to White families, especially at the high school level with tracking, and striving to create an inclusive educational atmosphere. There is a financial dimension to this complicated minuet, too. White families tend to have higher incomes than Black and Latinx families[3] and, therefore, they have greater capacity to enroll their children in private schools or even to move to nearby predominantly White and upper-income communities. In 2015, the median household income for non-Hispanic White households in Morristown and Morris Township was $109,869, while it was $133,633 for Asian households, $61,085 for Black households, and $54,523 for Hispanic households.[4] Ultimately, any outmigration of the White or Asian population could not only reduce student diversity, but also diminish resources for the Morris district schools.

Whites also dominate key leadership positions in the district, therefore enabling them to have greater influence on educational decisions. White mothers hold a disproportionate share of the leadership positions in the elementary school Home-School Associations and the Morris Educational Foundation, and on the school board. While part of the explanation is that White higher-income mothers may have more time and resources to volunteer in the schools, the fact remains that these positions allow them to influence policy and practice, which has been shown to benefit their children, often at the expense of others.[5] For example, tracking policies provide White students with differential access to high-level courses and programs. Not only that, but White students are the key beneficiaries of the honor roll and National Honor Society, STEM Academy, and admission to prestigious colleges.

As a Black social support staff member told us about Whites in Morris, "They have more power. They have the money. They have the Board of Education. They have the people in place who listen to them. That's why there's no need for White flight, because why would you move from a place where you have control?" This statement contradicts the culturally responsive educational leadership model, described in more detail below, as it shows that Morris is and has been controlled mostly by Whites. One might question whether diversity in the Morris schools "works" because White supremacy has never really been seriously questioned or threatened. Consequently, the burden on the school district is not only to avoid favoring White families, but also to encourage and support families and students of color that have been historically marginalized in the system to participate and have their voices heard when educational decisions are made.

It is important to note, however, that there has been some diversity in leadership over the years. For example, a Black woman named Linda Murphy, profiled in Chapter 4, was the Morristown High School vice principal and principal for the 10-year period between 2002–2012. She was instrumental in several policy changes aimed at increased equity and integration. Another example of at least some diversity in school leadership is the school board. Out of nine members, the longtime and current school board president is a Black male township resident, and there has been at least one Latina member represented on the board for the last 10–15 years.

The district has made several policy changes that are designed to lead to decreased within-school segregation by a student's race, SES, and perceived ability. A former teacher, parent, and current White school board member explained one way the district has increased equity:

> I've been on the board for 16 years and I've never heard anyone say,
> "Maybe we should separate this group or put them somewhere else."
> In fact, it's always the opposite. For example, we grouped [students] for
> math in 4th and 5th grades for many, many years and they said, "this
> doesn't make kids feel good necessarily," so we stopped that . . . and I
> still say that the way the creators started the Morris School District by
> integrating two school systems and switching the teachers around, it
> could have been very different, maybe just lip service, but it wasn't.

Indeed, the switch from homogeneous math groups that were racially identifiable to heterogeneous groups is an example of culturally responsive school leadership, as are the ways in which the district assigns students to elementary schools and the strong relationships forged between the community and the schools.

CULTURALLY RESPONSIVE SCHOOL LEADERSHIP

The lens of culturally responsive school leadership (CRSL) is useful for analyzing the diversity and equity work in MSD. Khalifa, Gooden, and Davis define CRSL as having several overarching goals, which are meant

to offset the tendency of schooling to dehumanize students and communities of color.[6] School leaders and teachers interested in creating humaniz-
ing educational environments must engage in and promote four tenets by:

1. participating in "critical self-awareness" of their own biases
   about race and social class, and requiring their teachers to do the
   same;
2. recruiting, retaining, and preparing teachers for culturally
   relevant teaching and curricula "in ways that result in improved
   student outcomes, but this must be done with cultural
   responsiveness;" [7]
3. promoting inclusive school environments where school staff
   "promote a climate that makes the whole school welcoming,
   inclusive, and accepting"[8] of all students; and
4. engaging in and maintaining relationships with community
   members and parents in culturally relevant ways.

Germane to the Morris context, leaders must strive to build their
schools and classrooms as communities of trust in ways that involve families and communities in the educational project. Educational leadership
and administration research recognizes that school reform (such as integration efforts) and community development should be aligned, and that
school-level leadership has powerful effects on student learning and on
staff motivation, especially in diverse settings.[9] Student achievement and
engagement are positively affected when school leadership actively works
toward the goal of being culturally responsive, "which include elements
of ongoing practices that address a continuing need and a changing demographic."[10,11] As Patrick Jenlink writes, equitable schools for all "are
those schools where race, ethnicity, gender, class, and sexual orientation
are recognized and valued as difference, rather than as a path to discrimination. Equitable schools are those schools where privilege is replaced by
social responsibility."[12]

Most literature, however, shows that *school leaders* and *teachers* respond to demographic shifts and increased diversity in race-neutral, and
oftentimes negative and divisive, ways toward students and families of
color.[13] Findings from this literature show that, as schools diversify, White
families use their privilege and power in the system to advantage their
own children by challenging school choice policy or attendance boundaries, by resisting de-tracking initiatives, or by influencing placements in
high-level courses or programs.[14] As Amanda Lewis and John Diamond
document in their study of a racially diverse high school, school district
routines (e.g., discipline) and taken-for-granted practices (e.g., tracking)
unintentionally lead to racial inequality within "good" schools. Lewis
and Diamond concluded:

[W]e have no doubt that most of those working in schools are operating with the best of intentions. Such good intentions, however, are not enough. The kind of impact broad cultural belief systems have on classroom dynamics are often at the level of the unconscious—only by bringing them to the surface can we begin to confront them.[15]

Where our study departs from Lewis and Diamond's research is that, instead of defending and protecting the system as it is, we found current district administrators who were talking in hopeful ways about change and a "commitment" to fix what is "broken." Indeed, while color-blind ideology and White dominance are still present, the Morris district is starting to move toward the goal of true integration by changing practices and policies that lead to inequitable access, opportunities, and outcomes by race and SES.

For example, when we asked a staff member of the Morris Educational Foundation about persistent racial achievement gaps, she responded:

I don't know the answer. . . .There's just something that has to be fixed but my perception is, let's look at the data and see why this is and fix it. I think there would be a commitment to do that. I don't think there's any sentiment of a lack of caring about it, you know? . . . . It's not like our community to be like, "We don't care."

The question is whether this deep caring about and commitment to equity and integration always gets translated into action.

In the next sections of the chapter, using the CRSL framework, we will illustrate our findings on school leader perspectives regarding what it takes to build a successfully diverse school system throughout the long and still ongoing postmerger period. That period had three distinct stages: (1) the initial phase-in of the new district and its newly constituted school board; (2) the so-called "race riot" in 1974 and its immediate aftermath; and (3) the long continuing journey toward "true integration" and its promise of redemption.

Early on, we seek to paint a balanced picture of the 1974 racial incident, referred to by some as a "race riot," which surprised and traumatized the Morris community. We also consider its enduring impact on the district's reputation, and the ongoing leadership work that promotes and advances the critical mass of community support for the district's diversity today. We show how these early events combine to tell the backstory of the district's historical and contemporary significance, and also illuminate how its legacy, both positive and negative, lives on in the community today. Woven throughout are examples of administrators' attempts to try to find a balance between (1) maintaining the White student numbers and prioritizing their needs and experiences (often at the expense of others), and (2) striving to create equitable access to opportunities with the goal of more integrated teaching and learning environments. In the Lessons Learned section, we provide useful strategies for school officials, education advocates, lawyers, policymakers, and others to draw upon when developing desegregation and integration plans in their own contexts.

THE POSTMERGER PERIOD

As we described in Chapter 2, the New Jersey Education Commissioner Carl Marburger ordered the merger of the Morristown and Morris Township school districts in 1971. The purpose was to prevent *de facto* segregation caused by housing patterns and changing demographics and to ensure racial balance in the schools. The merger was formalized in 1972, a school board for the new district was elected that same year, and the administrative work of getting the new district up and running was addressed.

The early years were not easy, though. *The New York Times* reported in 1973 on the "painful" and "agonizing" process of the forced merger, which the newspaper said had been "plagued by controversies and numerous [law] suits."[16] According to our interviews and to media reports at the time, there was certainly opposition to the merger and predictions of massive White flight—mostly from township residents. However, the township was actually more split on the merger issue than some reports have made it seem.

When we asked respondents about whether or not White flight occurred postmerger, no one recalled that happening. As a White Morris Township resident explained, "I think a lot of people that really believed in public school systems kept their kids in public school. A lot of them couldn't afford to do anything else and I don't think they were going to just up and move." A Black, longtime township resident concurred when she said White flight "didn't happen because at the time of the merger, industry was coming to Morris County—Bell Labs, AT&T, all of these other companies, and they were bringing Blacks in who could afford these houses" in Morristown. As Figure 3.1 shows, decennial census data indicate that the White population in MSD did decrease during the 1970s, but that it was minimal. In 1970, prior to the merger, 86% of the population in the area that would become the MSD was White. While this dropped to 83% in 1980, the reality is that the proportion of the White population was decreasing in neighboring towns as well. In fact, the proportion of White residents dropped from 97% to 95% across Morris County.

Respondents who experienced the merger firsthand spoke about the "fertile ground" in which the merger took place, both in terms of the

Figure 3.1. Population Change 1970–2010, Morris School District

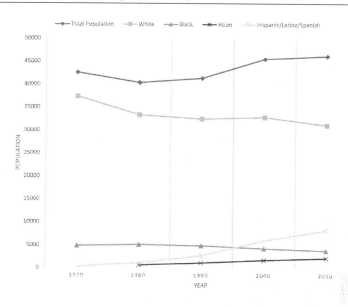

people and the place. At the time of the merger, an influential group of residents came together to support public education and spearhead the effort to regionalize the separate K–8 Morris Township school district with Morristown's K–12 district. This pro-merger group of residents feared that, if the mostly White township pulled its students out of Morristown High School, the school would eventually become an all-Black school. They worried that, if the township built a separate high school and stopped sending its students to Morristown, there would be rampant White flight. Steve Wiley, a pro-merger advocate whose story was highlighted in Chapter 1, was quoted in a 2015 local newspaper about the reason he pushed for the regional school district: "Separate, segregated high schools would hasten White flight from Morristown, dooming it to the same turmoil afflicting New Jersey's urban centers."[17]

Wiley's fears about high school segregation causing White flight from Morristown were not unfounded. The same White flight phenomenon was happening in other urban areas across the state. The federal government's 1967 Kerner Commission's report included a section on Northern New Jersey's urban "ghettos"—Newark, Jersey City, Elizabeth, Englewood, Plainfield, Paterson, and New Brunswick, saying, "In each of the ghettos the Negro felt himself surrounded by an intransigent wall of Whites" who were moving in droves to the surrounding suburbs. When White families left urban schools, the schools left behind often suffered from under-enrollment, less funding and resources, and less access to high-quality teaching and coursework. The Kerner Report made it clear that a main reason for the riots was the inequities Black residents faced in accessing high-quality education, jobs, and housing.

The Report for Action produced by the Governor's Select Commission on Civil Disorder in New Jersey (the "Lilley Commission" after its chair Robert Lilley) just a few months later in February 1968 took a related, but somewhat different, approach to the problem. Although it focused primarily on Newark and the causes, consequences and remedies of the civil disorders there, in its Introduction the Lilley Commission report ascribed the troubles in New Jersey to one core problem in American society—"the place of the Negro in American society."[18] In the Commission's view, immediate, serious, and sustained action was essential. And the Commission made clear what action NJ needed then and what action the state did not need:

- We need fewer promises and more action from political leaders and government officials.
- We need more principals, teachers, and guidance counselors who want their students to succeed instead of expecting them to fail.
- Suburban residents must understand that the future of their communities is inextricably linked to the fate of the city, instead of harboring the illusion that they can maintain invisible walls or continue to run away.[19]

In words that reverberate strongly today, the Commission stressed that "law and order can prevail only in conditions of social justice," and that "old and outdated approaches" must be abandoned and "new solutions sought in the metropolitan and regional context."[20] At the heart of the cure is to heal the divide between people because "inherent in these problems is the virus of segregation."[21] While there is no way to know if Wiley or his contemporaries were directly influenced by the Kerner Report or the Lilley Commission Report, the ideas behind his arguments to merge urban, Black and White Morristown with suburban mostly White Morris Township seem aligned with both.

Like other school desegregation battles fought across the country, the integration movement in Morris started with a strong group of supporters. This pro-merger group included fair housing advocates, the NAACP, the Urban League, school board members, educators, and the clergy. In Jennifer Holme and Kara Finnigan's recent book on regional approaches to solving school segregation, one of the main suggestions for overcoming political (e.g., suburban) support of some of the policies that maintain the status quo of segregated and unequal schooling is by building diverse coalitions in which there is a common vision and a redefinition of the problem. The most compelling recommendation in their book, and highly relevant to the Morris case, is to have influential community leaders and advocacy groups as the face of the regional movement, a strategy that has proven to be important to the success of other grassroots desegregation movements; Minnie Liddell, leader of Concerned Parents of North St. Louis in the 1970s, is one such example.[22]

Similarly, as we explained in Chapter 2, community and advocacy leaders, such as Steve Wiley and Beatrice Jenkins in Morris, were instrumental in the success of school district regionalization. We found that the initial and long-lasting success of a desegregation movement is predicated on the mobilization and cooperation of a visionary group of advocates that keep the momentum going for years to come—which we show in Morris is still going strong today.

Merger Order and Implementation

As we have described, the commissioner's order of merger was in 1971, and the merger went into effect the following year in 1972. Rick, a White male, was just hired as an administrator at Morristown High at this time, having been a teacher at the school for 11 years. When we interviewed Rick we asked him about his memories of the merger, and his recollection was that "there was some ill feeling at that time. Morristown had a growing Black population and it was projected that that population would increase." As we heard from many people who experienced the merger firsthand, he explained that "people from Morristown seemed to be accepting." Yet, in the township the White residents were split on the issue of building a separate high school with some wanting to "be with their own kind" and others advocating for the merger referendum.

Rick went on to explain that this period in our history had been marred by race riots and angry protests between Blacks and Whites throughout the country. Nevertheless, Rick said students at Morristown High got along well. He pointed out that one place in which students were truly integrated was sports: "There was a wonderful rapport, oddly enough, between Black students and White students at the high school. I think primarily stimulated by athletics. . . . But there was basically a good feeling, but I think everybody—adults as well as students—were exposed to all of these events taking place in the country and close to home as well."

These events that Rick was referring to included the 1954 *Brown v. Board of Education* decision to dismantle school segregation, and the White protests and violence that erupted in cities like Charlotte, Boston, and Louisville.[23] Closer to home, the 1967 Newark and Plainfield uprisings were fresh in the minds of many residents. As indicated previously, the federal Kerner Commission Report was released that same year with the following recommendation regarding schools: "to sharply increase efforts to eliminate de facto segregation in our schools through substantial federal aid to school systems seeking to desegregate either within the system or in cooperation with neighboring school systems."[24] In the fall of 1971, "dozens of school districts started the school year with new student assignment plans, most of them involving busing."[25] The result was massive White flight, especially in city school systems. For example, in 1973, the first year that Memphis began busing students to achieve integration, 20,000 White students left the city or enrolled in private schools.[26] Morris was ordered to consolidate districts for racial balance purposes during this same time period. Not surprisingly, the prediction from antimerger residents was White flight and a segregated all-Black district. Their predictions proved wrong, however, and it is important to understand why.

When asked about the reason Morris Township wanted to stop sending students to Morristown High and build its own high school, Rick responded that it had to do with several factors, including the 1972 end of the 10-year sending-receiving relationship between the township and Morristown, as well as the location and access to more acreage in the township for athletic fields. Another factor was "clearly" about race. As Morristown's Black population grew, Rick's view was that some township residents

> . . . clearly wanted their own area. I'd call it [Morristown] a ghetto, but that's probably inappropriate. They [White people] wanted their thing, and I think that the rise of the Black population was a threat. I personally believe that people in the township were concerned with how the Black population in Morristown was going to hinder the aspirations and growth, learning growth, of the students in the township.

When we questioned Rick on whether some township residents were actually concerned about the high school's educational quality or if it was really about the student demographic changes, he concluded, "the high school had a wonderful reputation with all sorts of programs and creativity. They just wanted to be with their own kind."

At the elementary school level, he remembered the schools as having, "a mixture [of students by race] and everybody seemed to be happy about it." Rick explained that, in Morristown and in the township, most students were already being bused, thus potentially dodging the antibusing protests that occurred in other cities after desegregation orders.

The Princeton Plan

After the merger was ordered, the newly formed district eliminated the neighborhood school student assignment policy in both the town and township, thereby breaking the ties between neighborhood segregation

Table 3.1. Black Student Enrollment in Morris Township and Morristown Paired Schools, 1971

School/Location	Percent Black
Woodland/township	0
Thomas Jefferson/town	48
Normandy Park/township	9
George Washington/town	45
Alfred Vail/township	10
Lafayette/town	42
Sussex Avenue/township	5
Hillcrest/township	1
Alexander Hamilton/town	35

and school segregation. The school board decided to implement the "Princeton Plan" to diversify elementary schools by pairing a primary (K–2) school with an intermediate (3–5) school—with one located in the town and the other located geographically close by in the township (see Figure 1.2). Another key aspect of the Princeton Plan was to reassign teachers to different schools. These decisions were made deliberately to avoid teacher bias in former Morristown vs. Morris Township school placements, and to avoid neighborhood school segregation—particularly in what used to be the all-Black central area of town that is now mostly Latinx, historically referred to as The Hollow. These historical decisions made by district leadership also tie back to the overarching argument in this book, namely that to produce and maintain stable and balanced integration across schools there must be student assignment policies that do not re-segregate students across the district's schools.

According to the *Jenkins* lawsuit, the urban-suburban neighborhood schools reflected a stark racial divide, with higher concentrations of Black students enrolled in Morristown schools than in Morris Township schools because of residential segregation (see Table 3.1 for the proportion of the Black student population at each set of geographically paired schools).[27] A point that the petitioners made was how geographically close the town and township schools were to each other to make the case that distance to school was a nonissue. See Figure 1.2, which shows that the distance between each of the paired schools is no more than one mile.

As the name suggests, in 1948 the Princeton Plan had been developed in Princeton, New Jersey. A year after New Jersey had incorporated into its new state constitution a unique provision barring segregation in the public schools, Princeton adopted this plan to foster diversity in its segregated elementary schools. Under the Princeton Plan, schools were grouped by grade level, rather than geography, as a way to achieve diversity. Albert E. Hinds, a Black activist and longtime Princeton resident, was interviewed for a documentary on the 50-year anniversary of the plan, and had this to say about the segregated school system: "The government realized that there was inferiority being placed upon us and enough in government had the conscience to say, let's change it and give the Blacks a better opportunity."[28] Howard Waxman was the principal of the segregated all-Black elementary school before the Princeton Plan began. His widow also was interviewed for the documentary and stressed how important it was for Howard to prepare Black students and Black teachers for what was to come in the integrated school environment:

> To him, this was important for him to prepare these young people, these students and teachers to understand what was happening. It was not going to be a very easy situation. It was going to be one of give and take, of compromise, but of trying to understand that being a part of this was going to lead to the welfare of all concerned.[29]

Many districts across the country adopted the Princeton Plan for cost-effectiveness rather than diversity purposes. Importantly, MSD augments the use of the Princeton Plan to achieve racial diversity in schools with a geographical dimension—by designating the center of town as an open assignment area because it was, and still is, where many low-income Black and Latinx residents live. Students living in this area are bused to various schools across the district to achieve diversity. Every other assignment area is zoned for a particular elementary school located within one of the attendance zones radiating out from the center like a pie. This means that many students are assigned schools that are typically not within walking distance, that are not necessarily the closest school geographically to their home, and that may require students to be bused or driven across town-township lines (see Figures 1.2 and 1.3).

When you compare other racially "diverse" districts in New Jersey, such as Montclair or South Orange–Maplewood, with Morris, they have a higher level of within-district segregation, as measured by the Theil's entropy index. This means that children in Montclair and South Orange–Maplewood are less likely to interact with children of different racial and ethnic backgrounds than children in the MSD. Furthermore, exposure and isolation rates (see Figures 3.2 and 3.3), demonstrate that children in MSD attend schools that are nearly perfectly representative of the overall district demographics; conversely, children across most of New Jersey frequently attend schools where their own racial/ethnic identity is disproportionately higher than the state average.[30]

Figure 3.2 shows that the average Black student in MSD attends a school that is 48% White, 39% Hispanic, 9% Black, and 4% Asian. The

Figure 3.2. Morris School District 2018–2019 Exposure and Isolation Rates

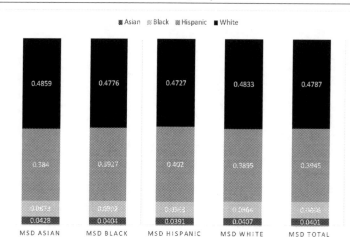

average Asian, Hispanic, and White students also attend schools that are nearly identical to this profile. However, Figure 3.3 shows that the average Black student in NJ attends a school that is 21% White, 30% Hispanic, 43% Black, and 6% Asian despite the State's demographic profile of 44% White, 30% Hispanic, 16% Black, and 11% Asian. It is worth reiterating that the district demographics in MSD closely mirror those of New Jersey as a whole.

As Rucker Johnson pointed out, "Any solution that attempts to address schooling without addressing housing is bound to fail."[31] However, this is not the case in MSD. We argue that school districts can, and must, circumvent neighborhood segregation by devising student assignment policies that intentionally result in integrated schools. In Morris, as one White parent said, "it is an effort here [to desegregate elementary schools], but it's not an effort on the part of the citizen. That's taken care of by the school district, so it's not at the burden of me, and everyone realizes that whichever elementary [school] your child goes to, there's a balance." In other words, the district bypasses residential segregation by utilizing the Princeton Plan and the open assignment area instead of relying on neighborhood school enrollments or allowing parental school choice. Even with the presence of segregated neighborhoods, demographic change, and gentrification, the Morris district elementary schools remain racially and socioeconomically balanced because Morris' geography-based student assignment plan can accommodate those changes.

While we did hear reports of families attempting to concentrate themselves in White and affluent neighborhoods within the district requesting school transfers or applying to the Normandy Park magnet school, the Princeton Plan is effective in stopping individual families

Figure 3.3 New Jersey 2018–2019 Exposure and Isolation Rates

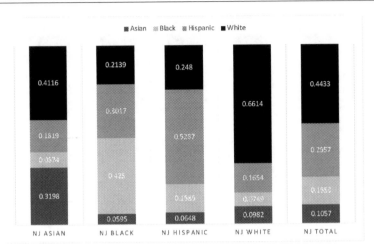

from self-segregating in certain schools because there is no neighborhood school policy. A current elementary school principal told us that she has heard that higher income families will try to move into the neighborhood closer to the elementary school on the township side. Yet, even if that is the case, she explained how the district achieves diversity in each of the K–2 and 3–5 schools:

> I've looked at the statistics and people keep saying "Oh, statistically that's not true, they [another school] have just as many free and reduced-lunch students as you do." There's an open enrollment area so that's how they try to balance it, so even if a whole bunch of people do move over there who are more affluent and White, then they'll send more people from the open enrollment area there. That open enrollment area tends to be an area I think that does have a lot of Hispanic members of the community. So I think it's this continuous balancing act because you don't want to get to a tipping point where you have so many poor students or so many minority students in one school and not another where people would not want to go to that school. Perceptions are pretty clear with that.

Indeed, school choice research clearly shows that when parents have deregulated choice options, without diversity goals, it leads to increased segregation and inequality.[32]

A major benefit of having diverse elementary schools is that students are exposed to diversity beginning in kindergarten. Research has shown that exposure to diversity at any age, but particularly at a young age, is vital for developing intergroup understanding, empathy, and breaking down of stereotypes. [33] Rucker Johnson's research found "that greater childhood exposure to individuals of other races can reduce the anxiety and stress experienced in interactions with members of those groups."[34] Racial identity affects school performance in a number of ways. Research by Pedro Noguera, Beverley Tatum, and others have shown that teacher-student racial matches influence how much students are engaged, whether they believe in their ability to achieve, and how they will be treated in the classroom.[35]

There are also academic benefits to attending diverse as opposed to segregated schools. For example, one study found that reading levels increased for kindergarten and 1st-grade students when the school had less of a concentration of low-SES students, and more racial diversity.[36] Another study found similar benefits for math skills when comparing students who attended racially and SES diverse schools versus students who enrolled in predominantly Black and/or Latinx, low-SES schools.[37] This level of exposure to racial and SES diversity at such a young age is not the case in most diverse districts; in fact, because of segregated neighborhoods that feed into elementary schools, the first exposure to diversity can be at the middle or high school level. We heard that Morris' situation makes for a smoother transition to middle school and high school because the students have been educated in diverse classrooms throughout their K–5 educational careers.

Racial Unrest Postmerger

According to teachers and administrators we interviewed, race relations after the merger were generally positive. The high school student population did not undergo substantial demographic change postmerger because the predominantly White students from the township and Morris Plains had already been attending Morristown High as part of each community's sending-receiving relationship. Despite the racial harmony, 2 years after the merger, in 1974, there was what most people described as a "race riot" at the high school. Teachers, students, and administrators at the high school that day explained to us that the fight happened because of an incident between some White and Black students at the Assumption Church annual fundraiser carnival on a Friday evening, which spilled over to Morristown High School on Monday morning. Rick remembered hearing that:

> There were words between some White kids and some Black kids. Now, there were several stories passed around at that time, one being that there was a friendship involving a young lady. So it was, "leave my girlfriend alone" kind of stuff. Then there was a little bit of a tussle there and I guess whoever was in charge—I don't know

whether it was police—calmed it down, but it . . . that was May the 3rd, which was a Friday. Then it seemed to escalate, or ferment, if you will, over the weekend, and then on the following Monday, the incident occurred.

He explained that the fight started in the cafeteria and then spilled out of the building to the front of the school. Apparently, some students had gone into the woodshop and gotten boards to use as baseball bats. Several staff members, including himself, were hit from behind with the boards, and a few students had minor injuries. The buses came and took students home right away, and the school was closed to students for the rest of the week.

The staff reported to school the next day to come up with solutions because, as Rick said, "We were really ignorant. . . . Everybody had their own opinion. Some of those opinions I suspect bordered on personal bias. Some of the resolutions on how to deal with this and how to deal with the kids were laughable. The one that sticks in my mind is an English teacher who said in a group meeting, 'We need to meet with the students, break them up into small groups when they return to school and go outside and plant geraniums.'"

The solution that they decided to implement when the students returned was to ask the coaches and their diverse sports teams to, as Rick commented, "release some of the tension." The White baseball and football coaches—Harry Shatel and John Chironna—who had helped their teams win many state championships were highly respected in the Black and White communities, and were charged with talking to their players about the racial uprising and getting the viewpoint of the student body. He explained, "We had the students go into the auditorium and the football players and baseball players basically said something to the effect of, 'We had a bad time here. There's a lot of reasons why it happened. We want to be sure that it doesn't continue and we want to do things differently.'" Perhaps not surprisingly, Rick described the aftermath as being "very awkward [because] there were people who felt that this never would have happened if the township had its own high school." He thought the delay in the racial unrest, 2 years after the merger, was due to the fact that they did not think they had a big problem with race relations so they did not confront race openly with the students. But they did have a problem, and it surfaced on that day in 1974.

This avoidance of discussing and dealing with race directly is an enduring problem that respondents talked about. As a current high school teacher of English as a Second Language said to us:

I think that if there's one thing I wish the district could do, I wish that they took the issue of race by the horns and really addressed it. You know, I wish they held race workshops. I wish that they made these numbers more public. I wish that they made the accomplishments of our minority students more well-known so that when there is a news article about a Latino kid or a Black kid that got into a fight, it doesn't scare everyone. But I know that those are very sensitive issues.

Indeed, what school leaders in 1974 did not expect was the long-lasting impact that the race-based incident would have on the school's reputation. Even today, we heard that real estate agents "guide away" potential buyers from the MSD, or at least they do not correct misperceptions that their clients might have of the district. Rick, whose wife was a real estate agent in the area for decades, told us, "I can tell you first-hand that incident influenced real estate big time. My wife who is now retired was an agent, and she's had many experiences where other agents will say, 'What was your husband's feeling about this? Who was right and who was wrong?' There were people who were guided away from buying in Morristown because of that high school incident, and the same thing for the township."

During our interviews with teachers, parents, and students, we heard stories about the negative outside perception of the district, mostly related to safety concerns. For example, an alumnus of Morristown High and current parent said that she went out to dinner recently with parents from other White communities who were shocked that she worked in Morristown. She said they thought there should be metal detectors at the high school.

At the end of the interview with Rick, we asked him to rate the success of the merger from 1 to 10, to which he quickly answered:

> I think the merger is probably a 12. I'm sincere about that. I think it showed the population in Morristown that we do care about students regardless of their color and regardless of their religious affiliation. I think it served as a lesson to the people in the township that were antimerger that you can have people who are diverse working together cooperatively and producing a product, and that indeed the *quality of the product in a school really depends on diversity*. That's a gift, not easily recognized because people I think have a tendency to hang with their own, whatever they consider, because that's easy. [Emphasis added]

Perhaps surprisingly to some, Rick had only good things to say about the high school's diversity and quality of education, despite being at the high school the day of the racial incident in 1974.

Changing Mindsets Postmerger

Three people from Morris Township that we interviewed who grew up being antimerger have since reevaluated their position on the matter. Even a former Morris Township mayor, named Tracy, who has grandchildren that attend the Morris schools, said that her father and husband were both against the merger at the time "because they liked how things were." She decided not to send her own children to the Morris schools because of the "turmoil" associated with the merger. However, Tracy characterized herself now as one of the district's "biggest cheerleaders, and you couldn't have told me that 45 years ago." She considered the merger as "probably the best thing to happen to our town and Morristown."

Tracy also said some people were upset about the busing and preferred neighborhood schools. Even though the farthest distance on the bus was 4 or 5 miles, people preferred to walk to school. This is a common excuse of many other progressive, suburban White parents who oppose urban-suburban school desegregation.[38] As Nikole Hannah-Jones recently wrote in *The New York Times*, "The school bus, treasured when it was serving as a tool for segregation, became reviled only when it transformed into a tool of integration. . . . Busing did not fail. We did."[39] Yet, in MSD it succeeded.

MAINTAINING A DELICATE BALANCE OF DIVERSITY: "I HAD TO WALK A FINE LINE WITH HOW WE PROMOTED THE DISTRICT"

What is it about the Morris district and the broader community that has kept it racially diverse for so long? Given Morristown High's negative outside reputation brought on by the 1974 racial unrest at the high school and the fact that many previously desegregated districts across the country have since re-segregated, MSD's continued commitment to integration is surprising. Thomas Ficarra, who served as superintendent in Morris between 2002 and 2014, told us that he laughed when people said, "It is something in the water." His story reflects the kind of culturally responsive school leadership behavior needed to attract and maintain a delicate balance of diversity in the schools over time.

Before his 12-year superintendency at Morris, Ficarra had worked in large school districts with mostly Black and Latinx students, such as Elizabeth. After retiring from Morris in 2014, he was hired as interim superintendent in the Hamilton Public Schools from 2015 to 2017 and in the South-Orange Maplewood district from 2018 until 2019. His strategy at MSD is reflected in the fourth CRSL tenet, namely, to develop strong community-school partnerships:

> I would say 30% of my energy, maybe more, went into caring for the community. . . . I used to have three and sometimes four Key Communicators dinner parties at my house [each school year] where we would invite over 100 people to my house for dinner . . . and

answer those phone calls when they came in and build those relationships and feed and care for every segment of that community
as best we could, keeping an eye on the fact that at any moment in
time it could all unravel.

It is true that, from the time of the merger until now, the White student population has remained the largest of any subgroup. This is a remarkable feat especially when compared to the larger context of New
Jersey where the White student population is currently 43%, and where
demographically changing suburban districts are often at risk of flipping
to become predominantly Black or Latinx.[40] In fact, everyone we spoke
to either explicitly or implicitly referred to White flight as a threat to the
community and to the overall success of the schools. Respondents talked about the fact that White, high-income residents have private school
options in the area. However, district and community leaders—from realtors to police officers to administrators and teachers—worked hard to
keep the diversity intact and going strong.

Threat of White Flight

Ficarra said that the district's middle school had been the point of exit for
many students and their families, possibly because some private schools
started at that level or because of the negative reputation the high school
had, or a little bit of both. During Ficarra's tenure, he turned those figures
around with his relationship-building outreach efforts. As a result, the
White enrollment in the high school increased by 18% between 2000 and
2015. He explained:

> There was White flight, and I'm not tooting my own horn, but I
> lived every day conscious that . . . every decision that was made was
> made knowing that I had a diverse community and I couldn't swing
> radically left or radically right. I had to walk a fine line of how we
> promote the district and one of the things that I got a wonderful
> response about was how we had one of the highest per-pupil costs
> around. I would stand up in front of the community when the bud-
> get came around and say our schools are a reflection of the commu-
> nity, we have kids that want to go to Harvard and we have kids that
> come in here where their parents do not speak English, and we have
> to provide a quality program for every one of them at every level
> and that costs more money than it does at the community next door,
> and they would support that.

The Key Communicators dinner parties are a prime example of building communities of trust. By inviting families and the community in to

make decisions about the schools, share successes, and build relationships and trust, Ficarra was embodying culturally responsive-sustaining leadership. According to Ficarra, local realtors were particularly important guests because they could spread the word about the benefits of diversity, as well as the great programming and special accomplishments at the high school. He even started inviting realtors into the high school during school hours for tours.

Realtor Program

One of the district administrators, named Helen, guides the realtor tours, works with realtors, and talks to families who are considering moving to Morristown—often childless couples moving from New York City, or families being relocated from other parts of the country for their jobs. To combat any negative perception of the high school, Helen provides these annual open house tours for local realtors; she said, "They seem to really get a tremendous benefit . . . because getting them in to see the high school while it's running is really important."

Helen's perception, though, was that the realtors are challenged by the fact that all of the neighboring communities have "lily-white populations and high SAT scores, it's easier to sell a house there and the houses are more expensive there. . . . I think when they're able to get them [prospective buyers] to call me, or the schools it's fine." She said it is tricky because realtors are not allowed to talk about schools subjectively because of the potential of violating steering and fair housing laws. They can, however, correct any misperceptions that incoming families might have about their school choices by referring them to third-party information. The reality is that many neighboring districts do have higher average SAT scores—MSD has the 11th highest Reading and Writing SAT scores in the county and the 13th highest Math SAT scores in the county of 39 school districts—but this ranking does nothing to adjust for the persistent racial and socioeconomic achievement gaps associated with the examination.[41]

Helen has heard, though, that at open houses potential buyers will ask realtors about the schools, and the realtor will say, "Well, they're fine, but there's plenty of private schools. There are plenty of private schools nearby that are great." She said that realtors assume that is what parents want based on the price of the home, and that there are seven private schools in the Morristown sending area. Helen also reiterated that longtime families who have been here for generations, some of whom were against the merger growing up, are realizing that Morristown High has a lot to offer the community and their own children and grandchildren and are choosing public instead of top private schools.

Realtors we spoke to talked about Tom Ficarra's efforts to communicate to the community about what was happening in the schools because of the negative outside reputation and rumors based on race. Diana is a realtor who sent her children to the Morris district. She described the superintendent's Key Communicators dinner party:

> He had a dinner once a quarter at his home where he cooked for 100 people. He's a great Italian cook. He would invite people from different walks of life. I was just the real estate person and [the] former mayor, policemen, teachers. . . . He would share with us what was going on in the district. The district has 11 buildings, so there's always a lot going on. The point was to get positive PR coming out of it because that's always been an issue.

When we asked Diana why public relations was an "issue," she said that it has to do with Morris' lower test scores compared to neighboring districts like Chatham, Mountain Lakes, and Mendham (see Table 2.1). She explained, "There's a lot of wealth here and there's a plethora of private schools, so, if you don't like the public school, you could go to any number of private schools. So a lot of the people in the [Morristown and Morris Township area] 07960 zip code want their children to go to those private high schools because they think that their chances of getting into better colleges are better."

As Helen, Diana, and others explained, relocation companies and people who work there will tell new families not to buy in Morristown "because of the schools—that Chatham and Madison were the safer resale towns and just focus there, particularly Chatham." Diana said that part of the realtor program at Morristown High School is to give them information about the schools to "dispel that myth." When we asked where the negative attitude about the schools comes from, she replied, "Because of the diversity and because of the press, because every time *New Jersey Monthly* or one of the newspapers comes out with these ratings, you really have to read between the lines." These ratings are often calculated using standardized test scores (ELA and math proficiency rates), which skew positively to the predominantly White, high SES schools/districts.

Ultimately, Diana believed that the district does *not* do enough PR. She asked:

> Does the average person know that Morristown High is the only place if you have a kid that wants to do fencing and be on a swim team? They have their own pool. And also, being involved in a radio station or a TV station. My daughter ran first the radio station and then the TV station! She produced shows. I mean, how many high school kids get to produce an actual TV show or radio show out of their high school?

George Jenkins, profiled in Chapter 2, whose mother was a major part of the *Jenkins* lawsuit, also spoke about the high school realtor tour. He has been a realtor in Morris County for decades. "I take a tour of the high school every 2 or 3 years because they offer that through [Helen's office]. She opens it up to the real estate community so that the other realtors who aren't as familiar with the system as I am will have a better perspective because oftentimes some communities get a bad reputation, but it's not based on anything. It's just rumors."

George told us that 50% of his business is with people who are moving in and around the area and are familiar with the schools. The other 50% are "people that haven't had a clue, never heard of Morristown before their company said 'you're being transferred out here.'" That population, George said, is the one he has the most difficulty convincing that being in the MSD is a good thing for them and their families.

> The people that grew up here obviously have a much better understanding of what's going on here, and very rarely do I find people who grew up here who have been in the area that have that same type of prejudice against the Morris School District. So I have to sell them not only a house, but I have to sell them on the value of living in this community, and I have to sell them on the Morris School District because they'll come to me with phrases like "we want to be anywhere but Morristown High School."

As we described in Chapter 2, George basically believes the realtor's role is to gather information designed to help clients achieve their objectives, not to steer them in any one direction. However, he strongly believes that, if someone's "perception is not consistent with what we know as reality, we think we have an obligation to let you know that, and you can make up your own mind what you want to do with it, but at least be factual." He explained that other realtors "fall into the trap" of just showing families certain communities on their "list." What sets him apart from his colleagues is that he has a "personal stake" in selling the community and the schools to families that are not even considering homes in the MSD. George goes the extra mile with prospective buyers, even driving them to the schools to meet and talk to the principals.

> There are people that are set and that's fine. But there are people who have said, "You know, we need to look into it further." And if I have people who I think are on the fence, I would just say, "Tell you what. Your kid's going to be in what grade? Let's go talk to the principal." Most realtors won't—they're interested in selling a house. The last thing they're trying to do is sell a community. I've always been taught to sell a community. It'll be easier to find them a house.

George feels like he has to "sell" the diversity in Morris to many prospective clients, and that, after they hear about all the benefits of Morris, some of them are in "awe" because "nobody told us that." In this way, he is an important member of the core group of visionary leaders practicing CRSL that do the work of helping to attract diverse families to Morristown and to the public school system.

When we asked the current superintendent, Mackey Pendergrast, if he has continued the realtor tours, he said, yes, they had 30 realtors come to their high school tour last spring. He also was invited to do individual presentations at real estate offices. Keller-Williams called him and said that the realtors keep getting questions about Morristown, and asked him to come and provide more information. Pendergrast said that school district rankings are his biggest obstacle. He said the rankings are good for comparing apples to apples, or ranking the best homogenous school districts where, unlike Morris, one-third of the students are not economically disadvantaged. The superintendent even went to *New Jersey Monthly* and advised them to compare across the same subgroups instead of between groups and to redo their metrics (they said no, they have to sell papers). He said you cannot compare a student who just came from Guatemala with a kid in a million-dollar home. Yet, he did say that the parents in Morris understand this situation with lower test scores and rankings. He boasted that, nonetheless: "We have more kids taking Physics and Calculus than other districts in Morris County."

Changing Perceptions of What A Good Community Is

We found a key component to the ongoing success of the district is the increasing belief in the benefits of diversity, especially by White families. Helen explained that over the years she has noticed a changing perception of what a good community is: "People have the opposite perception of what a good community is. [Instead of wanting a racially homogeneous district,] a diverse community is becoming something that people are intentionally seeking rather than avoiding." Helen believes that people are more "enlightened" today and "recognize how important diversity is for a strong community":

> People are slowly recognizing that this is a good thing, that a community is healthier and richer just like a garden is healthier and richer if you have different things there. I think in Morris County, probably more so than maybe upper Bergen County where most of this community is affluent and purely White, Morristown is . . . we're different. We're different, so if someone says, "I want to move to Morris County," and they're looking at SAT scores, average SAT scores, or "I want to walk past a school and see only kids that look like my kids"—it's difficult.

When we spoke with the current superintendent, he reiterated Helen's point that people choose Morristown intentionally for the diversity. They are seeking out a multicultural place to live, Pendergrast said. Parents will tell him that they chose Morristown because it is similar to where they grew up in Brooklyn or Montclair. People have lots of options, according to the participants in our study, but moving to Morristown is unique compared to the White communities that make up most of the county.

As one realtor told us, more and more parents are realizing that the "test scores [in MSD] are not the highest," as compared to "lily-white places like Chatham, Madison, or Millburn" because of the diversity. Parents also realize that test scores are not the only indicator of educational success. There are nonacademic outcomes that parents are also looking for. For instance, during the interview with Peter, a White father who relocated to New Jersey for his job about 10 years ago, he explained how he and his wife weighed the pros and cons of the Morris district when choosing where to live and send their children to school:

> I mean, if you think about the other places we were looking [at] before we bought our house—Randolph, Madison, Summit—places where the middle school and the high school tend to be smaller, they tend to be much less diverse racially, ethnically and socioeconomically. They're higher performing as a result because of the way those things correlate . . . but both for pragmatic reasons about buying a house and what we could afford and also a sense that there was a lot of virtue in having our kids go to schools that better reflected the real world that they would be entering and the diversity of the country, and that they had a lot to learn and benefit from that experience, [we chose Morris].

As Peter implied, parents understand that Morris is ranked lower by *US News* or *New Jersey Monthly*, compared to more homogeneous and majority White districts "where everyone is the same," because of its diverse context—and the fact that socioeconomics are highly correlated with standardized test scores.

Ficarra had a hand in changing the reputation of the district within the community. He also tried to create more equity across the elementary schools by limiting the amount of fundraising that each school could do, and also by not allowing one HSA to purchase technology, such as smartboards, and another school not to be able to afford it. At the time of his retirement, he was quoted in a local newspaper as saying, "Our community is thriving because our schools are thriving. They are successful and diverse and attracting families here in droves."[42] He also passed down a powerful tradition to the next superintendent, Mackey Pendergrast, namely the importance of collaboration and involving all community stakeholders in the school decisionmaking process. He set a clear precedent about the importance of community buy-in and support for the work of the school district.

SUCCESSES AND CHALLENGES OF SCHOOL DIVERSITY

What was remarkable to us was the strong similarities that emerged about the importance of school diversity when comparing the historical data with the current interview data. Just like the postmerger period of the 1970s, there is a strong pro-public school contingency in the community that supports the district today, even as demographics have shifted. Instead of White and middle-class flight, as other districts have experienced when student demographics have changed, MSD's White student population has remained quite stable over the last decade. This phenomenon was captured in an interview with a school administrator, who said:

> I feel like in some communities, when people feel like the school is becoming more diverse, you actually see White flight out of schools. That hasn't happened here and that's a great thing, so that the schools have stayed diverse and you're not seeing everybody like, "Oh, well, we're all going to go to this other district." I mean, that happens consistently in a lot of places and that hasn't happened here. Because of that, we have maintained a really nice, diverse group of students and people in the community. [43]

Respondents had many theories about the reasons why the diversity has remained stable. Yet, most respondents believed people stay, or move to Morris, because of the high-quality education that students receive. Diversity is seen as a benefit, not a detriment.

Despite all the accolades the district has received, there are also persistent challenges to having racial and socioeconomic diversity in schools. For example, a long-term challenge has been to require teachers to participate in implicit bias training, and to simply discuss issues of race in the classroom. When we conducted focus groups with teachers at each of the schools, they consistently spoke highly about diversity in the district, and at the same time talked about the challenges brought about by diversity. Teachers participating in focus groups at the elementary school level described the district/school by saying such things as "very progressive school"; "very diverse school which I think is amazing"; "one of the great things about our district is that we're so diverse"; "we're a cultural tapestry"; "diversity is the norm"; or, "a place where we all learn to exist together." They also explained that people who grow up in Morristown have tremendous pride in the community, remain invested, and want their own children to experience "the real world" of racial, cultural, and religious diversity in the schools.

Yet, as one White male teacher told us, there are challenges to diversity that teachers are still trying to overcome because of the "forced merger," and negative outside perceptions after the "race riot":

> I've always said I think our district is a microcosm of the real
> world. When we decided to purchase a home we wanted it to be in
> Morristown because, as you move to the outer boroughs, it's pre-
> dominantly just one race. I wanted our daughters to grow up in an
> environment where it was a great, multicultural diversity. Now just
> on the real side of that—and again, being born and raised here—the
> real world is great, but because there are so many differences, there
> are some challenges. Our goal that we strive for is to celebrate our
> diversity. However, sometimes there are issues. They probably have
> made you aware of some of the race riots here in the Morris School
> District as a part of that forced merger. So we've come a long way. I
> still think we have a ways to go, but just to give you the holistic per-
> spective, I think it's a great district, but obviously we're still trying
> to move towards greatness in just celebrating our diversity.

When asked what the district is doing to celebrate diversity, this same teacher said it is hiring more teachers of color and bilingual staff to reflect the student population.

During another teacher focus group, elementary school teachers were quick to point out the many ways in which Morristown stands out when compared to other school districts in Morris County that are racially homogeneous, mostly White communities. They described how challenging and rewarding the experience has been to teach racially and SES-diverse student groups from Morristown and Morris Township. One veteran teacher commented:

> It's quite interesting because the district is an amalgam between
> the town and the township, and if you look at the demographics
> between the town and the township, there's a $50,000 difference
> in median income. So right there most people who may not know
> anything about Morristown can certainly grasp that statistic and
> begin to kind of play with it. What you're hearing described from us
> so far is the context for teaching here is very different than it is in
> other places. That is such, for me, a gift through the years, because
> I've gotten to work with so many different kinds of people. So as a
> teacher, as you evolve as an educator, you just take on a different
> point of view. I would actually, if I were to work in, say [a White
> community nearby], I would blow my brains out literally if I had

to work [in that district] because it is such a monoculture, and here we have this . . . it's constantly changed through the years, too because of its socioeconomic structure, the area that we call where the Neighborhood House is—the Neighborhood House was founded by Italian immigrants. It was then taken up gradually by African Americans. Gradually, then, it became more of a Latino community, and that varied, too, if you look more closely. It was the Columbians that came in first and then there were Dominicans. It's just . . . now we got a lot of kids from Africa. These are not the same kinds of backgrounds and communities, and that's another thing that we've had to learn. From our perspective, we actually structure our school and our classrooms very differently to try to meet all of these different needs. If you go into each of our classrooms, you're going to see a very different set-up, and that's on purpose. I think that's such a unique strength of the town and the township working together and yet at the same time it's not a problem. It's not something that's ever going to be fully resolved, that you can walk in and go, "This is what you do. This is America. This is what we deal with in America." That's very different from most of the communities in New Jersey.

This teacher's quote reflects the on-going work that diversity and integration require. Teachers, particularly at the elementary school level, also shared that they do a lot of community building at the schools to ensure all children feel included and develop friendships across lines of race and SES. As one teacher described, there are children who are "dirt poor to very, very affluent, but they blend together very well. They don't even realize it, which helps create strong classroom environments."

Teachers also described the many benefits that students get from being exposed to diversity, such as learning to help one another and to make sure that everyone is happy and feeling included. They said there is less competition over academics compared to other more homogeneous districts, and more of a focus on developing well-rounded students. One teacher said, "I think the culture is more, 'Let's help each other, we're a unit.'" Another replied, "Be who you are. That's what I like." A third teacher followed up by saying, "And the kids celebrate each goal [of their classmates], even though it might be a goal that was reached by that child years ago. I think they're just very supportive of each other in the room."

The middle school was described by teachers as the point when students tend to separate by race in their classes (because of tracking) and during lunchtime. During one focus group, teachers described some of the tensions between Black and Latinx students, especially when there was an influx of Latinx families in the early 2000s. As one teacher explained, "I would say 5–8 years ago, there was a getting-to-know-you type of thing, more than it was, 'Why are you here? Go back to your home country,' type of thing. It was more of a space issue really because of housing and jobs." Another teacher described an internal hierarchy that was formed among the Latinx students during lunchtime:

> They separate by race and they come back together in the high school because I guess they put it behind them. The middle school a lot of times, the kids went up there and they'd break off by where you came from, which Central [or South] American country you came from. They kind of had the hierarchy of who's better. Columbia was on top and Honduras was the bottom. They had names for each of them. Each lunch table kind of sat like that. I think that has pretty much dissipated up there [at the middle school]. It used to be like that for several years.

Currently, teachers reported that, if there is any tension among racial groups, it is handled immediately. They have friendship groups through the counselors and are taught empathy as part of the curriculum.

Tracking vs. De-tracking

The district has an inconsistent record in terms of practicing homogeneous ability grouping or tracking versus heterogeneous grouping or de-tracking. This inconsistency happens between the elementary, middle, and high school buildings. In elementary school, starting in 2016, students are de-tracked in English Language Arts and math. Yet, in middle school and high school, students are tracked into Advanced (A-level), Honors, or Advanced Placement (AP) classes, and these tracks are racially, socioeconomically, and linguistically segregated. MSD is aware of the problem and has made efforts to progress toward true integration, which we explain in more detail in Chapter 4, including eliminating the lowest B-level track in high school, using multiple measures for course placement decisions in middle school, and hiring a high school counselor to support students of color and make sure they are on track for college. Yet, in many respondents' eyes, there remains much work to be done to achieve true integration inside school walls.

Tracking practices at the elementary school level were changed during Ficarra's and Pendergrast's tenures. An elementary school leader named Melissa explained why the district decided to de-track the math groups, and which group of parents were initially against the switch:

> We had homogeneous math groupings and we did notice that in our homogeneous math groupings we had a majority of White students in the top two math groups. This year [2016], we have moved to

heterogeneous math groups in the homeroom and there was some concern —I would say mostly from White parents—that if our kids are all going to be mixed together for math, is that going to affect my student's learning in a negative way? We said no. We've been doing this for language arts all along and we'll differentiate instruction. So that's new this year. The reason that we didn't move to heterogeneous math groups sooner was the concern of more—I would say probably White, affluent—parents that their children wouldn't go forward as quickly.

This same school leader said that the current superintendent, Mackey Pendergrast, has pushed them to differentiate instruction more and use formative assessments, "so kids aren't stuck if they weren't in the highest math group in 3rd grade." Melissa concluded that de-tracking the curriculum is a good thing because you want everyone to have more opportunity to achieve. We also heard how K–5 de-tracking has a cumulative impact on increasing the racial and SES diversity in the middle school and high school Honors and AP classes.

Teachers also told us about some of the current superintendent's initiatives "to level the playing field." Instead of de-tracking the curriculum and creating heterogeneous groupings in all middle and high school classes like he did at the elementary school level, Pendergrast has decided to expand access to Honors level courses and create more personalized learning in which each student "ascends" at his or her own pace. New initiatives included expansion of the middle school Honors math class by offering 70 more seats. When asked about whether or not the subject of de-tracking ever comes up in the district, some teachers gave colorblind answers, such as, "It's not based on race or socioeconomic status. It's based on who needs what. If they happen to be Black, White, Spanish, whatever, it doesn't matter. That kid needs help, or that kid is a high achiever."

A Black teacher described her two daughters' experiences with Honors classes some years ago, and said the racial opportunity gaps were "glaring," particularly for her oldest daughter because she was the only Black female student in the Honors track. Yet, she described that for her younger daughter there was considerable, although not yet adequate, improvements in Black representation in Honors and AP classes:

It's glaring when your children are in the so-called upper classes, gifted and talented, and they're the only one. My oldest daughter graduated in '92. She was the only one [Black student] as she went through. I mean, she had friends certainly in all grades and groups and whatever, but when she got to the high school in Calculus and Trig, she was by herself in all of the advanced classes. Whereas my younger daughter had a group of African American students—there was maybe 10 of them—who went through the district together kind of as a group. So it at least made it that you weren't the only Black kid in class, especially the only Black female in class.

At the leadership level, there is a debate about eliminating the tracking structure entirely versus expanding access and attempting to diversify high-track courses. This tracking debate, including gifted and talented admissions and programming, continues to play out in the district, and the nation.[43]

Superintendent Pendergrast has said that politically it is not the right time to de-track. He clarified that statement by also saying, "It is also not the right time educationally. De-leveling would require a significant strategic instructional shift and I believe we first have to continue to increase the rigor at all levels even more so than we already have before we de-level." He said he hopes that in 4 or 5 years they will do it when students are performing better across the board . . . "when Honors-level kids do much better and when A-level kids do much, much better. It's also that the gap between these two groups is too large now."

Pendergrast reported that 50% of Black students are in 8th-grade Honors classes today, and that was not the case 4 years ago, when it was only 25%. And, he said, they "deserve to be there because they are getting 4's and 5's on the tests." This increased representation in Honors classes is reflected across all racial subgroups, but there remain big gaps between them. Comparatively, only 20% of Latinx students were enrolled in 8th-grade Honors in 2016, compared to 32% in 2019; White students have climbed from 56% in 2016 to 76%; and Asian students up from 62% to 88% during that same time period.

The superintendent also believes that the A-level is the most challenging to teach because there are students coming straight out of bilingual classes that are sometimes two or three grade levels behind, and then you have students who are reading two or three grade levels ahead who are balancing out their schedules in those classes. When asked about whether teachers are being trained for differentiation, Pendergrast responded yes, and pointed out that teachers have also been trained to educate students from Central American countries impacted by trauma.

At the teacher-level there seems to be very little discussion about de-tracking (or de-leveling), and many teachers were puzzled when we asked about it during the teacher focus groups. Their bewilderment is probably because teachers believe the district is already "de-tracked" since students are given the choice to enroll in high-level courses (Honors or AP). Our findings, however, showed that teachers and counselors recommend students' placement in Honors and AP based on prior track placements, test scores, and grades. Research has shown that tracking students based on perceived ability is tied to race and SES.[44] Yet, the district continues to offer Advanced or A-level, Honors, and AP tracks, which leads to inequities and an inadequate education for some. As the White high school students explained during a focus group with them, they have had the same teacher teach an A-level class and an Honors class, and the way they teach each level is vastly different in terms of expectations and rigor: "So, in A-[level], basically they say, 'Here's an assignment, do it for the block [class period].' Honors, we go over it in depth and do an activity interactively with people." Also, Black and Latinx students told us that they are sometimes made to feel like they do not "belong" in the AP courses because they are composed of mostly White and some Asian students, which deters them from enrolling.

The Student Perspective

Another thing we heard during the interviews was that some students are not prepared to take high-level classes because they have been consistently "tracked" into the lower A-level. Studies show that students placed in low-tracks receive lower scores on standardized tests, and teachers have lower expectations.[45] This finding matched the experiences of students at the high school. Students described the teachers who taught AP and Honors as the very best teachers in the school "who were always on top of you," while the A-level classes were taught by teachers who were subpar and less demanding. During the focus group, one student from the high tracks commented, "I think that teachers that teach AP and Honors are kind of wasted for the kids that are in the A-level because they could benefit from them just as much as us, so it's kind of I feel like the A-level kids are missing out because the 'fantastic teachers' are teaching the upper levels." El-Haj and Rubin caution, though, that eliminating tracking completely is only the first step toward greater equity when they write, "We cannot simply expect all students to be subject to the same standards without also taking seriously the need to radically reimagine curriculum, pedagogy, and assessment in ways that tap into a range of experiences, expressive modalities, and materials available for creating meaningful learning opportunities for all students."[46]

Although there are efforts now to diversify the Honors and AP courses through expanded admissions criteria in the middle school and de-tracking at the elementary level, we found that tracking still exists, and this within-school segregation was not lost on the students. White students were fully aware of their privileged positions in the schools because they dominate high-track courses and receive prestigious awards. During the focus group with White high school students, one male student questioned how integrated they are when they are separated by race in their classes:

I think in terms of socially, that people really come together in this school. Race doesn't really put up too much of a barrier, but when it comes to academics I'm not really sure how integrated we really are, to be honest. I'm in a lot of Honors classes and a lot of kids in my class—the majority of them are White. I also have . . . I take Advanced History and that's my only . . . I don't know, regular class I guess you can call it. A majority of the people in that class are African American and Hispanic, so I'm not really sure what to say about that. That's just one thing I've noticed coming here is that most of the kids in my higher level classes are White and the few Asian kids that come here are in those, too, and not as many Hispanics or African Americans.

Another White male student pointed out that during the recent National Honor Society award ceremony:

We were at the National Honors Society induction last night and in my grade out of 150 kids there were 60 inducted and I think there were two Black kids and one Spanish kid out of 60. I honestly just think it's because of the difference in opportunities. I don't know if that's socioeconomic but that's just . . . they're not getting the opportunity to excel in the class that they're in. It's sad to see. My grandfather asked about it last night. He said, 'I really didn't . . . it seemed like it was all White kids.' We're all up on stage. It's easy to see. It's the first thing that stands out. Not being racist at all, it's just if you look at the stage you'll see that there's 57 White kids there out of 60.

Despite all of the challenges that diversity brings to the schools, however, from the teacher's and student's perspective they would not want to be in a mostly White school/district environment.

In fact, across all of the student focus groups with Black, Latinx, and White students we heard how much they valued the diversity in their schools. As one White student responded:

I think these issues we have, as difficult as they are, I almost feel blessed to have them because there are other schools who are just White. They don't even—they're just so ignorant. They don't even have a dialogue about it. They don't discuss the socioeconomic issues and the divisions. As bad as they are, at least we're exposed to it and we can try to do something to help it. There are some places that they don't even think about it. It's not even a problem in their minds . . . but just the fact that we're living here in one of the most diverse communities around and it's just right there in your face all the time, I just think that's a very good exposure. I'm happy I don't live somewhere where there's—I mean, it's better to have issues and to realize the reality of a situation than to just be living in a little bubble not even knowing that there is an issue.

A good example of the real-world environment fostered at MSD happened after Freddie Gray died while in police custody and the Baltimore riots ensued. Reportedly, after these incidents, there were some racist messages on social media posted by White students. The principal immediately responded by bringing students together as a "family" instead of allowing divisions to happen because of race and ignorance regarding the issue. The students explained that the principal got on the loud speaker and told them basically that they all belong in Morristown, they are part of a community, and they are all representative of Morristown High School. He said something like, "If one student has a problem, we all have a problem that we need to solve together as a family."

LESSONS LEARNED

We are always surprised by the fact that the story of how the MSD came to be is not more widely known and understood, even by education or legal experts, or scholars that study school district regionalization. Morris is rarely cited in books or dissertations on the topic, nor is the *Jenkins* lawsuit that brought the desegregation order about. A Black school official theorized that the prevailing attitude used to be that people did not know how to talk about the merger so they avoided the topic: "It happened and people say it's good, but I'm not so sure. I think one of the reasons why they don't want to talk about it is because they can't articulate why it was good. They can articulate what happened from a big picture standpoint, but when you really drill down almost 50 years later and start to question if the people before us would be proud of what has been accomplished, folks come up blank." This silence about merger is changing. Indeed, recent attention to the district, brought about by press coverage of our research study, has given district officials the opportunity to, as Mackey Pendergrast said, "reassess whether the people who started MSD back in the 70s would be proud of our actions today." He asked, "Are we fulfilling the vision they had 45 years ago? Would they be proud of where we are or would they want us to be further along?"

This is one of the reasons why we felt compelled to write this book, to share the story of the merger that occurred in an unlikely place and time. The 1954 *Brown v. Board of Education* decision was a long time ago, yet many U.S. schools still labor under the vise of segregation. The MSD is home to a hopeful, if incomplete, counter-story. We believe that the Morris remedy of school district regionalization could and should be used to achieve district and school-level diversity for the numerous academic and social benefits it bestows upon students. For example, in counties with high degrees of geographic fragmentation, such as Nassau County, NY, or Essex County, NJ, small, racially distinct, neighboring school districts could be targeted for regionalization to obtain racial and socioeconomic integration. In New York City, a similar process could be applied to merge racially isolated school catchment areas for integration purposes. In addition, districts could use the Princeton Plan that pairs racially segregated schools located across catchment lines to create more diverse K–2 and 3–5 schools. These school assignment policy changes would accomplish two things: One, it would send a clear message about the importance of having diverse neighborhood schools to maintain strong communities. Two, it would place more of the burden of school assignment and school choice on the district instead of on the parents whose choices likely contribute to segregation.

In Chapter 2 we illustrated how the merger and the resulting diversity came about through the courts and the final order by the commissioner of education. In this chapter, we described how diversity once achieved was maintained, not only at the district level but also at each of the schools, in the face of predictions that merger would result in massive White flight and, ultimately, a segregated district. Our findings strongly support the conclusion that stable and committed leadership at the community, school and district levels has been crucial to the success of the integration process in Morris. This multifaceted leadership—particularly the involvement of superintendents, school board members, teachers, alumni, local civic and religious organizations, and pro-Morris realtors—has served to nourish and support the commitment to diversity of the student body. Mackey Pendergrast made a point to say how important the stability of the board of education has been to the district. He came in with bold initiatives, and the board has stood behind him and, as he said, "they deserve a lot of credit for that."

What makes Morris stand out is the way in which educational and community leaders, from the time of the merger until now, have joined together to move the district toward the ultimate goal of school integration. In so many other city-suburban areas with regional equity plans, education is curiously left off the table, but not in Morristown. Genevieve Siegel-Hawley wrote that the power of the community to achieve regional school desegregation is to recognize "how decisions made about the education of children in smaller parts of a community impact the education of children across the larger whole."[47]

This chapter showed how district creators instituted the Princeton Plan to racially and socioeconomically balance the elementary schools. They had the foresight to know that keeping a neighborhood school policy would reproduce the status quo of parents choosing racially and SES–isolated neighborhoods that are then funneled into segregated neighborhood schools. The Princeton Plan decouples neighborhood segregation from school segregation. This chapter also showed how realtors, police officers, and other community members came together four times a year to have dinner at the superintendent's home to learn about what the district was doing well, and to turn negative perceptions into positive realities. We described how Pendergrast is continuing that community outreach legacy through his listening tour. In all, we illuminated the power of community in both creating the desegregated district, and making it work for almost a half century and counting.

In common with other diverse districts, however, the Morris district is still working to fully confront and address racial and socioeconomic disparities in academic outcomes and disciplinary rates, which we discuss in more detail in Chapters 4 and 5. Related to that is the daunting challenge of assuring that districtwide, and even schoolwide, racial and economic integration extends to the classroom and program level. Over many years, various forms of ability grouping or academic tracking had resulted in most upper-level courses being disproportionately populated by White and Asian upper-income students—which we have shown is partly because the district has catered to White families to retain them and keep the diversity intact.

Stamford, Connecticut superintendent Joshua Starr, in a recent Op-ed, wrote, "The most important lessons I learned from de-tracking the Stamford Public Schools: Leaders can't take something away from White people without giving them something better in return . . . so the question was . . . how to improve the system for everyone while forcefully dealing with the urgent need to get rid of tracks that were hurting kids of color."[48] What this superintendent did, according to the article, was get support from key stakeholders, including teachers who were resistant at first to teach heterogeneous classes. Then, he had "to build the infrastructure for improved teaching, learning, and professional development, all the while signaling to communities and families of color that tracking would be going away."[49] While it took 5 years to fully de-track, he said it was important to take the time to plan for the implementation, be fully transparent about the decision-making process, and provide details and research to back it up.

According to the CRSL behaviors, school leaders like Stamford's superintendent must constantly question which students are benefiting the most from the district's policies and practices, and which students are left out. In nearby South Orange–Maplewood, a Black parent advocacy group has filed a federal lawsuit, *Black Parents Workshop v. South Orange–Maplewood (NJ) School District,* citing "patterned policies and practices that discriminate against African American students."[50] These policies include "de facto" segregated elementary schools and differential access to high-level courses at the high school level, which leads to lower achievement. We recognize from the recent experiences of South Orange–Maplewood and Montclair that taking steps to bring full integration to every classroom and program can create a firestorm in the community. Yet, Stamford's experience shows that district leaders can overcome community resistance, and their story could be used in the Morris School District as it proceeds to reduce inequities in the tracking system.

A review of the de-tracking literature shows that students from high tracks are not negatively affected by heterogenous groupings, and that students coming from low tracks show improved outcomes from the reform. In Morris, however, the fact remains that White and Asian students are still enrolled in Honors and AP classes at disproportionate rates. Meanwhile, Black and Latinx students are disproportionately referred for discipline infractions, and relegated to lower level courses and programming. Curiously, the circumstances of Asian students and families rarely emerged as a matter of concern during our study, perhaps because they tend to be higher-achieving than even the White students, and most of their families tend to be relatively affluent. MSD also has a relatively small percentage of Asian students, compared to nearby upper-income suburban districts, such as Millburn and Livingston, and even compared to the state as a whole. Ultimately, these gaps in access and opportunity must change via sweeping de-tracking reform if true integration is the end goal.

The district prides itself on the "cultural tapestry" of students. Yet, for decades, the perceived threat of White flight and loss of diversity, as well as the avoidance of discussing or dealing with race directly, have led administrators, teachers, and parents to adopt a colorblind stance on the persistent achievement and opportunity gaps and disproportionate disciplinary issues. Since Mackey Pendergrast's arrival, and the adoption of the Equity and Inclusion Plan,[51] there have been some initial breakthroughs. For example, teachers have been participating in Implicit Bias Training, which, according to Mackey, has been one of the "toughest obstacles." This work began during the 2018–19 school year and is still a work in progress, but definitely a step in the right direction. Also, some of the taken-for-granted practices, such as homogeneous math groups in elementary school, have been questioned, reassessed, and changed for the good of the community.

National, state, and local educational policy officials have the opportunity to change the status quo of segregated schools, which has been shown to depress educational opportunity and outcomes for low-income, students of color, and English Language Learners, as well as to concentrate resources and opportunities for already advantaged students in top performing schools or high-track courses.[52] The Morris remedy to create racial and socioeconomic balance would move more schools toward a more equitable, just, and diverse educational system. It would create the conditions in which more community members would be able to proudly say *diversity is one of our greatest strengths* when talking about their schools and communities.

CHAPTER 4

The Black Student Experience in MSD

Linda Murphy is a Black woman who graduated from Morristown High School in 1972, which is historically right on the cusp of the merger. Linda grew up in the township, but instead of being middle-class, Linda's mother was a housekeeper, and she and her family lived on the property of a family who lived in the township. She said, "We grew up poor, but my mom connected me to all of the rich people because she worked for them, so I've lived in those neighborhoods. We became friends with them. I went to Frelinghuysen [Middle School]. I was in Butterworth Farms and all of those—I knew all of those people, became friends with them and I got to see people are people." Linda explained that some people in the township were nice, and some were not so nice, but in general "they all embraced us, embraced me and my brother as kids and as friends of their kids. I got to see all of that and I just came with a different perspective than a lot of people might have who only were involved in one neighborhood. I was involved in several."

This experience of being one of a few Black students who attended the mostly White and segregated Frelinghuysen middle school stood out to Linda as it prepared her for future experiences in diverse schools, classrooms, and work environments. Linda is what sociologist Prudence Carter might call a "multicultural navigator" because of her ability to cross different racial and cultural spaces, feel comfortable in those spaces, and experience a range of benefits as well.[1] In other words, Linda took advantage of the diversity in the schools because she had prior experience and felt comfortable navigating White spaces.

Linda's experience of growing up in a low-income, Black family in the township, according to her, gave her a unique perspective because she understood what "minorities are going through" and also the "very different world" of being raised in the White high-income township. She understood the wealthy family's perspective of "looking down their noses at parents who do not read to their children at night, or maybe are not thinking that their child has a chance of going to college." She explained, "I know that it's much deeper than that. There's a whole history behind what you see in people." Linda remembered that in the premerger year of 1969, after she graduated from Frelinghuysen middle school in the township and came to the integrated Morristown High School, "I was joined by all of the students who were in [the majority Black] Lafayette [middle school in the town], so I had to get to know that whole part of the class that I had not met yet. It was us coming together in high school" as part of the sending-receiving relationship premerger.

Linda described her high school years as "a very positive experience, we knew what was going on [with the merger] but it didn't really impact our world. Nothing changed. I think I was more shocked when I went away for college and heard about the riots." She told us how she was attending college in Ohio at the time, and when she heard about the riot:

I was shocked. More than surprised. I was shocked because—well, shocked and hurt because it was my high school and that was not the place I knew it to be. It was not something that was commonplace to have even fights, racial kinds of disturbances. It was just not what I remember about the high school. So to know that that had happened in the short period of time since I left was very surprising.

What was interesting about her statements about the high school's positive race relations, was what Linda said next about the threat of White flight postmerger. She noted that, while she was not around during the first year of the merger in 1973, the threat of White flight "goes on even today." Linda was a high school math teacher from 1980–2002, and the vice principal and principal at Morristown High from 2002–2012. She remarked that from the time of the merger to today people have been worried about White flight:

A lot is done to maintain the status of the White numbers there. There's a belief that the high school would not hold a standard that it holds now without the population as it is, meaning that you need the Whites there to maintain the academics and some of the other things, accolades, that the high school shares which creates an environment—and I agree with that. I think you need all of those people to create a place that is desirable to families.

However, she said there are White people who are "afraid of having their kids mix with diversity, but there are more people who really like the diversity because they can be—the trick about the high school is, it's an interesting thing, you can be in the school and not have to deal with diversity." Linda's statement is consistent with the research evidence that has shown how even desegregated schools fail to fully integrate students within classrooms because of racialized tracking and ability grouping.[2] Not having to "deal with diversity" is not the message that most district administrators conveyed when they spoke about the benefits of being exposed to diversity, nor does it match with the district's mission statement to "come together to learn with and from each other." Yet, we heard during our interviews and witnessed during our observations that within-school segregation is commonplace because students are still racially tracked by their perceived abilities into separate programs and courses.

Another thing that Linda discussed during the interview was how important parent advocacy was in the high school when she was the principal: "You have to get the parents. The parents can move mountains in a school when they say something, it becomes much more kind of—I never understood that, but if an administrator says it, it gets a certain amount of attention. When the parents say it and they're upset a little bit, it gets a whole lot of other attention."

Linda told us that during her tenure at the high school a group of Black parents shined a light on the gaps in test score data and opportunities. This group went to school board meetings and met with the superintendent and Linda when she was the high school principal. They asked for three main things to help close gaps, which we explain in more detail below. First, they wanted a separate high school counselor for the "minority students." Another thing they asked for was more diversity in the teaching staff. Third, the group wanted the lowest B-level track to be eliminated in the middle and high schools.

Despite the many challenges of working toward true integration, Linda emphasized the overall benefits. "I think regardless of the problems diversity brings, diversity is definitely better for all." Linda's experiences highlight the MSD's efforts to walk the delicate line between (1) fully confronting diversity by ensuring school programs and classes are de-tracked and racially representative, and (2) not dealing with diversity or talking about race and continuing to track upper-income, mostly White and Asian students into separate, specialized programs and courses. The first alternative is to be critical about the way things are and become change agents. The other is to accept the state of things because it has and continues to either benefit you because of your race and SES *or* disempower and marginalize you, which we heard sometimes leads to Black families' becoming resigned to the fact that the district is not going to change. Acceptance and resignation often cause people to leave the district or give up. As a Black parent told us, "So you do have that kind of sense of loyalty and people just love the town and it's growing. But I think you do also have that segment that feels a little disenfranchised from it all and almost like they're being pushed out." We believe that MSD has chosen a third option of trying to satisfy all parties.

As Linda's quote above shows, oftentimes, the district has been most responsive to parents demanding change. Because of the structure of leadership in MSD, White parents are most commonly making demands and serving on leadership positions to influence policy decisions. Therefore, their voices are the loudest and are heard the most often.

Indeed, when we interviewed a White administrator, named Teresa, whose job is to market the district to prospective families, she told us that an important part of her work is keeping in touch with alumni for purposes of fundraising and informing them about what is going on in the schools. She maintains a website and publishes fall and spring newsletters each year. Teresa was eager to tell us about how she "interviews alumni who have had some really great success in life. We try to just feature them and build pride in our community about what our graduates are doing." She said that a common response from the alumni is that when they get to college they feel just as prepared as their peers academically, but that they feel "*more prepared* than [their] peers for being able to work in groups and understand and respect the differences of others." One reason for the newsletters is to "brag to the community about what's going on here." Another is to showcase how vital it was for each alumnus to be exposed to diversity in their K–12 education for their future college and careers. In each newsletter, Teresa includes a featured alumni section. This section has highlighted alumni such as Carl Sparks, who is the CEO of Travelocity; Joe Daniels, who is the CEO of the 9/11 Memorial; Jill Abramovitz, who is a Broadway actor, writer, and singer; Jami Wintz McKeon, who is the Chair of the largest female-run law firm in the world; and Allison Hobbs, who is an author and Harvard graduate.

Building this sense of pride in the community and the perception that the schools are successful, Teresa explained, is what draws people, particularly middle- to upper-middle-class people who are mostly White, back to the community to raise their families. These alumni communicate the quality of an MSD education to parents; MSD is a school system that graduates successful, college-bound students who go on to have remarkable careers. In other words, the schools need to be seen as successful (e.g., they can help your child get into a prestigious college) in order for affluent people to buy into them and bring with them the resources needed by the public school system. This display raises the question, though, about who diversity benefits in the public schools.

Notably, most of the alumni featured in the newsletters are White, as are most of the staff who work for the Morris Educational Foundation, all of the superintendents, and most of the principals, teachers, elected school board members, and other community leaders through the years. For the first time in the town's 300-year history, Morristown currently has an acting police chief who is African American.[3] A Black social support staff member noted why she believes there has not been White flight from the district and highlighted the fact that ". . . we have 52% White and that's who governs the district. Look at our Board of Education, look at the people that make the decisions, look at the curriculum. If that population wants a particular AP class, they get it. It doesn't matter whether we only have two kids in that class. They get it. . . ."

Even the Black high school students that we interviewed noticed that "White people's presence is the majority in the classroom and wherever we are." "Look at the PTA," said one student. "Or the educational foundation," replied another student. "I have never, in any of those meetings, I have yet to see anyone of any minority [group] in any of those meetings."

The way in which Whites are able to retain power while also embracing diversity is explored by Robin DiAngelo, in her book *White Fragility*. DiAngelo writes about the ways that Whites continue to dominate privileged and powerful positions in the United States, and therefore make key decisions about policies and programs that serve to maintain the status quo. Some examples from DiAngelo's book include: the 10 richest Americans (100% White), U.S. Congress (90% White), U.S. governors (96% White), President and Vice President (100% White), U.S. presidential cabinet (91% White), teachers (82% White), and full-time college professors (84% White).[4]

When we asked Teresa about whether the district offers certain courses like Honors or AP to attract certain families and to deter White flight, like Linda she explained that avoiding White flight is part of the work that she engages in:

> We're constantly trying to celebrate and share with the larger community the successes that our students have because I think if those families felt like they couldn't get those experiences here they might . . . they certainly have the capability to make a lot of choices
> in terms of what they choose for their children, and if they don't choose here, our schools would look different. It's different in other communities that are less diverse.

When she speaks of "those families" she is referencing the mostly White, middle- to upper-middle-class families that have the option to move to other suburban districts or to choose private school. As Table 4.1 shows, White and Asian households in MSD are more likely to have higher income than Black and Latinx households.[5] While there is a small percentage of Black and Latinx families that are middle-class, most Black families are living in intergenerational poverty and many Latinx families are recently arrived immigrants with very few resources. Therefore, there was a strong theme throughout all of the interviews that the district chooses to offer separate, specialized programs to attract and retain White families in the schools, or essentially to avoid White flight and keep the "diversity" intact. Unfortunately, the singular focus on avoiding White flight seems to have led district leaders to overlook the Black flight highlighted by the 50% drop in the Black student population between 1999 and 2019 (see Figure 1.1).

Although she pointed to some challenges of meeting the diverse needs of the changing student population, Teresa was optimistic that the district will do the right thing for students of color in the schools. She said, "I think people are willing to work through challenges or work through issues or get to the bottom of things to break down barriers, to really try to make it successful." The fact remains, though, that there is a racial opportunity gap in the school district. There is a disproportionate number of White students in the gifted and AP courses, and in the STEM Academy, and until recently a disproportionate number of Black and Latinx students being given disciplinary infractions. Teresa believes that the schools have the resources and the people who can work at the same time with the students at the highest academic levels, as well with those struggling academically. When other parents ask her, "What's happening in Morristown with the high school students who just arrived in the United States and do not speak any English?" she tells them that MSD will take care of them." "There's a pride in just the fact that that person showed up here, that this is a good place for them to grow." Teresa said it's good for the recently arrived immigrant students and good for the student body overall to have that exposure to diversity. In a sense, this seems to be a way for her to sell the district's diversity to families from outside the district who have had no prior experience with diversity.

Questions remain, though, about how much interaction is really occurring among students from different racial and ethnic backgrounds, and who is really benefiting or being left out of the district's programming and opportunities overall. Teresa's perspective shows the shortcomings of the diversity discourse when not all students are given access to the full range of opportunities that the district has to offer. Linda's experience provided answers to these questions from her perspective as a Black Morristown alumna, longtime resident, and former MHS teacher and principal.

This chapter is focused on the Black student experience in the community and schools. In addition to individual interviews, we conducted focus groups, and classroom observations at the elementary, middle, and high school levels. We also engaged in several interviews with Black parents and clergy members, as well as Morristown High School teachers, administrators, support staff, and students about the successes and challenges of educating Black students.

This chapter shows that, for many years, Black parents and students have felt that the district has seemed to "cater" to White families, and even to Latinx families because of the additional resources needed for English language services. In the past, the district has been reactive instead of proactive when issues regarding racial opportunity gaps are brought up and questioned. We start by laying the groundwork of changes in

Table 4.1. Morris School District Household Income Brackets by Race and Ethnicity, 2017

		# of Households	Less than $25,000	$25,000–$49,999	$50,000–$74,999	$75,000–$99,999	$100,00–$149,999	$150,000–$199,999	$200,000 of More
White	Morris Township	7,383	8%	9%	11%	10%	19%	13%	30%
	Morristown	6,011	13%	14%	17%	17%	17%	7%	15%
	MSD	13,394	10%	12%	14%	13%	18%	10%	23%
Black	Morris Township	358	26%	26%	15%	19%	12%	0%	2%
	Morristown	938	22%	21%	8%	21%	22%	3%	3%
	MSD	1,296	24%	22%	10%	20%	19%	2%	3%
Asian	Morris Township	372	4%	5%	7%	11%	3%	18%	53%
	Morristown	325	0%	3%	34%	18%	31%	10%	4%
	MSD	697	2%	4%	19%	15%	16%	14%	30%
White (not Hispanic)	Morris Township	7,132	8%	9%	11%	10%	19%	14%	30%
	Morristown	4,641	11%	10%	17%	20%	17%	7%	19%
	MSD	11,773	9%	9%	13%	14%	19%	11%	26%
Hispanic	Morris Township	322	11%	21%	11%	4%	20%	12%	22%
	Morristown	1,800	19%	28%	22%	7%	18%	4%	2%
	MSD	2,122	18%	27%	20%	7%	19%	5%	5%

the Black student population, showing who's staying, who's leaving, and why. Then, for the Black parents who stay, we discuss their advocacy efforts to break down inequitable structures and policies, and we provide a picture of Black students' experiences in the high school in support of the parents' claims. We show that there is an "enigma of diversity" in the Morris district because of who benefits from the structures and policies in place (e.g., tracking and punitive discipline policies), and who is denied the opportunity to reach their fullest potential. We illustrate how this diversity discourse enables the "selective inclusion" of some Black (and Latinx) students in mostly White and Asian classroom spaces, but avoids a comprehensive program of justice that would break down the structures that keep the school community internally divided.[6]

In the final sections of the chapter we tell a far different—and much more optimistic—story about the district under Mackey Pendergrast's leadership and his 2017 Equity and Inclusion plan. In the Lessons Learned section, we look to the future and show how far the district has come on its journey toward true integration. We also provide recommendations for MSD, which include aspects of the Equity and Inclusion Plan, to answer the question "what would diversity that liberated everyone look like?"[7]

CHANGING DEMOGRAPHICS AND THE SUBSTANTIAL LOSS OF BLACK STUDENTS OVER TIME

The first two African American students in the area that would later become the MSD were siblings who graduated from MHS in 1897. Their names were Estella and Clarence Walker.[8] In the years following, the Black student population climbed to its peak enrollment during the time of the merger, with 48% of the total, and then steadily declined each year, with only 8.4% today. One thing we asked Black participants during the interviews was how they made sense of the changing demographics, and why they thought the Black population had declined so precipitously over time.

While the district started out in 1971 as a Black and White district, we know from census data that the Latinx population has been steadily growing since that time, and the Black population has been shrinking. When asked why the racial demographics of the district have changed, most Black parents said that the increase in cost of living was largely responsible for the diminishing African American population. However, what we found is that the declining numbers are also due to negative perceptions of the district by some Morris alumni who, for their children, have opted out of the public schools for private options. A few Black parents we interviewed were able to get scholarships for their children to attend private schools.

One of those parents was Latasha, a Black 1990 graduate of the Morris district who pulled her two children out of the district for private schools. She had this to say about the population loss since she attended school there: "I would say one main reason is that Morristown is very expensive to live in, living in the town. There's not enough affordable housing. Sometimes that pushes people elsewhere." Similarly, another Black mother, Denise, described the housing situation and the fact that as Black homeowners sell their homes, Latinx families are moving in:

> I've heard a lot of people say that younger people can't afford to live here. It's extremely pricey. New housing is extremely pricey. It's difficult to buy in, so if you don't have a family home, it's extremely difficult as a young person getting started maybe with their first job out of college or what not, to be able to afford to live here. So they're going other places, so we have seen even at our church how most of our members used to be from the immediate community but now it's . . . they're from everywhere, and people actually commute in from Mt. Olive, Flanders, Hackettstown, that way. We even have some members who, believe it or not, live all the way in Pennsylvania who commute and come to church once or twice a week for whatever may be going on. Some people who live in Teaneck and just different places like that. I still think that we have a good number of people who are here, but not as many as when we first came [in 1990].

Denise said that she is noticing about some of the older generations of Black homeowners in the historically Black neighborhood between Monroe Street and Martin Luther King that "in recent years, we've seen a lot of those homes be sold to more Hispanic families, just as they kind of come in. When we sold our home, it was a Hispanic family that bought our home . . . so the face of Morristown has definitely changed a little bit."

Denise described the Black population as being either (1) "solidly middle-class" residents who moved in from other places for their jobs, can afford to send their children to private schools if they choose, and do not have preconceived notions of the district, versus (2) "people who were born and raised here, who are 2nd- or 3rd- or 4th-generation Morristownians." Morristownians, according to Denise, were described as having negative "ingrained thoughts and attitudes about the district and they kind of have this attitude of almost . . . this is what's happened. This is what's always happened. This is what's going to be happening. So the only way to get away from it is to move away or send your kids to private [schools]."

As Table 4.2 highlights, there are dramatic achievement gaps in the Morris School District, particularly between Black and White MSD students. Black students are reaching math and English language arts proficiency at less than half the rate of White students in the district. Furthermore, only 85% of Black students are graduating, while nearly all White students graduate. It is worth highlighting that Black student achievement outpaces Latinx student achievement levels, and that Black student achievement is higher than achievement levels for students who are classified as economically disadvantaged. Additionally, it is essential to emphasize that there are high-achieving students of all racial, ethnic, and economic backgrounds in the MSD.

District and school leadership in Morris are deeply aware of persistent achievement gaps and actively working to combat them. In fact, data between 2016 and 2018 suggest that the district is making progress in closing these gaps. Despite these efforts, it is understandable that the group of private school parents discussed here want their children to have a different experience than they had in the Morris schools.

Parents like Denise and other Black residents we spoke to who were *not* born and raised in Morristown come into Morris with more of an open mind, and are more likely to "recognize it as a great district with a lot to offer, but at the same time say, 'well, we've got to work harder to make sure that our kids are taking advantage of all that the district has to offer.'" This second group of parents formed a committee to advocate for changes to the status quo situation of Black students being relegated to lower track placements, receiving disproportionate discipline referrals, and having lower college attendance rates than their White, Asian, and Latinx peers.

When we asked James, a Black parent who moved to Morristown from the Midwest, what he believed was the biggest challenge of the district today, he responded:

I think the biggest challenge and the thing that's frustrating for me as an active member in the schools and as a parent that has had two kids graduate from this high school . . . and as a grandfather of a child in the district, it's in many ways a district, to use the—I guess it was *A Tale of Two Cities*—this is a district of two groups of people. There's a population of students here, immigrants for the most part but also African Americans, many of whom are third-, fourth-, fifth- generation students in our district who academically are not performing on par with their White peers, who are not taking advantage or are being encouraged to take advantage of some of these great programs that I had talked to you about earlier on. That's been going on for as long as I've been in the district and from what I've heard from people who went to school here in the 1950s and the 1960s and the 1970s and the 1980s, it was going on back then, too. Unfortunately some of the people that kind of helped bring the

Table 4.2. Morris School District Achievement Gaps, 2017–2018

	Asian	Black	Hispanic	White	Econ. Disad-vantaged	Non-Econ. Disad-vantaged	English Learners	Non-English Learners	District Total	Statewide Average
% Proficient ELA Grade 3	*	35.0%	29.0%	74.0%	24.0%	71.0%	*	*	55.0%	52.0%
% Proficient Math Grade 3	*	24.0%	30.0%	73.0%	26.0%	68.0%	11.0%	61.0%	53.0%	53.0%
% Proficient ELA Grade 8	*	65.0%	55.0%	87.0%	51.0%	83.0%	*	*	75.0%	60.0%
% Proficient Math Grade 8	*	18.0%	16.0%	37.0%	13.0%	33.0%	*	*	25.0%	28.0%
% Proficient Algebra 1	*	20.0%	17.0%	72.0%	15.0%	61.0%	*	*	49.0%	46.0%
% Proficient ELA Grade 10	*	30.0%	15.0%	68.0%	13.0%	58.0%	*	*	48.0%	51.0%
Graduation Rate	100.0%	85.4%	57.9%	97.2%	63.4%	*	42.1%	*	83.7%	90.9%
College Matriculation Rate	*	80.6%	41.3%	90.6%	40.3%	*	7.1%	*	79.6%	72.8%
% Going to 2-Yr. College	*	28.0%	38.7%	7.5%	52.0%	*	100.0%	*	12.3%	27.6%
% Going to 4-Yr. College	*	72.0%	61.3%	87.7%	48.0%	*	0.0%	*	87.7%	72.4%

* Data Not Available

two districts together have either died or retired and moved away. So there is a lack of leadership in the community with respect to just sitting down and looking at some of the other issues. So our minority students, many don't do as well and the majority parents don't seem to have a strong interest or concern about that and the impact that that has on the overall institution of the district and the potential negative impact it can have on property values and the reputation of the school. What's made this district a great district is that people who seek a great place to send their kids and a great place to live come here, and we're starting to hear particularly among African American students that, where when I first came here 22 years ago, where this was kind of the place to go for diversity, that African Americans are now starting to look at other places that are maybe not so diverse [mostly White] because they're starting to question the value overall of Morris.

Ultimately, there was a collective feeling from Black parents that the district has, at times, systematically restricted and excluded their children from fully benefiting from all of the course offerings and opportunities that the district has to offer, which can have negative consequences for future opportunities and aspirations. James believed that "there's a degree of apathy that exists in the minority community overall." On the other side of the coin he reflected, "If you say, as we [high-income residents] often times do, 'This is a great community and I moved here for the diversity,' then you've got to do the work and we have people that don't want to do the work. They talk about it and they love living in an integrated place, but they don't want to look under the sheet and see some of the mess that we've got here." This same ideology was present during the time of the merger, as Wanda described in Chapter 3, residents either had status quo goals—that Whites should go with Whites—or integration goals regarding merger. The district is still grappling with the tireless work that is required to move it toward true integration; in this era, it would involve the district not allowing Whites to disproportionately fill high-track courses or enrichment programs. As we will show, district officials are working hard at overcoming obstacles and getting closer to the goal of true integration each and every year. We explain later how the administration was forced to confront these issues in 2017 when a racist image in a chorus spring concert program forced the superintendent and middle school principal to address the Black community and come up with a shared solution.

As discussed throughout this book, the work of integration taking place within the schools is trammeled by the persistent residential segregation as well as the reality that race and income remain correlated in MSD, as they are across the rest of the nation. Table 4.3 shows some of

Table 4.3. Morris School District Economic Disadvantage by Race and Ethnicity, 2017

	Morris Township		Morristown		MSD	
Unemployment Rate						
Asian	12	1.7%	0	0.0%	12	0.9%
Black	131	36.2%	24	2.6%	155	12.0%
Hispanic	21	2.2%	82	2.1%	103	2.1%
White (non-Hispanic)	443	4.6%	249	3.7%	692	4.2%
Poverty Rate						
Asian	37	3.3%	18	1.6%	55	2.4%
Black	303	35.2%	128	7.6%	431	17.0%
Hispanic	114	7.1%	734	12.0%	848	11.0%
White (non-Hispanic)	751	4.3%	481	5.2%	1,232	4.6%
Receipt of Food Stamps						
Asian Household	0	0.0%	0	0.0%	0	0.0%
Black Household	33	8.9%	148	20.5%	181	16.6%
Hispanic Household	22	5.9%	102	5.5%	124	5.5%
White (non-Hispanic) Household	83	1.2%	110	2.3%	193	1.6%

the stark economic differences among different demographic groups in the MSD. In 2017, Black unemployment rates, poverty rates, and rates of receiving food stamps far outpaced those of Asian, Hispanic, and White households. While 17% of Black households live below the poverty level and 11% of Hispanic households live below the poverty level, only 4.6% of White households and 2.4% of Asian households do.

Levels of educational attainment for the population over 25 in MSD mirror these economic trends. Table 4.4 demonstrates that Asian and White levels of educational attainment are significantly higher than that of the Black and Hispanic populations in MSD. Asian females have the highest level of academic achievement, with 49% of the population holding a bachelor's degree or higher. Between 35% and 40% of White males, Asian males, and White females hold a bachelor's degree or higher. While 16.8% of Black females have a bachelor's degree or higher, fewer than 10% of Black males, Hispanic males, and Hispanic females hold bachelor's degrees or higher.

Table 4.4. Morris School District Educational Attainment for People Over the Age of 25 by Race and Ethnicity, 2017

	Morris Township		Morristown		MSD	
Asian Male:	**387**		**315**		**702**	
Less than High School	6	0.8%	0	0.0%	6	0.4%
High School Graduate	13	1.6%	18	2.1%	31	1.9%
Some College or Associate's Degree	30	3.7%	10	1.2%	40	2.4%
Bachelor's Degree or Higher	338	42.1%	287	33.0%	625	37.4%
Asian Female:	**415**		**555**		**970**	
Less than High School	15	1.9%	0	0.0%	15	0.9%
High School Graduate	0	0.0%	20	2.3%	20	1.2%
Some College or Associate's Degree	61	7.6%	55	6.3%	116	6.9%
Bachelor's Degree or Higher	339	42.3%	480	55.2%	819	49.0%
Black Male:	**264**		**462**		**726**	
Less than High School	20	3.0%	67	5.4%	87	4.5%
High School Graduate	83	12.3%	200	16.2%	283	14.8%
Some College or Associate's Degree	74	10.9%	111	9.0%	185	9.7%
Bachelor's Degree or Higher	87	12.9%	84	6.8%	171	8.9%
Black Female:	**413**		**776**		**1,189**	
Less than High School	41	6.1%	72	5.8%	113	5.9%
High School Graduate	156	23.0%	323	26.1%	479	25.0%
Some College or Associate's Degree	97	14.3%	178	14.4%	275	14.4%
Bachelor's Degree or Higher	119	17.6%	203	16.4%	322	16.8%
White (non-Hispanic) Male:	**6,714**		**3,832**		**10,546**	
Less than High School	143	1.0%	72	0.9%	215	1.0%
High School Graduate	719	5.3%	376	4.9%	1,095	5.1%
Some College or Associate's Degree	519	3.8%	604	7.9%	1,123	5.3%
Bachelor's Degree or Higher	5,333	39.0%	2,780	36.3%	8,113	38.0%
White (non-Hispanic) Female:	**6,973**		**3,818**		**10,791**	
Less than High School	111	0.8%	169	2.2%	280	1.3%
High School Graduate	1,129	8.3%	547	7.2%	1,676	7.9%
Some College or Associate's Degree	849	6.2%	542	7.1%	1,391	6.5%
Bachelor's Degree or Higher	4,884	35.7%	2,560	33.5%	7,444	34.9%

(continued)

Table 4.4. Morris School District Educational Attainment for People Over the Age of 25 by Race and Ethnicity, 2017 (continued)

	Morris Township		Morristown		MSD	
Hispanic Male:	**672**		**1,958**		**2,630**	
Less than High School	130	10.7%	658	16.9%	788	15.4%
High School Graduate	97	8.0%	777	19.9%	874	17.1%
Some College or Associate's Degree	243	20.0%	282	7.2%	525	10.3%
Bachelor's Degree or Higher	202	16.6%	241	6.2%	443	8.7%
Hispanic Female:	**542**		**1,939**		**2,481**	
Less than High School	93	7.7%	779	20.0%	872	17.1%
High School Graduate	73	6.0%	723	18.6%	796	15.6%
Some College or Associate's Degree	170	14.0%	188	4.8%	358	7.0%
Bachelor's Degree or Higher	206	17.0%	249	6.4%	455	8.9%

These disparate levels of wealth and education have a wide range of consequences. Table 4.5 highlights one effect that is likely related to these racial/ethnic wealth and education gaps. In the MSD, access to technology correlates to race and ethnicity. While nearly all Asian and White households have a computer with a broadband internet subscription, only 70% of Black households and 76% of Hispanic households do. Such a disparity has a wide range of consequences given the opportunity and access that computers and the internet provide.

Given all of these data, MSD's achievement gaps—highlighted in Table 4.2—are unfortunate, yet unsurprising. One result of all the racial and ethnic gaps in education levels and economic levels is that Black and Latinx students—including high-achieving students—encounter the kinds of bias noted in many of our interviews. In the next sections, we go into more detail about why some Black parents leave the district for private school and others stay in MSD. For those parents who stay, we explain some of their advocacy efforts to level the playing field for Black students and create more access to opportunities through initiatives aimed at diversifying teachers, guidance counselors, and higher-level courses with the goal of improving outcomes and closing gaps. Woven throughout are student voices about their experiences in the schools.

BLACK PARENTS WHO LEAVE

While the term "achievement gap" is more commonly used in the educational world today, we prefer to focus attention on the "opportunity

Table 4.5. Morris School District Technology Access Data by Race and Ethnicity, 2017

	Morris Township		Morristown		MSD	
Asian Households	**1,098**		**1,131**		**2,229**	
Has a Computer:	1,091	99.4%	1,113	98.4%	2,204	98.9%
With Dial-Up Internet Subscription Alone	0	0.0%	0	0.0%	0	0.0%
With a Broadband Internet Subscription	1,079	98.3%	1,113	98.4%	2,192	98.3%
Without an Internet Subscription	12	1.1%	0	0.0%	12	0.5%
No Computer	7	0.6%	18	1.6%	25	1.1%
Black Households	**827**		**1,652**		**2,479**	
Has a Computer:	490	59.3%	1,421	86.0%	1,911	77.1%
With Dial-Up Internet Subscription Alone	0	0.0%	0	0.0%	0	0.0%
With a Broadband Internet Subscription	462	55.9%	1,277	77.3%	1,739	70.2%
Without an Internet Subscription	28	3.4%	144	8.7%	172	6.9%
No Computer	337	40.8%	231	14.0%	568	22.9%
White (non-Hispanic) Households	**17,400**		**9,064**		**26,464**	
Has a Computer:	17,112	98.3%	8,545	94.3%	25,657	97.0%
With Dial-Up Internet Subscription Alone	98	0.6%	13	0.1%	111	0.4%
With a Broadband Internet Subscription	16,755	96.3%	8,304	91.6%	25,059	94.7%
Without an Internet Subscription	259	1.5%	228	2.5%	487	1.8%
No Computer	288	1.7%	519	5.7%	807	3.1%
Hispanic Households	**1,514**		**6,122**		**7,636**	
Has a Computer:	1,452	95.9%	4,973	81.2%	6,425	84.1%
With Dial-Up Internet Subscription Alone	9	0.6%	0	0.0%	9	0.1%
With a Broadband Internet Subscription	1,437	94.9%	4,342	70.9%	5,779	75.7%
Without an Internet Subscription	6	0.4%	631	10.3%	637	8.3%
No Computer	62	4.1%	1,149	18.8%	1,211	15.9%

gap" because it is a more all-encompassing term that covers both inputs and outcomes. This term is what Gloria Ladson-Billings recommends that educators and researchers use because "it puts the onus of the challenge on educators (especially educational leaders) to directly address this issue by being conscious of promoting more opportunities for students to achieve."[9] Achievement gaps are focused on uneven outcomes, typically measured by standardized test scores, with the onus placed on the students themselves instead of focusing on the opportunities they are afforded or consistently left out of. "As a result, students of color continue to be framed in comparison to Whites; this comparison becomes normalized, as if it is a 'natural' way of thinking about achievement, rather than focusing on the excellence of students of color."[10] On the other hand, opportunity gaps create barriers to gaining access to educational resources within the school, which, in turn, leads to unequal outcomes that we see among racial subgroups. Opportunity gaps put the onus and responsibility on the educational system itself, not the student.

Some Black parents we interviewed who grew up in Morristown and attended the public schools have decided to send their own children to private schools because they had negative experiences related to opportunity gaps during their time at MSD. Latasha explained that even though she attended the Morris district and believes it is a "decent district," she does not believe it serves everyone well. When we probed her about that comment, she explained that while the course offerings at the high school are "rigorous," not everybody "is prepared" to take advantage of them. Her belief, like that of others we spoke to, was that teachers in the elementary schools are not always "catching" students' academic issues early on, particularly African American students, and this creates gaps in achievement that eventually become opportunity gaps when students advance into the high-level middle and high school courses:

> So that's where I believe there's an issue early on that someone somewhere is not catching, especially for African Americans, whether it be that they catch it and offer some extra assistance or however it is I believe it's being missed, because I believe by the time you get to high school, there are some basics that you should already know. If any kids get to the high school and don't have the basics, that to me tells me that something got missed early on. I know that for sure because it happened with my son. I would say that's why I'm a firm believer in that, which is one of the reasons why I have a 9-year-old that goes to a private school.

Latasha explained that her son fell behind in math by 3rd grade, and did not learn the basics, so she pulled him out of the Morris district in middle school and had the opportunity through a scholarship to send him to a private school. She did not want the same thing to happen to her younger daughter, so she sent her to the same private school for elementary.

While Latasha was considering enrolling her daughter at Morristown High, it's only because of her private school education that she said, "I am confident that if she does have to go to the high school, she will go to the high school in those upper classes, in those Honors and AP classes. I do believe that would happen. I think that would happen because she's getting the foundation to prepare her to be in those classes without any issues." Based on her prior experiences in Morris with her son, Latasha believed that private K–8 education would better prepare her daughter for the high tracks in Morristown High School. Latasha explained that there's never been a situation in her private school "where my daughter was made to feel like if she couldn't do it, it was okay. The expectation was set at the very beginning and there are no excuses from there, you know? If she is having some issues, they give her some extra help"— implying that some teachers have low expectations for Black students in the Morris schools.

James said he hears the same thing over and over from Black parents in the schools and at his church: "I hear this today, that their [Black] students—they weren't getting the encouragement there. It wasn't a situation where they were being discouraged. They just weren't being encouraged and feeling supported. For those kids that were going to those schools, these are parents that saw that and in turn said, 'Let me do something about this' and they either moved or pulled them out." He explained further that he thinks that teachers "have been so accustomed to a kind of benign-ness that exists in the minority community," that it has created a situation in which if parents speak up and advocate for their children then they will get pushed into the higher-level courses, but if parents do not do that, their children get left behind. He commented, "We have African American parents that feel that their kids qualify for advanced placement and were told, 'No, they didn't.' [Certain high-income parents] and other people in this community started speaking up about it to the district and they said, 'Oh, okay' and they moved them in."

An example of teachers' low expectations was the way in which Latasha described being treated during Back to School Night. She said her son could have "failed a bunch of math tests," and the one thing that the teacher stressed to her was, "He's just so respectful. I can't get over how respectful he is." To which Latasha responded, "Well, what do you expect?" She said there was this expectation that because "he's an African American male, he will come to school and start wreaking havoc. Well, that's not what I teach my kids. It's almost like he gets lumped automatically into a group." Latasha explained that there was a real disconnect between expectations that teachers had for her son's behavior versus academic achievement, which relates to racialized disciplinary policies and outcomes. She described that she would get the "runaround" when she tried to get him help. Latasha knew that there was something wrong with his performance in math, but all the teacher had to say was, "Oh my gosh, he's so respectful." Latasha had one teacher tell her that maybe her son had a learning disability, and another teacher tell her that his scores were not low enough to qualify for extra help. She kept asking, "Can somebody help me?" While Latasha did not describe her problems with the district in explicitly racial terms, she certainly implied that the way her son was treated was because of race.

Like other parents who opted out of the Morris schools or were critical of them, there was still a strong sense of loyalty and pride for the diverse district. In fact, Latasha said that she "would never tell anyone that MSD is a bad district because I don't think it is. I really don't. I know myself that I've had some really good teachers. I know my kids have had some really good teachers. But I think if you have a couple of bad ones, you may have some problems, especially in those early-on grades. If the expectation is not set real high in the very beginning, we need to set those expectations. I don't care who—White, Black, yellow, orange, pink, green—everybody should be expected to perform, and if you have some issues then that's when you surround that child with the help that they need."

She concluded the interview by telling us while there's a perception that MSD is a great district, "when you start pulling things back and getting underneath some of the numbers, I'm just saying it has some work to be done. . . . There's a lot to offer at Morristown High School, but I think if you get on that right track then you're good. But if you get on a different track then it's like you're just there. . . . They have AP, Honors. I think they're in a good position, it just depends on who they're in a good position for, who can benefit from it."

With good reason, most of the parents we spoke to had the perception that the district was doing very well overall. Unlike predominantly Black and Latinx low-income urban districts in New Jersey characterized by large class sizes, ineffective teachers, and less access to courses and programs, suburban districts like Morris have abundant resources and course offerings. According to a recent MEF newsletter, Morris has "dedicated teachers and counselors, small class sizes, and comprehensive academic and extracurricular programs . . . [including]

- 8 AP classes
- 5 world languages
- Humanities Academy
- 40+ extracurricular programs
- 36 Honors-level classes
- STEM Academy
- 27 varsity sports." [11]

The question is, how racially representative are these tracks, courses, extracurriculars, and specialized programs? For example, are all students given access to diverse, high-quality classes? The answer is no. Tracking continues in the district, even though de-tracking improves educational outcomes for students historically tracked into low-ability classes, and does not affect the outcomes of higher-achieving student outcomes.[12] The reason there are gaps in opportunity and achievement is because of the tracking structure that keeps the boundaries among racial subgroups intact.[13] Indeed, when we interviewed administrators and teachers, they fully admitted that there was a representation problem in the high-track courses. Yet, mostly for "political" reasons and because of the threat of White flight, the district's leadership has remained unwilling to fully address the problem by de-tracking the curriculum. As one administrator told us, "Unfortunately, my superintendent asked me to put my de-leveling plan for ELA on the back burner. He does not feel it is the right time politically to make that change. In the meantime, we are making other efforts to increase representation of Black and Hispanic students in our honors and gifted classes."

Black parents said that they were most frustrated when they approached leadership about the "achievement gap," and the typical response they received was that the school leaders were aware of the problem and they were trying to fix it. Yet, the Black parents felt there was little action behind their words and promises to close gaps. For example, Latasha remembered a time when someone on the board of education said that they had made progress because there used to be 3% of Black students passing the tests, and now it's up to 35%. She thought that was not progress because there are still 65% not passing. She replied, "So the fact that . . . some think the little progress enough is acceptable is not good, which is why my daughter is not there. I just won't allow that to happen to her."

BLACK PARENTS WHO STAY: "WE'VE GOT TO WORK HARDER" TO ADVOCATE FOR OUR CHILDREN

The second group of Black parents whom we interviewed opted into MSD and chose to work together to help close racial opportunity gaps. In 2012, a group of concerned Black parents formed a committee to address the "45-year achievement gap" that has existed between African American and White students. The committee noticed a "huge disparity" between where Black students are performing on test scores and the classes that they are getting placed into versus White students. As Denise, who was one of the leaders of the committee, explained, "We had some success with working with the district in terms of getting some changes implemented and sort of bringing it [the disparities] to their attention, although from their perspective they told us that it's not something new and that they were very aware of it and that they were working on it. We just felt like they weren't working hard enough on it." This messaging from the district sounds very similar to Teresa's explanation of how the district is "willing to work through the challenges"; yet, from the parents' side, they overwhelmingly felt there was a lot of talk, but little action.

Denise said that Linda Murphy, the high school principal at the time, and a couple of other educators got together and decided to try to do something about the achievement gap. They had a meeting at the high school where Linda invited Denise, other parents, and "a couple of clergy persons to look at the data which they had gathered and put together. The data showed the huge gap between the performance of a majority of African American students and Caucasian students." She said from that initial meeting the movement grew by forming a group and attending home and school meetings and board meetings. They also met with principals and Superintendent Ficarra "to bring to their attention the data . . . and it was kind of like, 'This is what this says, what are you doing about it? What are the initiatives that are going on? What are we going to do to turn this around?'" The district's response was basically to avoid the topic of race in their discussions, which, according to Khalifa, Gooden, and Davis's CRSL behaviors, is not productive when districts try to tackle gaps in achievement and opportunities. This example illuminates the two sides of the district's response to diversity. On one hand, district uses racial diversity to sell the district to prospective families, but on the other hand they historically have claimed colorblindness when confronted with any racial inequities.

Increasing Teacher Diversity and Implementing Implicit Bias Training

The first two tenets of CRSL, explained in Chapter 3, are to be critically self-aware of your own biases, and to recruit and prepare teachers for culturally relevant practices for the purpose of increased outcomes. What the Black parent committee noticed was that there were not many "faces of color in the schools," so they were initially met with resistance about closing the gap. Indeed, the district's response to parents seemed to vary by race. Our data show that when White parents come and ask for things from the district, it is framed as a benefit. When Black parents do the same, they are perceived as troublemakers. As we will show in the next chapter, the district considers Latinx families as absent and apathetic.

James's quote exemplifies the disproportionate number of White parents who volunteer at the school, and the district's uneven response to parental demands because of that involvement:

Our parents who are Yale, Duke, Columbia, Princeton grads who live in this community in million-dollar homes are executives on

Wall Street and other places . . . they start programming, advocating, partnering, collaborating with our district day one of kindergarten. They do. They're just there. They're active. They're active at home and in school. Many of the moms don't work. They are very supportive of the schools. When we had elections before the systems were changed, they were the ones out front. Playgrounds look great. All of the stuff that you . . . read [about] all of the kids are comfortable there, whether it's their kid or somebody else's. But in any kind of system, if you're a teacher or a principal of a school like that and you've got a group of kids whose parents are showing up, volunteering, serving as room moms, then those are the kids that you're just going to pay more attention to.

The bottom line for Black parents was that they were just trying to help their children and get more parents involved in the fight, and not stir up trouble as the district thought they were doing. In fact, increasing the level of staff diversity came up as something the group recommended to the district, and many school staff concurred with that recommendation. Participants believed that if there were more diverse teachers and administrators to match the diversity of the student body, there would be more understanding of the different racial and ethnic backgrounds of the students, higher academic expectations, more diversity in the higher level tracks, and more relationship-building efforts. As Latasha commented, "I think there's something to say about kids learning from someone that looks like them."

The Black parent committee formed sub-committees and parents worked on advocating for more diversity in leadership positions and professional development to prepare teachers for educating diverse learners. As a result of their advocacy work, Denise explained that the district also instituted "some diversity training amongst the staff," although that did not go as far as the group would have liked. She explained, "They brought in an independent consultant who did a study and did questions and so forth, and they came in and did training for teachers. It was very expensive and I think there [were] some money issues. . . . So it was supposed to span out across the district. It didn't quite make it that far. It kind of stalled out with just the high school teachers who had the initial training." The group believed that one of the main issues was that because most of the staff were White, they did not understand some of the cultural differences that the Black and Latinx students were presenting in school. Denise said they were disappointed that more teachers did not get trained. A social support staff person explained to us that the cultural diversity training was met with a lot of resistance from teachers "who viewed it as, 'Oh, people think we're racist.'"

Black parents had reason to be concerned about the lack of teacher diversity and training on implicit bias. Research consistently shows that there is a strong link between teacher-student racial and gender match and students' academic growth and social-emotional well-being, particularly in the younger years. Consider these two statistics from the literature: First, "Black children are, on average, two grade levels behind White children in terms of academic achievement."[14] Second, Black students are 39% more likely to complete high school if they have at least one Black teacher from 3rd grade to 8th grade.[15] Additionally, Black teachers have been found to set higher standards and expectations for Black students than White teachers.[16] Black male students who have a Black male educator perform higher on standardized tests.[17] Black teachers also are more likely to form positive relationships with Black students. This is important because research has shown that Black students learn best when they form relationships with teachers.[18]

However, MSD's teacher force is unfortunately very similar to the national teaching demographic in which 82% of teachers are White, only 5% of teachers are Black females, and a mere 2% are Black males. In the Morris schools, 80% of teachers are White and only 5% of teachers are Black.[19, 20] In the Morris schools, 80% of teachers are White and 5% of teachers are Black. During our observations, we consistently noted in our fieldnotes how most of the teachers were White, and most of the food services staff were Black. Research has shown that when there is a racial mismatch between teachers and students of color in diverse school settings, it can lead to challenges in developing strong teacher-student relationships, with implicit bias being a driving factor.[21] Therefore, it is important for teachers, particularly White teachers, to not only understand their own implicit biases, but also how these biases may affect the teacher-student relationship, as well as how teachers view Black and Latinx students' ability to learn and succeed in school.

Teachers in diverse school settings often hold colorblind ideologies. As one teacher proudly told us during a focus group, "I don't see race, I just see children." When teachers and administrators are colorblind, second-generation segregation in racially diverse school settings can occur. Racialized tracking is often the result of teachers disproportionately placing students of color in lower academic tracks,[22] labeling them in need of special education services,[23] and/or giving them harsh disciplinary referrals and school suspensions in comparison to their White peers.[24] As Amanda Lewis and John Diamond write in their book *Despite the Best Intentions*, "confronting implicit biases, cultural beliefs and racial stereotypes is not a simple matter of changing minds, but a matter rather of contending with the full structural and ideological effects of the racialized social system." Therefore, if we believe schools are the "great equalizer" in society, teachers and administrators must interrogate and change any racist structures and hierarchies in schools while simultaneously addressing implicit bias. One way to address the problem of second-generation segregation, and any implicit bias that occurs when teachers and counselors assign students to classes, is to hire Black and Latinx academic counselors who encourage students of color to enroll in higher-level courses, and make sure they are on the right path to college and beyond.

Hiring a Guidance Counselor for "Minority Students"

Another big ask from the achievement gap committee was for the district to hire an academic support counselor for minority students, who, as Denise explained, "would do nothing but be a person that students of color could go to for help with college readiness–type issues: doing college applications, filling out forms, whatever they needed to do." During meetings with Black parents, the committee learned that their children were not always being encouraged to take classes that would prepare them for college, or to work to get a high enough grade point average and apply for colleges—even if they were high school athletes who everyone expected to play college sports. James described the problem and the solution:

> [The district] created a position in the high school that is geared towards seeking out and assisting those [Black and Latinx] kids who are, I would say, academically on the line. I don't mean on a line of dropping out, but they're on the line of being a good student, a good-to-average student to being a great student. When you look at the numbers of minority kids, particularly African American kids that go to college, it continues to go down. When you look at where those kids go to college, it's nowhere close to the kinds of schools that some of our best White students are going to. When you hear some of the stories from their parents and kids about not being encouraged, supported, either at home or in the district or in the school, then this position was created to kind of help close that gap.

The other issue was that some Black students and parents "felt very intimidated" talking with support staff about the college process. Therefore, what they needed was a point person in the high school whose main job was to walk students through the college application, follow up "and kind of keep an eye on these kids to see that if there was someone who wanted to go college."

Denise told us about her oldest son who was a student athlete but did not have a high enough GPA for college recruiters to look at him:

> What we're finding is that it's almost as though they're being—and I don't want to say that someone is telling them this purposely—but I'll say that they're being led to believe that they have a real chance

of being able to play in college because this is what happened with my own son, my oldest son. Very good in football but he had a learning disability and he struggled in school almost his entire life, he struggled. As a result, he did not have the GPA for the recruiters to really look at him in that way. Talent-wise, he certainly could have gone and played, but we did not really realize that that was going to be a major issue until it was almost too late. I'll say it like that. I think that's what happens with a lot of our kids is that they're coming along and they're almost being sold a pipe dream: "You're good, you're great, you're doing well, you're going to play in college," and they believe this, but the academic piece is not really there. It's not where it should be and it's not being stressed that, hey, you've got to get it together if you have any hopes of wanting to play on a college level. You can't go with a 1.5 GPA. So the recruiters are taking initial looks, but once they look at those grades they're out the door. There's nothing they can do with that . . . so the kids are finding themselves kind of in this vacuum where they're great, they're getting all of this press, their name is in the paper, they're being interviewed, it's phenomenal, it's just awesome, and then the next thing is, "Well, whatever happened to so-and-so and so-and-so? Where did he go? Did he go? He didn't go?" And it's all this conversation that's like, "Well, why didn't he go? What happened?" You see him walking up and down the street or working at Walmart. Not that working at Walmart is a bad thing. If that's what you choose, great, but this is somebody who we thought had all of this talent and was surely headed for a college scholarship and it didn't happen.

As a result of students like Denise's son falling through the cracks, the district hired a Black MHS graduate named Robert to be the new Academic Support Counselor. Robert was already working at the high school as a Social Studies/History teacher. He also speaks Spanish, which helps him connect with Latinx students, as well. Linda Murphy told us during the interview, "So I hear he's doing a phenomenal job with the Hispanic students that want to go to college, that he's actually helping them fill out applications and according to what I'm hearing those kids would not even be thinking about going to college without him. Therein, that's a success story, that there are some kids being reached. What I would have liked was to see African American kids being reached."

Before Robert, in 2008, the district hired its first Student Support Coordinator, named Selena, because the district was classifying too many Black students for special education services. Selena explained that her job description was to "put support systems in place and kind of make

sure that the kids who were falling between the cracks had support systems in place so they didn't have to be classified and could be successful
here." According to Selena, ever since she started in the district 17 years
ago, the African American population "doesn't seem to be the population
that the district puts its resources in."

When we interviewed Robert, he told us that the question of "why
aren't there more Blacks and Hispanics in upper-level classes" has been
plaguing the district for 20-plus years, and "the numbers haven't increased all that much." He explained, "I look at it as, we still pretty
much promote a system of internal White flight where a lot of parents
will send their kids here because they know that if you're in AP or Honors
classes, you don't have to sit with the Black and Hispanic kids." Robert
and Selena both explained that this opportunity gap is due to teachers,
who Robert said, "view people like me differently . . . and we have very
little programs that are helping them [Black and Latinx students] with
anything except graduate from here and hanging out near my house."
When we asked Robert what he would change about this situation, he
quickly responded by saying that the district needs to "get teachers that
are truly relatable to the kids they're going to teach. . . . We don't have
enough adults in this building that can deal with a diverse population in
front of them; I don't think they're comfortable building relationships."
And while there are "many Caucasian teachers here that can relate," he
said there are not enough "who are willing to accept the differences culturally." He lamented, "I went through this district having no Black male
teachers at all, and it's not that different now, and when you don't see
anyone at all that looks like you or has been down the path you've been
down, you don't really buy into that. You're like, 'It's not really for me.'"

Like Robert, Selena told us that her role is to be the point person
in the district for students and their families. She said that for a lot of
Black students, "they need the support of knowing that somebody was
watching them, somebody cared, somebody was there for them . . . and
for parents, not knowing how to navigate the system for their kids to take
advantage of what's here for them." Selena also pointed to the problem
of teaching staff who have lower expectations for Black students, and
"when you have that perspective of lower expectation, you don't demand
that kids meet their potential because you don't think there's potential
there. You're not trying to pull that out." The other problem is that when
one or two Black students qualify for the Honors or AP track, "there's
not a lack of ability that makes them want to switch into a lower level, it's
a lack of comfort; a lack of teachers believing that they should have been
there. When a student walks into class and a teacher says, 'Are you sure
you're supposed to be here, this is an Honors class, are you on my roll?'
that sets it off in a negative tone."

The Black Student Experience

During our focus group with Black students, they agreed that the biggest problems in the school stem from the lack of diverse students in the upper-level courses, and the lack of diverse teachers. However, the "number one problem" that affects their collective experience in MSD is the fact that, as one Black student explained, "People don't talk about race. We're not pushed to have friendships or discussions with other races in this school." Another student followed up by saying, "Race has always been a really taboo topic so no one likes to talk about the fact that minority students don't have as many outlets and they don't have the support systems that a lot of White students have . . . it's not that Black students are not capable of doing it. They just don't have the resources." A third student said, "We don't have any classes to learn about other cultures, so then we become ignorant and that's when there's this gap between the two different groups [Black and White]." They felt that the school was "so divided." The Black students in the group who pushed themselves to try Honors or AP courses with mostly White students credited their counselors for encouraging them.

As for teacher diversity, Black students shared stories of lower teacher expectations, from elementary school through high school. One Black female student commented, "I feel that as an African American female in this district, less is expected of me. On many accounts, I've walked into an AP or Honors class and the teacher has checked the schedule twice, [asking me] 'Are you supposed to be here?'" These students said that they have internalized the low expectations from teachers over time. They are reportedly asked to be African American historical and Civil Rights "experts" by some teachers.

On an early June day, our research team was invited to the high school for a panel on the merger history, organized by the League of Women Voters. Fifty students were in the audience, eager to hear about how their district and schools became racially diverse. After the panelists spoke, it was opened up for questions and answers. Notably, the 15 Black students sitting in the back two rows were the most vocal. One Black female student raised her hand and said "they" have to act as "experts" on the history of slavery and Civil Rights because White teachers do not always know the history. Another student commented that the only class that is "integrated" is chorus (which we also noted in our fieldnotes). The Black students in attendance that day came up to us afterward and said they formed the Melanin Minds group after Trump was elected president and "a few White students thought they could speak their mind about what they really thought of diversity." The Melanin Minds group has been going to school board meetings to voice their concerns about racism in schools. They successfully got the Advanced-level African American

History course switched to Honors level, and told us that they wished that all students were mandated to take that course to help with intercultural understanding.

At the heart of the discussion to diversify upper-level courses was the suggestion of an alternative approach, namely de-tracking the curriculum by creating heterogeneous classes. Although the achievement gap committee was advocating for diversifying Honors and AP, Robert seemed to think that classroom integration might be the better option because that is what the students are used to in elementary school. His reasoning was:

> When we say, "all right, we have to put a few more African American or Hispanic kids in AP" there are long odds for success in that class for a number of reasons because now you're going from these classes that are really diverse into these classes that are very White. Again, just sitting in those classes is a difficult thing. You've never done that before. You've spent your whole life in this district thinking it's diverse because you've been in these A-level or whatever classes, and now you're in an Honors class and it's all of the kids that live in Summit—that's the wealthy neighborhood in town. You're just like . . . you don't want to speak in those classes. You feel uncomfortable and you're really not prepared.

Robert concluded that for some people the district is "fantastic in every way, but there's also the other side. I think for years and years we've cared more about what it looked like than what it really is." According to Robert, people say about MHS, "this is diversity, wow, no it wasn't, I remember being a student here consciously thinking about the fact that no one Black has ever taught me anything. That's pretty profound in such a diverse district."

The Black students whom we talked to echoed the sentiment about how great the district is overall. Most rated the district a 7 or an 8 on a scale of 1 to 10 because of the cross-cultural friendships they have made. A Black female student explained:

> I give Morristown an 8 because I was fortunate to be able to go to all of these schools and have the people, the outlets to push me as far as I can. . . . I just feel like I'm very hopeful. The school is the most unique out of all of the districts, and I just feel like if they just do more stuff to engage the community as a whole and learn more about each culture, I feel like we could be a 10. There's no question in my mind. It's just all about taking that first step.

Taking that first step meant talking about race in schools. Students told us that they are taught not to talk about race. However, we know that culturally responsive school leaders build bridges among diverse families, students, teachers, and staff within the school to "deconstruct borders that keep school community members divided."[25] This type of leader understands that students and staff come with different racial identities and backgrounds, and that these positionalities relate to political and social hierarchies in society. Instead of subscribing to colorblind ideology, or the belief that treating people as equals regardless of race will fix discrimination, they understand that race matters in the teacher-student relationship.

Another Black male student explained why he rated the district a 7: "If we're talking about diversity, I'm glad to go to this school. Mo-town till I die [laughter]. But I do believe that it is not a perfect school district. It's put on a pedestal because we are diverse and we have had some success, but we're a long way from where we should be at this point in time." This feeling of division within the school extended beyond Black and White. For example, when we asked about how the presence of a growing number of Latinx students had affected their schooling experience, the students basically said it hadn't: "Nope, there are classes that are all Hispanic. If you can't speak English, you're going to be thrown in together." Ultimately, they felt that there are a lot of classes that are inaccessible to certain groups because of perceived ability, language barriers, and comfort levels when the class is mostly White.

In sum, the student support counselors for Black students were considered to be, as Latasha described, "a huge support for our children, especially African American children, by just following up with them and being genuinely concerned about their well-being." This is not to say that only Black teachers and staff can and will help Black students succeed. Indeed, Robert told us that two of his favorite teachers in the Morris district were White. Latasha also told us about a "Caucasian teacher" who helped her son with math: "Beautiful person, but she understood the struggle and helped him through it, you know, and didn't let anything come between her taking the time out, whether it be in the morning or in the afternoon, working with [my son] and helping him get there."

Eliminating the B-Level Track, and Having to Teach "Those Kids"

The third CRSL tenet, according to Khalifa et al., is to promote inclusive school environments where students feel welcome and secure. Tracking students into separate courses seems antithetical to culturally relevant leadership practices. Indeed, another ask of the parent committee was for the district to eliminate the lowest B-level of the tracking structure. At the high school, they used to offer B-level, A-level, Honors, and AP. According to Linda Murphy, during her tenure the parents came in and said it was not fair to have students in the B-level. Looking back, Linda said theoretically she was "fine with that," however the problem was that the district would make these decisions without providing training for the teachers. She said, "if you're going to eliminate the B-level, prepare your teachers for how to teach to a more diverse class so that the kids who get put now in with A-level students aren't either lost or the course isn't watered down or whatever. They didn't do that. So now you get teachers dealing with it." Linda explained that she had some teachers who resented "those [B- level] kids that don't belong here [in Level A]."

Linda said the teachers would "water down the curriculum" in the A-level course, and "then everybody's upset because the White parents whose children are in there, they don't want the curriculum watered down. Their kids are coming home saying, 'This stuff is so easy, I had all of this stuff last year, blah, blah, blah', because those teachers are doing it the same way even though it's an A-level class." The result of eliminating the B-level, which was supposed to be a positive thing, was that everybody was mad. White parents came in and told her that they wanted their kids in Honors. They assumed that because there were more Black and Latinx students in the A-level now, that automatically the teaching was going to be poor quality. "So everybody's mad, so everybody wants to move their kid up," Linda responded, "and my thing is everybody deserves quality teaching and kids who aren't in the same place level-wise, we just need to know how to teach them. If you want to put them all together, you need skilled teachers who know how to do that. There is a way to do it, but you've got to know how to do it."

While we acknowledge that the district was falling short, they were still leading the way by de-tracking the lowest level when most districts would not move in that direction. Indeed, the district could have been proactive by training teachers for heterogeneous classrooms. They also did not follow through with needed resources and supports after the programs were put into place. One thing that was needed was implicit bias training. Linda believed that for de-tracking to work the teachers also need to

> like kids who are diverse, and I don't mean that to be negative. I just mean that if I resent you [Black and Latinx students] because you are bringing my grades down from whoever's observing me and I'm dealing with you and you don't act like you want to be here anyway and you have this attitude and you're this and you're that, then my feeling and view of you is very negative. That permeates the life of that child. There are several teachers who would say to me, "Now, let me tell you about this kid." And then it becomes, "THOSE kids."

She explained that in a diverse public school building, it's normal to have all of these different implicit biases and perspectives going on.

Research consistently shows that if teachers and staff do not talk about race then these feelings permeate the culture and community in negative ways.[26] She said, "What we don't do is acknowledge it and say, 'Here's what we're going to do to work on it' and continually work on it because it's worth it. At the end of the day, it's worth it and the kids who you think can't succeed, you'd be surprised how much they can do with just a teacher who cares. Even if that kid is failing, but they feel like you care and you try with them, you'd be surprised. It may not click this year, but somewhere down the road they may get it."

When we asked Denise to comment on the racialized tracking system and trying to diversify higher-level courses and advocate for more students of color to qualify for them, she responded that what the district noticed was that "along the way, African American students will start to fall behind, and I think what happens is that obviously by the time they get to high school where those higher level courses are, of course they don't qualify to be in there because they've been lagging behind since the 3rd grade or the 4th grade or whatever the case may be. Obviously, you're not going to pop up into 9th grade and all of the sudden be taking AP level courses. That's just logic." While teachers will say that students have the choice of which courses to take, what they neglect to say is that students have to qualify for them. Denise said what she thinks is happening is that there are lower expectations when children are younger, and "I just know that it's not always expected that a child is going to be on a certain level or is able to do a certain level of work."

Denise and other Black parents we spoke with told us about teachers and counselors pushing their children into lower-level courses, or simply not suggesting that they try higher-level classes, particularly in math. For example, Denise's daughter was on the honor roll throughout middle school, but when it came time to plan out her high school career the counselor did not recommend her for 8th-grade algebra, which Denise knew would not get her on the right track to take calculus in 12th grade. This was the case, she said, with "several of the African American students, I [was] told by other parents, . . . even though their child was doing well in math. And my daughter has always done well in math. Math is one of her best subjects. She was not recommended for algebra in 8th grade. Now, was that purposeful? I don't know. I'm not sure." Her daughter ended up taking algebra in 8th grade because of her mother's advocacy. However, she later found out that all her daughter's Black friends were taking geometry, and she was in an algebra class with mostly White students.

These perceived lower expectations for Black children were pervasive and something the committee brought up to the district. One interaction between a teacher and Denise's daughter caused her to go in and talk to the teacher about it:

The teacher literally said to her, "You won't have to work as hard—
it's the same work, but you won't have to work quite as hard." So
of course, I was not happy about that and had to go over there and
have words because this is somebody who's saying it to a 12-year-
old. Of course, if you tell a 12-year-old that they don't have to work
that hard and that it's going to be easier for them, what do you
think they're going to pick? So I'm like, how dare you? Why would
you say that to a 12-year-old and why would you say that with the
parent not present? Why would you even put that idea in their mind
that they don't need to work hard? So there are a lot of subtleties
and things that it's hard to pick out. It's hard to then come back and
say, 'This is happening, this is happening, this is happening' because
it's hard to really just kind of see it and call it out, you know what I
mean? So you have a bunch of individual little things that happen.

These cumulative choices about which track children get enrolled
into add up over time, and disadvantage Black and Latinx students the
most. Denise said it could be unconscious bias of the teachers when students are placed or recommended for certain classes, but that of course
in 9th grade students cannot enroll in Honors or AP courses if they did
not have the preparation for those classes in middle school. The result is
racialized tracking in the middle school and high school. As Latasha explained, "You could probably talk to anybody and they'll tell you that it's
diverse, but when you actually go into the schools, it's not."

Another issue that we heard from parents and students is that if they
get into Honors and AP, then they are one of the only Black students in
the class. Parents and students told us that Black students are told, implicitly or explicitly, by the teacher or other students that they do not belong
there. They are also not given supports to help them academically or
social-emotionally in those classes. Latasha told us that when her oldest
daughter went to Morristown High,

You've got the B-Level, you've got the A-Level, and then you've got
the Honors and the AP and the Quest [Gifted and Talented]. If you
take a peek—the sad thing is, if you go—if anyone was to walk into
the high school and go into one of the classes and you see all Cauca-
sians, you'll get the indication that that's probably an AP class, you
know what I'm saying? I mean, my daughter took Honors—I think
it was Chemistry or something, and she was the only African American in her class and was also made to feel uncomfortable about being there, you know what I'm saying? So there's some changing that
needs to happen. That's why I say it's diverse from the outside until
you really start peeking behind the curtain.

Similarly, Denise thought there should be "more of a push" to get more students of color in those higher-level classes, "especially a kid who's maybe on the border who could go either way. They could be pushed to do more." When asked if the new support counselor is doing that work with the students, Denise said, "Absolutely—I think he does a lot of that. I think he tries to challenge the students, to say, 'Why don't you take this class? Don't take this one, take this one. You're going to have to work a little bit harder but I'll help you. If you have trouble along the way, I'm going to be here for you.' I think we need more of that. I think if the students felt that they had some support and felt like they were going to be able to have someone in their corner, so to speak, I think that they probably would try in a lot of cases." ." These themes from our interviews with Black staff members, parents, and students regarding racialized tracking coincide with the tracking/detracking research. For example, Yonezawa, Wells, and Serna (2002) found that simply allowing students to choose track placements does not have the desired outcome of greater diversity in high-track courses, particularly for Black and Latinx students, because of organizational barriers (e.g., information about options), student's future aspirations (e.g., based on prior track placements), and wanting to learn in respectful classroom environments (e.g., places where they felt they belonged).

As we explained in more detail in Chapter 3, it is important to note that the district recently implemented a detracking policy in the elementary schools. Instead of homogeneous ability grouping in math, they are using heterogeneous groups that are not racially identifiable anymore, with the hope of more student diversity in the Honors classes in middle school and high school. Indeed, as part of the 2017 Equity and Diversity Plan, the district is making a serious effort to diversify middle and high school upper-level classes by using multiple criteria for course placement decisions.

THE DISTRICT'S RESPONSE THEN: "GOOD INTENTIONS" BUT "IT NEVER FELT LIKE PRIORITY #1"

The district's response to the achievement gap committee showed good intentions, but there was no perceived urgency to the situation. Denise said she had several meetings with Superintendent Ficarra and the director of curriculum, and at first they seemed to be interested in helping to remedy the situation. However, after time she became frustrated with the lack of follow-through to their promises, and reportedly said to them, "If the situation were reversed and Caucasian children were failing and not going to college and their test scores were so low and yet another group of children were and they were doing great, how would you feel? You're both parents. How would you feel about that?" While they tried hard to convince the parents that they cared and were trying this and that, Denise recalled, that "the scores were just miserable and the gap was just so wide. It just felt like . . . [when] . . . we would come up with suggestions for things, it just felt like it was met with resistance." The group also got excuses, such as when district leadership would say, "Well, we don't have money" or "We don't have this" and "We have to see about this, we'll get back to you on this." Denise said, "It was a lot of the rigmarole, the runaround I kind of felt. It was very discouraging." The group felt that the superintendent should be concerned about all of the students, and if there's a segment not doing well, "then it seems like it would be priority #1 and it just didn't feel like it. It never felt like priority #1."

Denise and Latasha both explained to us how the district did initiate some of the programs that the group suggested, as outlined above, which was a win for them. Latasha said there was also a lot of "uncomfortableness" around race when they had the discussions with the superintendent, and everybody seemed worried about ruining the image and reputation of Morris. She believed that "if people could just be honest, I think that's the biggest thing. Let's just be honest. It's not about hurting anyone's feelings. The facts are facts, now let's move to honesty so we can move to some action."

The group was astounded when they went back and looked at the data from 10–15 years prior, Denise said. "A lot of it didn't look good. So it was very discouraging and frustrating working with them or trying to work with them. Like I said, we did make some gains so I was definitely proud of that; the counselor and the new preschool spots and some other things that got done. But just by and large, it just felt like drips."

When a new school administrator arrived in Morris in 2017, he told us how he was initially attracted to the district because of the "achievement gap, discipline gap. It was all here, yet for some reason I wasn't certain of until I got here, it was more under the radar than it was at [my previous district] whereas that was their narrative. . . . The whole community was engaged in the dialogue about it." On the other hand, at Morris "it was something that was sort of not discussed here. . . . I felt that this was an incredible opportunity to come in and dramatically improve a school for kids who are, if you look at the data, are really struggling." This administrator came from a multiracial district where de-tracking was being implemented and the community had heated debates all the time about race, SES, equity, access, and opportunity to learn, which is important and very uncommon for districts to do at this moment.

On the other hand, Morris has until recently avoided the topic of race and equity. Interviewees talked about the civility of the district. Yet, for this brand-new administrator that was both a blessing and a curse because, as he explained,

I can tell you that I don't hear in this district discussion of achievement gaps and equity. I don't hear those words. It doesn't seem to be part of the conversation. . . . To me, my early assessment is that there is a wonderful feeling in the building and in the district and at the board meetings of, "This is a nice place that does nice things for kids and we're happy here. We're a wonderful district." The challenge, though, is that it's hard. You know, in order to bring about change, people have to feel and see the need for change, and if in your mind we're doing great and kids are happy, there's all the way up to the board level a feeling that the status quo is great, then it's harder to bring about that change. . . . I'm looking . . . [if] is there a way to keep the stability, keep the positive atmosphere, but at the same time have people dig in and understand that we're the great equalizer and we have work to do because what we're doing right now is not working for all kids.

For good reason, his concern stemmed from troubling patterns in the data in which the opportunity gap is widening as kids move through the school, particularly for Black and Latinx students.

THE DISTRICT'S RESPONSE NOW: EQUITY AND INCLUSION

The district has moved past the old way of being silent about the gaps and being uncomfortable and avoiding any discussion about race. The new and improved Morris district focuses on the gaps and has become more comfortable talking about racial subgroup data and building positive relationships between teachers and students. Their focus now is building a shared definition of what it means to be a "healthy community" in a truly integrated school district.

In 2017, the administration was forced to address race and inequality with the Black community when the middle school used a racially "offensive" image for the spring chorus concert. The cover image of the pamphlet was described in the local newspaper as: "a pen-and-ink cartoon of children singing in a chorus. The lone black child has spiky hair and is completely black, except for cutouts for his or her eyes. It almost looks like the youngster is wearing a dark ski mask."[27] When we spoke to Mackey Pendergrast about how they handled the incident, he explained that it "exploded in the African American community." The first five phone calls after it happened were from Black community members. They said, "Is this a Trump thing?" "Is this, trying to Make America Great Again?" They reportedly felt assaulted by the racist image.

The middle school principal and Superintent Pendergrast immediately held a Town Hall Meeting, which lasted 2 hours and was attended by 150 people in the community (100 or more were African American). Although some people in the town advised Pendergrast not to do it because it might blow up, he felt strongly that they needed to "reassert values [of diversity and integration] and regain trust." During the meeting, Black parents and community members said that no one has ever said "I'm sorry" before. Pendergrast described the comments as "real and earnest about wanting what's best for kids, and trying to stop microaggressions that take place." Looking back, the superintendent felt that it was a great night. He stressed the need to build a healthy community when he replied, "we need to forget Washington DC and create our own culture and community."

After the town hall, he met with Black leaders from Black Lives Matter, churches, the NAACP, and the Urban League. Pendergrast and his staff developed a 3–5 year plan for Equity and Inclusion. He also hired a Diversity Network Coordinator to do outreach in the community and keep developing trust with parents of color. He said that "today's leadership is different than 10 years ago, you need to take risks and to be successful you need a combination of community building and transparency, with metrics that will hold you accountable."

One key policy change in the middle school—where behavioral referral rates from teachers and discipline infractions overall were disproportionately given to Black, Latinx, and low-income students—was to rethink their discipline policy entirely. Instead of giving suspensions, students are sent to group talks, and they are given rewards for positive behavior. Restorative justice practices have replaced punitive discipline. The middle school and high school teachers and staff have been trained in implicit biases and cultural differences. In other words, teachers have been trained to understand their students better and to detect if there has been trauma. They came up with a new code of conduct and strategies to use when students misbehave in class. More social support staff were hired to help support students' social-emotional learning and their feeling of belongingness.

The results have been very positive, including fewer suspensions, fewer students missing class, and higher academic achievement across the board. According to the district, from 2014–2018 at the high school, behavioral referrals dropped from 2,754 to 748 and out-of-school suspensions declined from 198 to 87. At Frelinghuysen Middle School, behavioral referrals decreased from 788 to 134, and out-of-school suspensions fell from 175 to 18. While racial discipline gaps still persist, these reforms have worked and will hopefully have a bigger impact in the coming years.

Overall, the district's Equity and Inclusion Plan is aimed at "promoting lifelong success for each student." The district engaged in a series of dialogues with community stakeholders and came up with several categories that worked toward their main goal of embracing education as a "right to which all humans deserve equal access." The plan is composed of social as well as academic goals, such as getting students to practice "empathy and kindness" and to "respect the dignity of all people through their words and actions." Not merely a rhetorical commitment, the district plan includes reforms to curriculum and instruction, the department of human resources, professional development and training, community relationships, and social networks. The Equity and Inclusion plan explicitly includes a section on culturally relevant teaching. General goals include a social studies/history and humanities curriculum writing project that solicits student input, and a teacher training workshop in culturally responsive curricula and the development of an "intercultural mindset."

A key contributor to the plan was the Morristown High School's Melanin Minds African American Culture and Social Activism Club, which was formed in 2017, after Trump's election. Its mission is "to stimulate dialogue and understanding of important social issues among and across all cultures and encourage students to use their voices to make positive changes within our schools and the greater community."[28] Melanin Minds was featured in the Spring 2018 MEF newsletter because of its multicultural day program, which celebrated and spread knowledge about the diversity within the student body.

More concretely, the plan tries to equalize opportunities by providing free SAT/ACT test prep for students who can demonstrate economic need, and by considering the adoption of an AVID program (Advancement Via Individual Determination—a college-prep program that targets low-income students and provides them with support to help become college and career ready) or similar program to help support students. In terms of measurable outcomes that attend to the problem of tracking and student standardized test achievement, the district has set an ambitious goal that, by 2022, 50% of each race/ethnic and socioeconomic group will participate in at least one AP class by 12th grade and that non-ELL but economically disadvantaged students will have the same pass rate on the ELA-NJ standardized assessment as the NJ average.

Other goals include hiring more diverse faculty and staff through a diversity recruitment job fair; analyzing hiring data to look for trends; preparing a 3-year plan for Equity and Inclusion, which will be submitted to the Board of Education; and creating a community partnership committee that will help plan and solidify community-school relations. In terms of the development of student social networks and cultural capital, the plan targets student participation in extracurricular activities, aiming for the measurable goal of having 80% of each subgroup in the 6th grade participate in at least one extracurricular activity each year.

A faculty presentation of the plan given in May 2019 drew on the rich history of MSD, including sepia-toned pictures of schools from the late 1800s as well as a picture of a group of Black and White MSD students from the turn of the 20th century, showing integration as a long-standing tradition. The presentation then explored the *Jenkins* decision, comparing the growing pains of the merger with a hopeful 2016 *New York Times* article that featured our research team's interim report published by The Century Foundation: "As Other Districts Grapple with Segregation, This One Makes Integration Work."

The presentation went on to explore what integration meant to the community and asked faculty several essential questions in break-out groups in order to begin to do this work: "What is diversity? What is true integration and what does that look like in a school district? What questions do you think we need to be asking to reach the goal of true integration?" Attendees were presented with data, maps, and charts that showed test scores, student and faculty demographics, and socioeconomic data. The presentation addressed several of the concerns that Black parents had come to the district with in 2012, including disproportionality of discipline, the gap in student achievement, and the within-school segregation that occurred as a result of academic tracking and special education classification.

LESSONS LEARNED

Future work must include the voices of Black and Latinx parents and students to understand what is working and what concerns they still have about the education their children are receiving. While the Equity and Inclusion plan is still in the beginning stages, it indicates several shifts from earlier eras. The first thing that it does is explicitly address race as well as social class, and it makes provisions for emergent bilingual learners. By doing this, the plan responds to the earlier colorblind ideologies that have permeated the district. In this vein, the emphasis on culturally relevant teaching and the proposal to engage in collaborative curriculum reform in cooperation with students show that administrators are aware that the implicit bias of teachers and the curriculum are two obstacles to true integration. It begins the work of changing mind-sets about each student's potential to achieve, and what responsibility administrators, teachers, and staff have in a diverse school district with diverse student needs. Additionally, the plan calls for the allocation of resources to help students, faculty, staff, and administrators in meeting their shared goals— the subsidization of testing, the openness to AVID, both demonstrating a financial commitment to goal completion.

Returning to the question that we asked at the start of the chapter, "what would diversity that liberated everyone look like,"[29] the answer definitely starts with the Equity and Inclusion Plan. Pushing the plan even further, we would recommend that the district de-track the curriculum. This would end the practice of students competing for privileged spots in the tracking structure, and would stop requiring parents to advocate for their children to obtain those high-track seats. Integrated, mixed ability classes would also prepare students to be multicultural navigators, like Linda Murphy. Other diverse districts could learn from MSD's successful practices by hiring academic support counselors for Black and Latinx youth, and maintaining strong community-school partnerships. They also could switch from punitive discipline to restorative practices. Other districts could learn from MSD's challenges, too, by ensuring that teachers uncover implicit biases and are prepared and supported to teach in culturally relevant ways to help all students reach their fullest potentials in school and beyond. Latasha's wish for MSD was for them to acknowledge, "The facts are facts; now let's move to honesty so we can move to some action." This is the key for moving the district forward to true integration.

CHAPTER 5

The Latinx Student Experience in MSD

Manuela Villanueva, now in her 40s, immigrated to the United States from Venezuela when she was 7. She spoke no English when she arrived in New Jersey in the early 1980s and her family settled in the northern part of the state. She remembered being pulled out of the classroom for language instruction, but recalled that she would return at the end of the day and sit with her classmates ready to learn, as a fully included member of the class. As she spoke about her time teaching in MSD, she bounced back and forth, between her first years in the country, decades ago, and her daily experience in the district as a Spanish teacher, community liaison, and parent. When she was in elementary school, she remembered feeling included socially by her English-speaking peers because she was one of a few Latinx students in the entire school back then; but she also remarked that she learned English in a safe, exclusive environment outside of the classroom. Manuela evoked a contrasting image between her current position as community liaison working with the district's increasing numbers of Latinx families (now at 39%) versus her own recollections of schools when she was in a small minority. She said that when she visits elementary schools today, she often sees a whole separate English Language Learner (ELL) class full of little Latinx kids filing down the hall.

This chapter focuses on the importance of fully addressing the challenge of educating the recent influx of mostly low-income Central American Spanish-speaking students and their families. Rising to that challenge, the district leadership has given priority to hiring a Latinx parent liaison, bilingual educators, and social support staff to try to build relationships with the Latinx community. Culturally Sustaining Pedagogies emerge as a form of building and sustaining integration efforts across time. Yet, as we will show in the sections below, there are obstacles to full integration of MSD's Latinx population broadly, and the ELL students specifically, because of bilingual education policy that segregates learners and often leads to social exclusion and misunderstandings among English-speaking peers; President Trump's election and the subsequent anti-immigration rhetoric that has led to discrimination inside and outside of schools;

and the underrepresentation of Latinx students in Honors and Advanced Placement courses. We decided to begin the chapter with a vignette of Manuela's story because it reflects the changing times—demographically, academically, and socially. It also encapsulates the shifting nature of bilingual education policy, discussed next.

THE FEDERAL/STATE/LOCAL POLICY LANDSCAPE OF BILINGUAL EDUCATION

Bilingual education was legislated in 1968 under Title VII of the Elementary and Secondary Education Act, which was the first moment when linguistic rights and needs of students were acknowledged.[1] Though in a post-*Brown v. Board* world students are entitled to equal protection under the law, pinning down what "bilingual education" really means is difficult due to the multiple variations that it takes, especially across different states, districts, and schools.[2] In addition to the elusive nature of a unitary definition, there is great diversity in its implementation, which further complicates it.[3] Bilingual education can be broadly separated into three models: transitional bilingual education, maintenance bilingual education, and two-way enrichment bilingual education.[4]

Until the late 1960s, transitional bilingual education was the standard protocol for school districts that attempted to educate their non-English speaking students. Transitional bilingual education draws on students' native languages to facilitate learning in academic subjects.[5] Student mother tongues are used to introduce content and to help build comprehension, after which students are then mainstreamed and their native language is no longer used as a medium of instruction.[6] Transitional bilingual education has an assimilative goal—it is not meant to produce bilingual adults, but rather aims to raise English proficiency and to help students become members of (English-speaking) monolingual classroom communities.[7] Limited period native language instruction is criticized for not helping develop academic fluency in students' native languages, and often not even adequately preparing students to become academically successful in English.[8] Additionally, transitional bilingual approaches often tend to segregate students in an attempt to use native language as a form of instruction.

Federal legislation and case law in the late 1960s and early 1970s challenged the assimilationist underpinnings of English-only instruction and transitional models of bilingual education. In 1968, Title VII of the Elementary and Secondary Education Act (ESEA), known as the Bilingual Education Act, recognized the unique needs of non-English–speaking students and provided funding to districts to develop programs to help students access public educational services.[9] In 1974, the U.S. Supreme Court found, in *Lau v. Nichols,* that the San Francisco Unified School District had violated the Civil Rights Act of 1964 when it failed to provide instruction for non-English speaking students. English-only instruction, the Court found, was discriminatory.[10]

After *Lau,* school districts began to experiment with different variations of bilingual programs; maintenance bilingual education and two-way enrichment bilingual education were two such programs.[11] In a maintenance bilingual education program, students receive intensive instruction in their native language along with English; students who become proficient in English continue to receive instruction in their native language so that they can become conversationally and academically proficient in two languages.[12] Two-way enrichment bilingual education programs, on the other hand, place speakers of both languages in the same academic setting.[13] Two-way bilingual programs move beyond a compensatory model where non-English speakers are seen as being in need of assistance, and instead conceive of bilingual education as an enrichment activity for all of the students involved.[14] While these are only two of many variations, these programs share a common goal of drawing on the native language as a resource.

If bilingual education is difficult to define, so too are its alternatives. Gándara and Hopkins use the term "restrictive language policies" to contrast bilingual education with other forms of teaching ELL students.[15] Several states have banned bilingual education in favor of English-only instruction. The most prominent example is Arizona, which has implemented a Structured English Immersion (SEI) model.[16] SEI is one of two immersion ideas, revolving around the concept that students are not to use their native language and a thorough amount of time on task in English will result in proficiency in the new language.[17] The SEI model is a counterpoint to bilingual education programs and emphasizes English language development through the use of block scheduling.[18] SEI is the model that most opponents to bilingual education put forward as a viable, if not research-proven, alternative.

English Language Learners are entitled to educational access, regardless of immigration status, and are protected under the Civil Rights Act of 1964 and the Equal Educational Opportunities Act of 1974.[19] Districts must establish procedures to identify and assess English Learners and must provide language assistance to ELL students to help them become proficient in English. However, they are given broad latitude as to which sort of instructional program they choose. A district's program must allow students to have meaningful access to curricular resources and extra-curricular activities and cannot result in unnecessary segregation in school.[20] Accountability mechanisms state that districts must monitor the progress of ELL students and must support them to achieve "English language proficiency and acquire content knowledge within a reasonable period of time."[21]

New Jersey statutes provide that all ELLs are entitled to a free, appropriate public education.[22] In keeping with federal guidelines, New Jersey districts must identify students who speak a language other than English, develop a screening process, and establish and provide required courses and support services in order to prepare students to meet high school graduation requirements. The level and intensity of support services are determined by the number of ELL students in a district. New Jersey districts are required to establish language services when there are at least one but fewer than 10 ELLs enrolled in the district, are required to create an English as a Second Language (ESL) program when there are at least 10 ELL students, and are required to establish a bilingual education program where students are instructed in their native language and in English when there are 20 or more ELLs in any one language classification.

MSD offers an ELL/Bilingual curriculum across the grade levels, determined by student language proficiency and the number of students eligible for services. However, as per NJ state policy, depending on the number of ELL students in each grade level per school, students are offered language support in self-contained classrooms (>20 students) or integrated classroom settings with push-in or pull-out support (<20 students). In grades K–5, the district offers ESL[23] for students who are still learning English—students receive mainstream instruction and are pulled into a small-group setting where they are given specific language and academic support.[24] In grades 6–12, ESL is divided into four self-contained English language levels, ranging from a prebeginner level through an advanced level to Heritage Spanish. The leveling helps address the needs of recently arrived immigrant youth who may have limited native language literacy as well as interrupted educational experiences in their home countries. ESL satisfies graduation requirements for English Language Arts. The district also offers a bilingual education program in Spanish and English at the elementary and secondary level. At the secondary level, ELL students take bilingual math, science, and history courses. Speakers of Spanish who are still in the bilingual track also take Heritage Spanish in grades 9–12, which focuses on developing academic literacy as well as on social and emotional learning goals.[25] Once they have passed all four levels, students can take mainstream English-only classes.

In 2016–2017, MSD centralized its school registration, a move that made identifying non-native English speakers and properly serving them substantially easier. In addition to establishing residency, students are required to fill out a home language survey. If they indicate that they speak a language other than English, they are then assessed by an ELL/Bilingual director depending on their grade level. If they are elementary-aged, the ELL/Bilingual coordinator for K–8 determines their level and assigns them to a school that can properly serve them; not all of the elementary schools have bilingual tracks, some only have "high intensity ESL" that would not be appropriate for a student who has no English language proficiency. The district arranges transportation and the students are assessed using the WIDA Model (Measure of Developing English Language) once they are at their school. High school–aged students are assessed informally through a diagnostic conversation with the ELL/Bilingual director after their home language survey indicates that they speak a language other than English. They then take the WIDA assessment and are referred to guidance counselors to be placed in an appropriate classroom setting. The major difference between elementary and high school is that students are older and are closer to aging out of the system. One ELL/Bilingual Coordinator who worked at the high school level, remarked, "We don't have the luxury of time. Most of the students that come to us are over the age of 15 and we basically have 3 years to get them [to satisfy] a tremendous amount of graduation requirements to get them walking down that aisle."

There have been a number of shifts in the way curriculum and instruction are coordinated across schools in the district. MSD recognized that the job of supervising curriculum for ELL/Bilingual students was too much for K–5 principals, to whom curriculum decisions are normally left. It was too large a job for high school administrators as well, and it required expertise that many administrators do not have. At one point, the district employed a K–12 ELL/Bilingual Director, but returned to having a K–8 Director, and a high school Director. Curriculum reform has been a constant process of working with students, teachers, and other stakeholders to identify the best practices that help balance language acquisition, mastery of academic content, and social and emotional development.

The district has focused on minimizing social segregation through reworking schedules so that ELL and general education students can socialize and be together in electives or specials, like physical education. Most significantly, the district recognizes the need for native language proficiency and language maintenance and it has identified the dangers of prioritizing English Language Acquisition over all else. One of the administrators involved in the ELL/Bilingual program reflected that without these measures, "You end up having segregated classes in a school and they're not getting to be friends with all the other kids and they just go up from one year to the next together. We don't want that." But another administrator emphasized what the balancing act that ELL/Bilingual education entails: "Does the integration piece supersede what we know is right? We have admitted to ourselves at this point that not all electives lend themselves to language learning environments. Emotionally it can be difficult for them to walk into a room where they're alone."

The Political Landscape of Immigration

Recently, immigration debates have focused on the influx of migrants from Central America; a full 8% of the 43.3 million U.S. immigrants are from Central America.[26] Central American immigration, largely the result of political violence and instability, increased in the 1980s as direct and clandestine U.S. involvement in the region helped escalate civil conflicts. In 2016 alone, U.S. Customs and Border Protection (CBP) intercepted nearly 46,900 unaccompanied children and more than 70,400 families from El Salvador, Guatemala, and Honduras arriving at the U.S.–Mexico border.[27] Haunting images of separated families, of children torn from their parents, led President Obama to declare an "urgent humanitarian situation" in 2014.[28] President Trump continued the Obama-era focus on the border, instead framing the migration as a security threat, remarking about the unaccompanied minors: "They look so innocent. They're not innocent."[29] A lack of rootedness, the absence of parents, and the direness of their economic situations led Deputy Attorney General Rod J. Rosenstein to make the argument that allowing these children into the United States would make them easy marks for gang recruitment.[30]

This openly hostile political climate regarding immigration, as well as the presence of immigrant youth in schools, complicates the federal, local, and state policy landscape that structures the availability of programs, supports, and curricula for ELL or emergent bilingual youth. Language policy is one part of this debate. The controversy over bilingual instruction is marked by competing discourses on assimilation and diversity. On the one hand, Donald Trump led the Republican field in 2015 on an anti-immigrant, English-only platform, declaring in a presidential candidate debate: "We have a country, where, to assimilate, you have to speak English. We have to have assimilation—to have a country, we have to have assimilation."[31] On the other, educational researchers speak of " . . . making our schools safe and affirming places for all children and youth, including those who have the gift of speaking more than one language."[32]

Much is lost when educators frame emergent bilingual youth as social problems or from a deficit perspective, when they fail to acknowledge the uniqueness of Latinx students' life experiences and cultural funds of knowledge, and when schools discourage or do not help to cultivate meaningful peer group identifications.[33] Yet, schools, including MSD, continue to be challenged by the best way to educate Latinx immigrant youth. This is the case, as Ovando and Collier acknowledge, because there is " . . . more written material concerning the politics of bilingual education than there are resources for teachers in the classroom."[34] The nationalism embedded in the polemics over bilingual education is the third rail that often distorts the debate and pulls it away from classroom practice and educational outcomes. Linguistic needs are but one part of the imperative that schools have; ELL students must also be able to demonstrate proficiency in the content areas, a competing need that positions language acquisition and access to content knowledge at loggerheads. Additionally, ELL students, like all children, have social needs, but often attend either linguistically isolated schools because of high levels of U.S. school segregation or are linguistically isolated within a school.[35] Balancing direct language instruction (which necessarily involves being separated from English-proficient peers), the building of meaningful peer relationships, and the instruction of academic content, is the central challenge for school administrators.[36]

In attempting to equip students with language skills, English Language Development (ELD) has historically been stressed over academic literacy and social and emotional learning. The current political climate and the empirical failings of ELD-centered instruction have led to changes in the view of what constitute "best practices" from a view that emphasized the importance of language above all else to one that is focusing on implementing strategies that situate language development within academics.[37]

MSD aims to strike a balance—the curriculum attempts to meet students where they are and to help them develop a number of competencies. The course sequence for ELL students balances English language development, the development of academic literacy in English, the acquisition of content knowledge, the maintenance and strengthening of native language literacy, and social and emotional learning and growth. In striving to address these varied and layered charges, MSD tries to, in each course, help students access the course material and to view themselves as members of the school community.

Immigrant Youth and School Leadership

Indeed, migration from countries with political, economic, and social instability brings with it several challenges that school leaders must address. Many immigrant youth present with limited or interrupted formal education.[38] For students with limited or interrupted formal education (SLIFE), basic literacy in even their native languages might be a struggle that makes attaining academic literacy in a second language a formidable obstacle. In fact, many Central American students may not speak Spanish as a first language, instead speaking an indigenous language. Migration itself can be a traumatic experience—separation from family and caregivers, the stress of fleeing, and months-long journeys often beset with violence and instability, leaves a mark on the lives of children and influences their ability to adjust to new social communities.[39] Furthermore, the structure of U.S. schooling with its emphasis on individualism, can be alienating to children from other cultures, especially to older students who bring a wide range of pragmatic life experiences, but are being called upon in classrooms to perform in largely academic and objective ways.[40]

Trauma, interrupted and limited education, poverty, a lack of support structures, and a hostile political environment form the milieu into which immigrant youth and school administrators and teachers step. Charged with the task of helping students develop their language proficiency, coupled with the moral imperative of helping students retain and develop their own unique cultural resources and social worlds, administrators and teachers look to a variety of sources for best practices. One such framework, culturally sustaining pedagogy, described in more detail in Chapter 3, builds upon earlier culturally relevant teaching models.[41]

A central theme in the research on school leaders in schools with emergent bilingual youth is that they engage in key leadership practices to help create inclusive learning communities for all students. First, educational leaders are most successful when they see the work of educating emergent bilingual youth as the work of *all* faculty and staff not just the work of ESL teachers, who are often relied upon to act as intermediaries between the community and school.[42] Second, leaders can also be deliberate about constructing spaces for educators to have deep and meaningful conversations to examine their own perspectives on immigrant youth culture, language, and experiences.[43] Third, the most effective administrators also move beyond surface-level conversations about emergent bilingual students, seeing the project of inclusivity as not merely being about translating documents but rather about how to integrate culture into the curriculum, how to develop heritage Spanish, and how to consider external factors that influence ELLs belonging in school.[44]

EMERGENT BILINGUAL STUDENTS IN MSD

In the next sections of the chapter, using the concept of CSP, we will illustrate our findings on student, parent, educator/social support staff, and school leader perspectives on the Morris schools. Our qualitative research primarily focuses on the lived experiences of immigrant youth at the secondary level. In addition to Spanish interviews focus groups, and classroom observations in the ESL, Bilingual, Heritage Spanish, and Honors/AP levels, we also engaged in two focus groups with Latinx parents, and several interviews with Morristown High School teachers, administrators, and support staff about the successes and challenges of educating ELL students.

We begin with an overview of quantitative data relating to the emergent bilingual population in the MSD. Afterward, we turn to a discussion of students thinking about the concept of diversity and inclusion—considering how recently arrived immigrant youth in the ESL track and Latinx-identifying youth in the mainstream understand their community, themselves, each other, and their place in school. We then consider how Latinx parents experience school and community outreach and collaboration. Finally, we turn to Morristown High School faculty and support staff to think about how they understand their role in creating a safe and inclusive Latinx community within the school, as well as how they touch the lives of Latinx students outside of school and in the community.

Overview of the Latinx and Emergent Bilingual Student Population

As previously highlighted in Tables 4.1 and 4.3, race and ethnicity have a strong correlation with economic levels in MSD. While lower than that of the Black population, the Hispanic population in MSD has poverty levels more than three times that of the Asian population and more than double that of the White population. Furthermore, while more than a third of Asian households and non-Hispanic White households have an annual income that exceeds $150,000, only 10% of Hispanic households in MSD have attained that level of economic wealth. Instead, 45% of Hispanic households make less than $50,000 annually, with 18% making less than $25,000 annually. Additionally, Table 4.4 shows that the Hispanic population in MSD has the lowest level of educational achievement of any racial/ethnic group. More than 15% of MSD's Hispanic population over the age of 25 does not have a high school degree.

The achievement gap in MSD's schools is stark for Hispanic students. As Table 4.2 shows, across all measures (with the exception of grade 3 math proficiency scores) Hispanic students in MSD have lower levels of academic achievement than any of their peer groups. While 100% of Asian students, 97.2% of White students, and 85.4% of Black students graduate, only 57.9% of Hispanic students do. Notably, far fewer than half (42.1%) of ELLs in the district graduate. Relatedly, only 41.3% of Hispanic students and 7.1% of ELLs attend college.

Table 5.1 highlights some essential demographic data about the Hispanic population in MSD. First, it is important to note that the proportion of the Hispanic population is generally largest in schools serving younger students. This correlates with data showing that a larger proportion of children in lower grades come from families where Spanish is the primary language spoken at home. These data, in part, explain the higher rates of students classified as English Language Learners in lower grades. Collectively, these data highlight that in the coming years the middle school and high school in the MSD will likely have an increasing number of Hispanic students in need of English language acquisition assistance.

Table 5.1. Morris School District Hispanic Origin and Language Data, 2017–2018

School	Grade Level	Hispanic	English Learners	HOME LANGUAGE		
				English	Spanish	Other
Lafayette Learning Center	Pre-K	59.8%	NA	54.3%	44.9%	0.8%
Alfred Vail School	K–2	39.4%	17.8%	68.4%	28.5%	3.1%
Hillcrest School	K–2	48.6%	26.0%	57.2%	39.7%	3.1%
Woodland School	K–2	39.8%	23.2%	69.2%	27.5%	3.3%
Normandy Park School	K–5	41.4%	19.5%	64.6%	32.5%	2.9%
Alexander Hamilton	3–5	43.0%	13.7%	65.8%	31.8%	2.4%
Sussex Avenue School	3–5	36.5%	9.3%	78.3%	20.7%	1.0%
Thomas Jefferson School	3–5	39.2%	15.6%	65.2%	31.7%	3.1%
Frelinghuysen Middle School	6–8	39.6%	8.3%	81.2%	16.7%	2.1%
Morristown High School	9–12	34.7%	10.5%	85.6%	12.9%	1.5%

Recently Arrived Immigrant Youth: "We all Form the World"

During the Spanish focus groups with recently arrived immigrant students, many of the students in the ESL class and students in the bilingual class expressed how much they liked Morristown as a community because it was *safe, tightly knit,* and *supportive.* They emphasized the difference between their home countries and Morristown, in particular with regard to safety and violence. One student remarked, "Morristown is a really great town. It is not too crowded and noisy. It is not too quiet and alone. . . . You can go anywhere and it is safe." Another student agreed, "It is very quiet, very calm. Everyone knows each other. If you go to the store, you will see your neighbor, so it is very close like that." This generally positive view of Morristown was tempered by several comments about discrimination on the basis of immigration status that students had experienced in the broader community: "Sometimes they treat us bad.

Discriminate against us because we are illegal. They make remarks about deporting us. They make threats. For example: you are getting paid less and you say it is not fair, they threaten by saying you are illegal and don't have your papers. They even say: 'We will call the police.'"

In particular, students pointed to the 2016 presidential election as a tipping point. One student recounted graffiti that had been scrawled in the bathroom that said, "Go Back to Mexico." Students were surprised by this outward display of hostility. A student recalled: "I never heard anything like that in my life. I have never been exposed to racism and then with the election, his [Trump's] views, people felt open and they felt like they could say what they really feel. We saw a lot of that in the school." Spanish-speaking students felt powerless, as a student explained: "One of the most important things for me . . . is [learning] the [English] language. We all have the capacity to do everything. The language impairs us. It is the lack of communicating. Sometimes we have the idea, but don't have a clue of how to explain ourselves." Students expressed that the school had addressed the incident and that teachers had tried to control it. But the anti-immigrant sentiment cut deep and led to both a sense of powerlessness and a theorizing about the nature of difference. Said one student, reflecting on the graffiti: "I believe in . . . demonstrating to the United States that we all form the world. The only frontiers that they have are the spaces we put each other in. We are all the same. There is nothing different. Except that they are White, but we are all the same, we can all speak."

Several themes emerged from these focus groups with regard to recently arrived immigrant youth understandings of community and diversity. On the one hand, students overwhelmingly described Morristown as safe, quiet, and a nice place to live. On the other hand, they also described incidents of discrimination in their daily lives both in and out of school. They saw these incidents, perhaps somewhat naively because of how new everything was to them, as being outside of the norm for the community. Two students in an ESL class described their frustration and their lack of ability to address complex social issues, one on the basis of language, the other as a result of postelection anti-immigrant sentiment that manifested as racism. In particular, the student understandings of diversity indicate an as yet incomplete culture of diversity at the high school level for newly arrived immigrant youth, if we look to CSP as a set of aspirations. In particular, the emergent bilingual student describing her own experience with language as something that "impairs," suggests that she feels herself on the margins of her schooling community, without a voice. The student who pointed to racism as the biggest problem felt the need to prove to his White peers that "we are all the same," taking a slightly assimilationist tack as opposed to reframing the issue as one of structural racism and the systematic devaluation of immigrant contributions.

Spanish Heritage Track: "How Does MHS Fit Into My Community?"

In 2015, MSD articulated its commitment to maintenance bilingual education when it rewrote its Heritage Spanish curriculum for grades 9–12. The courses offer students access to literacy in Spanish in order to help them develop overall literacy. The course sequence introduces students to "various themes related to the life of an American high school student." The course writers aligned the Heritage sequence with the New Jersey Core Curriculum Content Standards and the Common Core State Standards in Literacy. In addition to conducting the courses in Spanish, the philosophical tenets of the course sequence emphasize the importance of helping students understand issues related to their experience as immigrants. In addition, a stated goal of the Heritage sequence is to help students "develop a sense of pride in their Hispanic heritage and the Spanish language."

The Heritage sequence begins with a unit that helps students begin to understand themselves as high school students, introducing them to classroom policies, rules, the school environment, and graduation requirements. Essential questions include: "How do I familiarize myself with my school environment and important people?" and "How does MHS fit into my community?" The course, however, is academic and culturally relevant. As students discuss broad themes regarding how to "do school," they also read the graphic novel *Diary of a Wimpy Kid* in Spanish and reflect on topics such as bullying and friendship. Literacy skills include the identification of text features, analysis, and critique of information; distinguishing between facts and opinions; and the analysis of historical and political contexts. A final project requires them to imagine themselves as exemplar students who have been asked to create a presentation for new Spanish-speaking students. The first year of the Heritage series continues to use young adult fiction to provoke conversation about identity—"who am I?"—immigration, and future lives in the United States.

Heritage 2 embeds literacy skills in questions of identity, asking students to think about what makes a good person, requiring students to analyze the way in which gender is shaped by cultural norms, using students' own experiences with migration as a place of reflecting on larger issues of social inequality, and teaching students how to engage in self-reflection. Students read short stories in the original Spanish as well as several translated young adult novels. Heritage 3 deepens these same areas of inquiry, trying to get students to think about character and citizenship, as well as what it means to live as a member of a community. Students also explore the concept of dreams, learning how to realistically set personal goals.

On a late November day, we observed a Heritage I classroom. Students filed in as the *Haz Ahoras* (Do Now) was up on the screen with two questions for students to reflect on: "How did you spend Thanksgiving?"

"Did you go out on Black Friday?" Students completed the assignment on their Chromebooks as they quietly talked. They sat in groups of three at tables. The objective for the day was to "Work cooperatively on a presentation about how to have success at MHS." As students finished the *Haz Ahoras*, the teacher, Ms. Aguilar, asked students to volunteer their responses to the question about how they had spent their Thanksgiving. "I spent it alone" said one student. "You didn't eat turkey?" Ms. Aguilar asked. Addressing the whole class, she queried: "For how many people was it your first time celebrating Thanksgiving?" More than half of the students raised their hands, as Ms. Aguilar opened the conversation: "Is it different from how we celebrate things?" "It's different," said one student. When prompted to explain, he continued, "Because it's not the same." Students laughed, then began to list some of the things that seemed different to them about American Thanksgiving.

Students marveled at the strangeness of eating turkey, and how bizarre it was that people had chosen to go to Walmart to buy things instead of spending time with their families at home. Ms. Aguilar guided them through the strange rituals of the holiday season, remarking to students, "Now, the Christmas spirit starts! In the United States right after Thanksgiving, we're in the Christmas season. It's part of the culture." Students transitioned into the work period of the lesson as Ms. Aguilar told students that they needed to put away their phones to work on their project. Someone complained about the group work. Ms. Aguilar smiled, "Outside of here, you have to work with people. Learn how to do it now."

We pulled several students aside to conduct a focus group, asking them questions about their experiences in school. One question that we put to them was, "What would you change in this community, if you had the opportunity?" A student smiled and quickly responded, "The language!" The surrounding students laughed. We tried to clarify: "You mean, everyone should speak Spanish?" The student considered this for a minute and responded, "Not to try to change them [English speakers], but . . . because if they don't understand us and we don't understand them, then we are at a standstill." After a series of questions about favorite classes, we asked, "What are some of the obstacles you encounter as students?" One student reflected:

> The biggest obstacle is speaking, English. I speak English, but I get embarrassed. I only speak English when it is necessary. I have friends who speak English, but if they speak Spanish, I will speak Spanish to them. If I am with someone who only speaks English, then I have to speak English.

Students of Latinx Descent: "I'm Just This Spanish Girl"

The focus group of Latinx-identifying students who were from second- or even third-generation Latinx families and thus had lived in Morristown longer did not spend as much time thinking about Morristown as a community; they focused on the school and on their liminal position as being perceived of as "Spanish" while also, in some cases, not actually speaking the language and having more in common with their White and African American peers. In general, these students put forward a slightly more critical view of diversity, its promises, and its dilemmas.

The first topic that emerged during the focus groups was the under-representation of students of color, in particular Latinx students, in AP classes. When asked to hypothesize a reason for this underrepresentation, a student theorized that this view came from their implicit bias:

> In this country, I'm not expected to succeed because of my back-ground, because . . . both of my parents came over here from poor countries and really, really started at the bottom. Fortunately, I was given this opportunity where I can climb the social ladder and I can climb this, but I'm not expected to. I'm not given the same expecta-tions you are, simply because the color of my skin or simply because of my background, you know what I mean?

Another student elaborated that the school had not fulfilled its respon-sibility to help communicate with students about opportunities: "I was never told by my guidance counselor, 'This is what you need to do.' I'm not handed this information. It's something I have to work for." A student took a critical historical perspective as she explained the structural nature of this local inequality of opportunities and expectations: "The history of our country kind of dictates that. With African Americans, they just didn't have it and us Latino-Americans—again, the history with our differ-ent cultures and backgrounds in this country kind of dictates that. When we're at the bottom, no one tells us how to climb the ladder, so we stay at the bottom, you know what I mean?" The students further complicated this idea of inequality by bringing up immigration status and the way it limits student opportunity, security, and ability to access educational re-sources at the postsecondary level.

In addition to this view of student opportunity being limited by a suite of individual actions on behalf of administrators and teachers, as well as the larger political climate in the United States, students pointed to segre-gation in school as a co-constitutive element of school diversity. Students of mixed-race background, as well as U.S.–born Latinx students suffered from being in between—as one student put it "I'm more like a floater, really." One girl explained: "Yeah. I'm a gringa because I understand

Spanish, but I don't speak it. That's also a major problem—well, to some people it's not a problem. Then with White people, I'm just this Spanish girl. I'm automatically ghetto because I'm Spanish and I don't know certain things. I don't match up to them because they think I don't have the same financial standard as they [White kids] do." As a result, several members of the focus group explained that U.S.–born Latinx and Black students tended to group themselves together. A student accounted for this: "I feel like Hispanic kids and Black kids comingle more than you'll see any other race comingle just because they have that common understanding of being kind of pushed away from other Whites in the school."

A bigger divide, however, was the separation in experience among students who had grown up in the United States versus recently arrived immigrant youth. Multiple participants expressed emotions ranging from pity to sadness in their descriptions of students in the ELL/Bilingual track. Said one, "I think the kids who have just come to this country, I think they're slighted even more than we are. We speak English. I feel like they're judged, even by the teachers. I genuinely feel bad for them because I think that—I mean, sometimes a teacher can't really help them."

For first- and second-generation students of Latinx descent at Morristown High School, language, race, and cultural practices form part of how they understand themselves and their identities within school. Distanced through language proficiency and distancing themselves through social practices, these students do not feel connected to recently arrived immigrant youth. They do not socialize with them in school, do not attend classes with them, and, with the exception of electives and physical education and a select number of extracurricular activities, students of Latinx descent feel more American than anything else. Their feeling of being more American than Latinx, however, does not insulate them from the very real barriers they still face, despite language proficiency. These barriers include immigration status, structural racism, stereotyping within school by students and teachers, and diminished access to more selective curricular tracks. The obstacles students face are slightly different than their parents' experiences with the school and community of Morristown, which we illustrate next.

PARENTAL INVOLVEMENT

Parent involvement influences the experiences of students in school although the relationship between parent involvement and academic outcomes is not yet completely understood.[45] Theorizations regarding parental environment divide parental involvement into several types: basic obligations of parents (e.g., food, shelter); school-to-home communications (e.g., report cards, newsletters); parent involvement at school (e.g., volunteering); and parent involvement in learning activities at home.[46] Additionally, parents often set expectations and help students set educational and occupational goals for themselves.[47] This communication of academic goals among family members is often referred to as *academic socialization*.[48] The connection between parent involvement and educational outcomes has implications for how any school approaches its relationship with the community. This, in turn, affects how students are socialized into academics—how they view their place in the school and their role in their own learning.

Structural barriers that disproportionately affect lower-income families and parents and students of color complicate parental involvement and academic socialization.[49] Barriers to parental involvement for Latinx parents in particular concern negative experiences with school governance, balancing demanding work schedules, a lack of English proficiency, legal status, and an inability to provide assistance with home-based learning such as homework.[50] In research conducted on African American families, researchers found that parents often feel that they need an invitation to become involved in school activities, and that establishing a welcoming school environment helps invite this sort of open participation.[51]

Best practices for encouraging family involvement in schooling include taking into account scheduling difficulties by scheduling outreach at a variety of times to help make school events more accessible.[52] The involvement of school counselors and other support staff can also help increase and sustain parental involvement both by helping teachers better understand the context of the families they serve and by directly reaching out to parents themselves.[53] Most importantly, schools can strive to be present in the community in ways that encourage involvement through a history of positive interactions with the school.[54]

MSD's outreach to Latinx parents aims to mitigate barriers and to do so deploys a variety of techniques. Aside from translating material into Spanish, the high school has hosted several parent sessions to help educate parents regarding graduation requirements. The high school has gone out of its way to employ bilingual social workers, bilingual guidance counselors, and a parent liaison. These staff members provide a number of invaluable services—they help address acute mental health crises, help students schedule classes, talk to parents, and are visible in the community. In terms of proactive community building, the high school has held a yearly *Noche de la Hispanidad* in which Spanish-speaking students and families come together with other members of the community to celebrate their heritage with food, dress, and cultural performances. One administrator we spoke to remarked that at the high school and elementary level, there has been an ongoing and targeted effort to recruit child study team members, nurses, teachers, and guidance counselors who speak Spanish. As part of its outreach, MSD sends Spanish-speaking people out into the community to help with kindergarten registration and to screen preschool–aged kids to anticipate their need for services.

Supplementary programing encourages the building and strengthening of school-community relationships. The district has participated in the Latino Family Literacy Project and has a program established at the elementary and secondary levels. The program invites parents into school to read with their children. The K–5 level focuses on literacy where parents are invited to come in and read a story with their kids. Every book that is chosen for the program includes an activity, and at the end of the program they create a family scrapbook. For the upper grades, parents and kids focus on the college application process, gaining awareness of how to navigate the process. This program deepens school and community relations and helps families become aware of educational resources and processes that might have previously seemed difficult to access.

At the high school, the Latinx parent outreach coordinator has been successful in making a space for bilingual and ELL youth in a long-standing program—PGC, or Peer Group Connections. PGC is a mentoring program in which high school seniors are selected to co-lead a classroom of 1st-year students. To participate, students must apply and take a class led by the guidance department. PGC, a course meant to help new students adjust to the high school experience, originally had not included any bilingual youth, which created an environment of exclusion for non-English speaking students who were being led by co-leaders who could not communicate with them. Teachers recognized this need and began to recruit high achieving ELL students to apply to the program.

Despite these attempts to encourage parent involvement, some barriers do persist—much communication is conducted via online platforms, which makes access difficult for those parents who do not have internet or who struggle with computer literacy. Many parents, particularly those who do not speak English, struggle with accessing school resources and information. Irregular work schedules, concerns about child care, and the difficulties of living between two cultures all complicate the involvement of Latinx parents and the efforts that MSD engages in to help bridge school and community life.

MSD, however, is aware of these challenges and has endeavored to address them. When it became clear that internet access was a barrier to parent involvement, Manuela realized that communicating with parents via text was an effective work-around. She signed parents up for remind.com and Constant Contact text so that they could be informed about various events at school. The MSD website itself has a translate option that allows parents—once they learn about it—to access the majority of district materials and contact information in Spanish. Even report cards are translated. But one principal remarked that translation itself is not enough: "Even if you do a presentation and have someone translate it, it doesn't work as well as having a separate presentation for your Spanish-speaking population." Instead of inviting Spanish-speaking parents to English-speaking presentations with a translator, she and Manuela scheduled a series of presentations on the new report card format with Spanish-speaking parents. The presentations and Q and A were in Spanish, and parents were able to bring their children's report cards or look them up on their phones and ask about anything they found confusing. For Bilingual and ESL classes, teacher comments were made in Spanish, communicating student progress.

Latinx Parents: "We Are Like a Small Society"

Sitting around a table with several parents at the Neighborhood House, a community-based organization described in more depth in Chapter 3, part of whose mission is to "help new immigrants and other families who are confronting economic challenges and fostering cross-cultural acceptance,"[55] we drank coffee and ate cookies as we began with a question in Spanish: "Why did you come to Morristown?" Parents nodded, and emphasized the town's safety, the ability to walk to work, and how quiet and clean the community appeared. One parent elaborated: "This is the only town where we have a sense of community, that diversity. Lots of times when you have people coming from other countries, they go to the big cities and yes, there is a lot of diversity, but I like it here. We are like a small society."

The group contrasted Morristown with Newark and other urban environments and also emphasized the differences between their home countries and their new home: "The difference is, there are more opportunities for our kids. In my country there aren't any opportunities. There are many kids who do not go to school. This country requires all kids to go to school. In our countries there are no requirements." Although they praised the plentiful nature of opportunity, especially for their children, in contrast to the poverty and violence they described in their home countries, one woman emphasized a problem: "This is what I believe is a problem. Living two different cultures at the same time is difficult for the identity."

As we branched into questions about their interactions with school, parents again emphasized opportunity and the availability of help for their children when they needed it. What stood out was the very real barrier that language posed and the difficulties with being present at school activities due to the demands of their jobs: "I come to a meeting, which I want to attend, but then I could lose my job. I need to feed my kids and that is my priority. Sometimes, people forget the life of an immigrant," said one parent. "There is a system to check the grades, but that is a problem, too, because the kids know their parents don't speak English. So they don't tell their parents." When we posed a question about one thing they'd like to change, we heard: "Well, I would like for them to explain in Spanish what is happening."

The parents rooted their immigration narratives in a shared sense of struggle punctuated by the deliberate choice to remain in Morristown, in large part because of its acceptance of difference. They also emphasized the plentiful nature of educational opportunity, referencing the difficulties with educational attainment in their native countries due to violence, cost, and the necessity of child labor. But the parents' perception of the availability of resources for their children was also accompanied by a belief that their inability to speak English and advocate for their children left them outside of the system.

We turn next to the district's efforts to strengthen the bond and increase communication between the school and the Latinx community via better district outreach, parent workshops, and Spanish translation services. Interviews with six high school educators analyzed below reflect the ways in which the district is responding (or not) to the influx of Latinx families in the schools.

TEACHERS AND SUPPORT STAFF

Manuela

Manuela, highlighted in this chapter's introductory vignette, is a Spanish teacher who works at Morristown High School. She also coordinates parent outreach to the Latinx community. Joking about being present in the community, she talked about the way she tries to get the word out about her position and feel for the pulse of the Latinx community: "I've gone to two Sunday masses, one at St. Jerome's and the other at Iglesia Alto Refugio. Sometimes my husband jokes around, like, 'You're like a politician.' I feel sometimes like I am. I'm putting myself out there. I'm shaking hands." Her on-the-ground efforts have helped make her a familiar face to Spanish-speaking families in the community. Her most recent victory was the way she had successfully used the existing Honeywell automated phone system to contact parents in Spanish. In addition to compiling a list of phone numbers by hand, she made the rounds—attending church, putting up flyers, getting the word out at various neighborhood organizations. She routinely holds a special workshop in Spanish before Back to School night in addition to planning outreach events about student GPA and grading, graduation requirements, and technology. Manuela contacts parents and has invited them to the superintendent's presentation, translating for them over sets of headphones that she handed out.

These efforts come out of Manuela's own life story, as the opening vignette of the chapter suggests. Her own experiences as an immigrant student who was undocumented until her sophomore year of high school, her history with the community, and her experiences as a parent all shape her approach to the Latinx community. While Manuela's parents were both Chilean, her husband is American and also attended Morristown schools. Her daily experiences with emergent bilingual youth have made her think a great deal about how Morristown serves its Spanish-speaking population.

Pausing in the corner of a Heritage Spanish class to talk, Manuela shook her head as she recounted the story of a bilingual student she worked with who spoke English as a first language. Manuela remembered that the student had been given an assignment where he was required to present on a list of historical figures; the names given had all been White men, like George Washington and Thomas Jefferson. Manuela deadpanned: "Come on, can't you throw in a Chávez, or a Rodriguez, or a Domínguez?" Instead of waiting for the school to address the lack of diversity in the assignment, Manuela took it upon herself to introduce this student to the work of César Chávez. Manuela reflected on how if she had not had as much education, time, or relative privilege, she would not have been able to open the assignment up for this student to explore other perspectives.

Another story that informed her perspective on the students and families she serves related to language learning and self-image. Her anecdote embodied a conflict over how to conceptualize bilingualism as an identity. She recalled how one of the elementary schools had decided to purchase Rosetta Stone Spanish; the students universally hated the platform and, by extension, learning the language. Not soon after, she was speaking with a parent whose daughter came home and told her grandmother, "Stop talking to me in Spanish, everyone hates it." Manuela spoke with the student about why she did not want to speak in Spanish, trying to understand where the feelings came from. She finally figured out that it was because of Rosetta Stone: "Imagine if I hadn't known to ask . . . the self-loathing that that would create in a child."

Manuela has a conceptualization of diversity that is consonant with CSP—she is critical in her understanding of the history of race and racism in the United States, she is aware of issues of representation in the curriculum, and she understands the complex issues regarding identity that accompany the project of bilingual education. Furthermore, her efforts as liaison have aimed to not simply translate documents, but to actually create a positive presence within the Spanish-speaking community so that the school can be responsive to the questions and concerns parents bring. She sees the relationship between school and community as dynamic rather than a unidirectional unloading of resources and information. Manuela is aware that the work of educating Spanish-speaking youth is not simply the work of a few teachers, but rather the work of the entire school community.

Alika Robinson

When we arrived in Alika Robinson's classroom, the room smelled of empanadas and there was a slide projected on the board in preparation for the LUNA (Latinos Unidos de Norte America) club. The slide, written in Spanish, read:

> LUNA club is a club for Latinos and all those that want to know more about Latin American culture! In this club, we try to provide support for the school and for the community. This year we have many plans and new events for all of you. We hope that you're excited and that you support our club. We have to be united and show that we are good people and that we can have a positive influence here at Morristown High School.

Robinson, advisor of the club, purchases empanadas each week as the club meets during lunch. LUNA holds two sports tournaments each year, volleyball and soccer, and sponsors dance lessons. The majority of those present were mainstreamed students who were not in the bilingual education track. The students spoke in English with each other, throwing in a few words of Spanish. Meetings generally consisted of updates followed by socializing through the lunch period. Two things that they were preparing for were a backpack drive and a bake sale. The backpack drive was inspired by the father of a student who frequently travels between the United States and Guatemala. He noticed that there was a need for backpacks in Guatemala and LUNA decided to hold a backpack drive to which students could donate. The group also prepared for the bake sale—they would be selling empanadas from a restaurant in town next Tuesday. They would use the money to help them take trips and hold other social events.

Alika, a young African American woman, had been teaching for three years at Morristown High School as a bilingual science teacher. She taught herself Spanish, and before coming to Morristown, Spanish had just been a hobby. She recalls:

> When I was looking for a teaching job, I was looking to switch districts, so I applied to this school district just as a chemistry teacher. I just put my application there. There wasn't even an opening posted. I just put it there in case an opening ever occurred or existed. I was thinking, "Okay, they have my stuff." So anyway, the supervisor contacted me because at the very bottom of my resume I put, "Proficient in Spanish." It was at the bottom. I was like, "If they ever kind of need it . . ." but I'm a Chemistry teacher so I did not see any sort of overlap with that. But, yeah, they called me in and they just said,

"We saw that you can speak Spanish. Would you be interested in a bilingual science teacher position?"

Robinson seized the opportunity and, since starting, has availed herself of all the professional development opportunities she could—exploring restorative justice, and creative uses of technology. Despite the interest in professional development at the district level, Robinson commented, "I do wish we had more kind of culturally . . . I don't know, I guess relevant, professional development. I will say that our last professional development day—last week—our Supervisor for Bilingual and World Languages actually presented to the entire staff about our ELL population. I thought that was amazing." It was the first time, Robinson remarked, that the school had done anything specific regarding that population, "So, it's steps headed in the correct direction, I think." Seeing the district's efforts with bilingual students as a work in progress, Robinson noted that:

I think even if I compare myself to when I didn't speak Spanish and my worldview then, and now, I think a lot of the teachers who don't speak the language, you're a little more distant from those kids and distant from that population. You almost don't care. It's harsh to say you don't care, but I could see my old self having a couple of kids in the back who didn't really speak the language and you do what you can but it's very easy to kind of overlook those kids and to almost not feel as much ownership for them, whereas now a lot of the ELL and bilingual teachers, we really feel like those are our kids. We really want to go to guidance if something is messed up in their schedule, whereas I think a lot of mainstream teachers wouldn't even notice that something is wrong with their schedule. They just don't have that same relationship with the kids. They feel that they can't connect with the kids as much because of the language barrier. It is an extra effort to try. There are some teachers that do a great job that really go above and beyond even though they don't speak the language. But those are few and far between for the most part. It takes extra effort and extra care to do that, and I think the teachers that teach the bilingual/ELL population feel a little bit that this population is neglected in the school.

Robinson's description of the divide between bilingual faculty and staff and monolingual faculty and staff plays out in the access that emergent bilingual youth have to advising, course material, and school community. Extracurricular activities and whole-school events are spaces in which emergent bilingual students struggle to be included. But Robinson remains hopeful, referencing a new event, Hispanic Heritage Night, as well as the presence of a parent liaison and bilingual homework tutoring provided during lunch or after school.

Tiffany and Diane

Social Workers Tiffany Luxardo and Diane Smith are White and learned Spanish as a second language, filling a Spanish translation gap in the school before Morristown High School officially could support a bilingual program. We met with them at the end of the school day, after they had spent much of the afternoon trying to help a bilingual student access mental health support because of self-harm. After calling several hospitals, they found one that would be appropriate for a Spanish-speaking teenager in crisis. This day, they remarked, was not atypical. They often struggled to find mental health, substance and alcohol abuse, and other resources for Spanish-speaking adolescents. Together, they do the hard work of addressing the effects of trauma and out-of-school pressures, the legal obstacles, issues of homelessness and food insecurity, and the mental health struggles of recently arrived immigrant youth.

While their main preoccupation and job responsibility center on helping the student as social workers, they see the importance of approaching students holistically and in relation to their families and their immigration histories. The nature of the job dictates this approach. Tiffany explained:

> I mean, our focus is always going to be on the child, but sometimes there are issues that come up with their parents. You could have a child, for example, who is born here, but their parents are undocumented and that creates a lot of uncertainty in terms of whether their parents could be deported or not. So it creates just a lot of anxiety, a lot of secrecy around letting people know, a lot of embarrassment.

While the majority of their job responsibilities involve locating appropriate resources for students, both women also see part of their role as one of building community, of penetrating the varied layers that constitute trauma and struggle, and of helping students adjust to a new school, a new country, and a new life. To those ends, Tiffany created a mutual aid program dubbed "Colonial Closet" (the Morris mascot is a Colonial soldier), which is a store room of free clothes, food, and other supplies. They reported that students of a variety of races, linguistic backgrounds, and socioeconomic levels have been enthusiastic about contributing to the store, donating used items, and helping organize the space. What is remarkable about the Colonial Closet is that it has become a social activity in a way that has helped, in part, to eliminate the stigma of what could be perceived as charity. Although it is still disproportionally utilized by Latinx students, Tiffany is working on spreading the word. She reflected on the balance of creating a community of mutual support in a school with relative affluence:

> I feel that with our Hispanic population, my impression is that even though they still might feel a little uncomfortable it's become more of a social thing . . . a good number of our Latino students are taking advantage of the closet, so it almost becomes a social experience when you walk in there sometimes. There's like 10 kids in there, you know, and they're all going through stuff. Some are helping [with] sorting. I honestly think it has become a social experience to go there after school.

Together, Tiffany and Diane attempt to triage the complex demands of the emergent bilingual population. They coordinate mental health services, help students find legal representation with regard to their immigration status, and they deal with the everyday challenges that students encounter in school. They are committed to seeing students in relation to their immigration histories, and as part of not only a schooling community, but also as adolescents in the flux of learning who they are in a new place. While Tiffany and Diane ensure the social-emotional needs of Latinx students are met, Sabria Candela, highlighted next, assists students in meeting their academic goals as the bilingual guidance counselor at Morristown High.

Sabria Candela

When students come to enroll at Morristown High School, they fill out a home language survey, they complete a language test to determine their level, and they are placed in a bilingual or an ESL-only program. In addition to their coursework, they are also assigned to a bilingual guidance counselor—the school has four bilingual counselors in total, in addition to the two bilingual social workers on staff. Sabria Candela's family emigrated from Spain and settled in the Ironbound section of Newark. With a caseload of nearly 40 students, Sabria relies on making herself available and visible to all students who might need her assistance. The nature of her work, in dealing with student educational aspirations, means that she must help students apprentice themselves into the American educational system and that she assists with setting students up for success in post-secondary education.

Sabria remarked that her position had to be negotiated from a place of trust: "I think that with any community and with there being a language barrier, there has to be a level of trust there. So the fact that the district is looking toward hiring more Spanish-speaking staff makes our services more accessible and then they start to find the people that they connect with." Like Tiffany and Diane, Sabria tried to make herself as visible as possible, and in creating vast support networks via interaction, make it so that students and their families would eventually feel comfortable with her. The biggest barriers to properly serving the Spanish-speaking community, she explained, often come down to a lack of resources available in the region in general—it is nearly impossible, for example, to find a Spanish-speaking psychiatrist, or bilingual drug and alcohol services. Together with the school social workers, the counseling department absorbs these problems. In addition to her one-on-one work with students, Sabria is the local Harassment Intimidation and Bullying officer, and is responsible for conducting training on bullying—what it is, and what the laws are. This, she says, is complicated by language proficiency and different cultural norms regarding what constitutes bullying. She has made efforts to translate the HIB material into Spanish and has gone into the bilingual classes to conduct workshops about bullying with recently arrived immigrant youth.

When asked about Morristown as a place to live and work, Sabria, who has worked in the district for many years, smiles. "I would say we're very unique in that there's such . . . there's a big representation of all different classes, right? It's a very wealthy town, but it can also be a very poor town as well. So there's a little bit of everything and that's really what I think attracts me to live in town and work in town, . . . that you have an accurate reflection of the U.S. and the world."

Sabria's commitment to building trust in ways that help her become a confidante and advocate are related to a CSP conceptualization of school-community relations. She is interested in learning about each of her students as individuals and in figuring out exactly the services they need to flourish in Morristown High School. She holds a realistic and complicated view of the diversity of the district, acknowledging the broad spread of experiences and backgrounds—what that can offer and what challenges that poses.

SCHOOL LEADERS

Mackey Pendergrast, the superintendent, has worked in education for more than 28 years. Coming to MSD was a challenge he was well-prepared for and eager to take. Mackey's interest in the district was personal. "Here, my feeling was we can get there from here within my lifetime assuming I live a decent amount. So for me, it was very important. It can be done here. In Morristown, it can be done where maybe it's not being done anywhere else in the country." Still, he acknowledged the reality of the gap in test scores:

> We've got kids coming in—and here's where it gets muddy. We've got these kids coming in, especially over the last couple of years.

They've let some kids in without their parents, right? It's all murky to me. We have kids coming here. I think the stat that the high school told me—there's 70 kids that came here, right? Without parents. A great majority of them, or maybe not a majority, but a large number of them hadn't been to school in a few years.

Mackey's vision is data driven, yet he acknowledges that test scores do not tell the whole story. He went about trying to get teachers to employ a variety of instructional methods, to integrate technology, but most important, he believes, is prioritizing human relationships. As a leader, he has done excellent work pulling together resources and stakeholders, and being vocal about his vision for the district.

LESSONS LEARNED

ELL/Bilingual Education in MSD reflects several of the projects that culturally sustaining pedagogy engages. But it is an ongoing and evolving process that still has many things to improve upon, as one administrator commented during an interview: "I'm realizing how far we've come." MSD's successes include its commitment to encouraging cultural pluralism, its concerted effort to engage in proactive community building, and its commitment to diversity in its hiring processes.

Heritage Spanish represents the biggest success of the district. As one Assistant Principal put it: "[We want to] leverage children's literacy in their first language." This move away from English Language Development toward maintenance, two-way bilingual education signals an awareness of the unique cultural and linguistic practices of immigrant youth in schools. The Heritage Spanish course sequence helps make immigrant youth feel more part of the community around them without asking them to abandon their identities. Community building itself is also a strength of MSD and one that reflects some of the priorities of Culturally Sustaining Pedagogies. Translation, dissemination of materials, and the number of bilingual faculty and staff help create the possibility for robust school-community relations.

Despite its successes, MSD has several areas on which it still needs to focus. CSP reminds us that ELL students are most successful when all of the faculty and staff view their education as a shared project. Despite a large number of bilingual faculty and staff, there is still a sense that ELL/Bilingual students are in a separate sphere. Comparing another district that had had success with educating ELL students to MSD, one ELL/Bilingual coordinator remarked: "[There] the whole school is involved in the same effort, where we're more like an academy type situation." This separation is, of course, mitigated by efforts to schedule ELL students in electives with general education students. But there is still, in many ways, the sense that ELL students are separate. A final area of focus for MSD would be on some of the more difficult elements of CSP—the elements that would require faculty and staff to engage in self-examination so that they become more aware of implicit biases and develop a critical view of U.S. history with regard to race and privilege. This is a longer-term charge, and one that would require a shift in perspective and consciousness. It would also help MSD move toward true integration and to a school system in which each child, regardless of race, culture, or linguistic background, could be fully included.

Moving from Desegregation to True Integration

Although the United States Supreme Court's iconic decision in *Brown v. Board of Education* has had enormous symbolic importance, and for a time led to significant desegregation in the southern states, its practical effect has waned even in the South.[1] In truth, *Brown* never had a major impact on school segregation in the rest of the country because it was limited to de jure segregation, which required either formal state statutes mandating racially separate schools or a showing of school segregation resulting from provably discriminatory intent.[2] While many scholars [3] and several U.S. Supreme Court justices[4] have rejected the idea that there is a meaningful distinction between de jure and de facto segregation, a majority of the federal justices has held firm to that distinction and refused to find that, when the segregation before it was deemed to be de facto, it violated the U.S. Constitution and justified a federal court–ordered remedy. The federal courts also resisted remedies that had regional or metropolitan dimensions, especially in northern states. Most state courts followed those approaches. Yet, New Jersey was a notable exception, as we described in Chapter 2. The commissioner-ordered merger that led to the Morris district would never have happened without the strong action taken by the New Jersey Supreme Court in the *Jenkins* case that departed from the federal court approach to remedying school segregation and thereby broke through the sanctity of district lines to make integration possible.

The reality throughout most of the country is that school segregation still persists even though there is substantial evidence that educating students in a diverse setting can have a powerfully positive educational and social impact, and especially on the educational achievement of low-income students of color.[5] Instead of giving primacy to desegregating, let alone integrating, our schools, we have devoted time, attention, and money to other techniques designed to improve student performance and to narrow opportunity gaps[6] across racial and socioeconomic lines. These techniques have included equalizing funding, expanding school choice options, and penalizing teachers, administrators, schools, and students for low test scores or rewarding them for improved scores. The truth, however, is that these approaches have ignored the segregated status of schools. Indeed, they actually have used segregation as a justification for employing some of those other techniques. Perhaps, in significant part because of that, they have fallen short of creating equitable educational opportunities.

In this book, we have sought to draw a clear distinction among terms such as "desegregation," "integration," and "true integration." While the predominant focus in the media and in research has been on versions of desegregation, in this book we focus much more on the integration end of the continuum. As Rucker Johnson wrote, "Moving from desegregation to integration means moving from access to inclusion, and moving from exposure to understanding."[7] School integration, and especially what has come to be called "true integration," goes beyond the creation of racial, ethnic, and SES balance of the student body in districts and schools, and even in tracks and programs. Integration infuses student diversity into every aspect of the school, including "its cultural climate, and the educational processes and contents employed in it."[8] We also draw on the definition that the New York City Alliance for School Integration and Desegregation (ASID) published, which defines school integration as "The pedagogical, curricular, and cultural mechanism(s) inside of schools that support racially integrated student bodies. Integration is about de-centering Whiteness—creating educational opportunities and spaces that are affirming and empowering to all students." Ultimately, the creation of diverse and integrated schools and classrooms should be considered an important educational resource that confers mutual benefits to White students and students of color in terms of increases in academic outcomes and social mobility, and a reduction of racial prejudice and implicit bias.

Yet, in most of the country Black, Latinx, Native American, and low-income students are systematically denied the academic benefits of high-quality and diverse schools. These "opportunities to learn are most often denied to students of color and to students who come from impoverished homes."[9] The problem is related to segregation across neighborhoods, schools, and even classrooms via tracking. Indeed, in the Northeast, interdistrict segregation is on the rise because of concentrated poverty in cities and housing segregation between cities and suburbs.[10] Predominantly White, high-income schools are often characterized by high test score averages and college-going rates, abundant resources, and highly qualified teachers and social supports. In comparison, in most states low-income schools that are predominantly Black and Latinx have fewer resources and less access to challenging courses and opportunities and effective teachers.[11]

New Jersey, where this case study on MSD took place, is something of an outlier in terms of resources as a result of the longstanding *Abbott v. Burke* litigation. *Abbott* resulted in greatly increased state education aid being directed to the so-called Abbott districts, 31 poor urban districts with a large number of the state's at-risk students. Still, despite *Abbott*'s positive effect on equalizing funding, schools that are predominantly Black, Latinx, and low-income still lag behind schools populated by White and higher-income students.[12] Students in the Abbott districts continue to be educated in extraordinary isolation where they seldom, if ever, come in contact with students who look different from them, and who come to school with different perspectives and backgrounds.

At the same time, there are hopeful signs that schools are becoming more diverse as national and statewide demographics shift. Suburban areas that were once predominantly White are experiencing influxes of students of color, and certain urban neighborhoods are undergoing demographic changes due to gentrification.[13] The White school-aged population in the United States has continued to decline and has been surpassed by the growing number of students of color. New Jersey reflects this national trend since there is no racial subgroup in the majority and students of color make up 52% of the K–12 school-aged population.[14] These natural demographic changes have resulted in a quarter of all school districts, roughly 160 out of 674, whose student populations are relatively proportional to statewide averages. This demographic transformation across the state provides a far broader field in which the lessons of the Morris district can be brought into play. After all, once there is diversity at the school district level, far greater opportunities exist for it to be extended to individual schools and eventually to courses, programs, and classrooms.

Even when diverse districts and schools exist, however, a common critique is that they are not fully integrating all students into every aspect of the school community.[15] Within-district segregation tends to occur because of segregated neighborhoods and attendance based on the neighborhood school concept. Within-school segregation is prevalent because of tracking or ability grouping that sorts students into classes or specialized programs by perceived ability, which is often tied to race and class.[16] Students of color are also disproportionately referred for disciplinary reasons and are given stricter punishments compared to their White peers—taking time away from teaching and learning, which can eventually lead to the school-to-prison pipeline.[17] Teachers often hold colorblind or deficit-based views of students of color, which can have negative effects on short-term and long-term academic outcomes and aspirations.[18] Ultimately, education leaders and teachers must embrace culturally responsive and equity-oriented policies and teaching practices that do not systematically exclude certain student subgroups from opportunities and resources in diverse school settings.[19]

That is the current focus of the Morris district's continuing efforts to achieve true integration. As we have emphasized throughout this book, however, the district must sustain those efforts, even if they are proving successful, over the long term. For example, as we describe in Chapter 5, MSD is working hard to educate the large number of newly arrived low-income Latinx students, mainly from Central America and in a surprising number of instances arriving as unaccompanied minors. As many respondents stated to us, the Trump administration's immigration policies and attitudes have made that work more difficult by increasing the anxiety levels of many Latinx students.

While much is known about the status quo of school segregation and inequality, there is very little guidance about what schools can do to create more equitable and integrated school communities. Unlike in the case of *desegregation*, there are no laws or policies that exist regarding *true integration*; there is no guidebook for districts or schools that want to do this work. One aim of this book is to provide New Jersey policymakers, school leaders, and other education professionals, parents, and the broader community with legal, policy, and educational practices to foster integration across all communities and schools. This is a particularly important and timely effort to undertake in New Jersey given the statewide school desegregation case, *Latino Action Network et al. v. the State of New Jersey* (LAN case), which was filed on May 17, 2018, the 64th anniversary of *Brown v. Board of Education*.

In this concluding chapter, therefore, we will tackle these questions: (1) What can be done in MSD to complete the job of achieving "true integration," diversity not only at the district and school level but also in every aspect of the students' school-level educational and social experience; and (2) what can we learn from the Morris district that can contribute to progress in addressing the larger issue of school segregation and inequality in other school districts across New Jersey and, for that matter, the rest of the United States? To deal with the replicability issue, we consider whether there is something about the Morris district and its community that makes it "unique" or whether "fertile ground" for the Morris remedy or other remedial steps can be found or cultivated elsewhere. As part of addressing these questions, we will review, and expand upon, the Lessons Learned that complete each of Chapters 2 through 5.

WHAT HAVE WE LEARNED IN MSD?

Our study has taught us a great deal about how a school district, once it has become diverse, can work persistently and single-mindedly to maintain that diversity over time, and to extend it from the district as a whole to each of its schools, and eventually to the courses, programs, and classrooms offered in every school. Each of those three levels—district, school, and classroom—has its own challenges and its own techniques for meeting those challenges. To be successful, a district almost certainly will have to skillfully combine and coordinate legal, policy, administrative, pedagogical, community-building, and grassroots mobilization efforts, and to sustain them over the long term. A successful district will have to assure that its staff is trained in dealing with those manifold challenges and is truly committed to bringing out the unique talents and gifts in all its students.

More specifically, we have summarized an array of lessons we have learned from our study of the Morris district and from the growing research and literature about true integration. To make them more useful to readers, we have grouped them into two broad categories: (1) those internal to the district and its immediate community; and (2) those involving external or outreach efforts beyond the district and its community.

Internal Lessons

To launch a serious effort to achieve true integration, there must be key leaders who have a deep and long-term commitment to that effort and are willing to come forward in a highly visible manner. Although such leadership may come from school leaders in the district, more commonly the original impetus is from advocates in the broader community. Certainly that was the case in the Morris district where eight residents of Morristown and Morris Township, including Beatrice Jenkins whose son George was the subject of Chapter 2's vignette, took initial ownership of the integration effort as petitioners in the *Jenkins* case. Steve Wiley, the lawyer for the Morristown Board of Education in that case and the focus of a Chapter 1 vignette, became an even more visible leader. The fact that he was a prominent White resident of Morris Township, as well as the son of a popular former superintendent of the Morristown district and a product of the Morristown public schools, added to his credibility and influence. Leadership was, in a sense, shared with several prominent civic and advocacy organizations active in the Morris community, including the local Fair Housing Council, the Urban League, and the NAACP.

As it happened, during the merger period the Morristown superintendent was a strong supporter, and the Morris Township superintendent was an equally strong opponent of merger. The former's support was helpful, but probably not decisive. Subsequent superintendents of the merged Morris School District, and especially Tom Ficarra and the current superintendent Mackey Pendergrast, both profiled in Chapter 3, played more prominent and important leadership roles as the focus shifted from creating the merged diverse district to operating it. Indeed, Pendergrast's ongoing leadership is especially important as MSD seeks to realize true integration.

Important as leadership is by the superintendent and other influential school district officials, including members of the board of education and the teaching staff, the leadership cadre must be much broader and more diverse. It must extend to municipal, county, and state officials. It must extend to significant civic and religious organizations in the community, local businesses, and real estate agencies. Even more importantly, it has to include parents and guardians of the district's students and, at a certain point, the students themselves.

To invite and encourage meaningful shared leadership, we found that the district must commit itself to real openness and transparency, not just in terms of sharing data and other information about the district, but also in terms of sharing decisionmaking itself. That involves serious outreach to the broader community, consensus building, and facilitating the community's identification of its leadership, which is fully representative of the entire community. High on the list of items requiring a broad community consensus are (1) the belief that a healthy school district and healthy community are inextricably linked and you cannot have one without the other; (2) the most important measures of what makes an effective school system extend well beyond scores on standardized tests; (3) all students must be viewed as capable of achieving their fullest potentials; (4) the enactment of culturally responsive school leadership and teaching is necessary to realize true integration and reap its full benefits; and (5) all students benefit in important ways from full and meaningful educational diversity.

This expanded view of a school district leadership team must be willing to address the district's hardest questions, and find an effective way to do so. These questions include the impact of race and social class on how the district operates and on how it should move forward to achieve true integration, as well as how to find the right balance among being responsive to White upper-income families. decentering Whiteness, and providing the educational services and full access to all of the district's educational opportunities and full access to all students and their families regardless of race or SES. Dealing with such questions in an open and productive way requires careful preparation since, as we have shown, they have the potential to deeply divide even the most committed communities if they are raised in a less thoughtful and less careful manner.

District leadership also has to be intentional when tending to the details of effectively organizing and overseeing the district's day-to-day educational program to advance true integration. That involves a number of important components. The district's formal policies and practices must align with and support that overriding objective, and be flexible enough to adapt to changing circumstances. The district's staffing must be as compatible as possible with the demands of true integration. That means the district's hiring practices must give priority to racial, ethnic, and social class diversity, and to the skills, professional and life-experience, and personal outlooks most likely to mesh with the district's student body and with the achievement of true integration. All the district's employees—whether newly hired or longtime administrators, teachers, and support staff—must undergo serious sensitivity training to root out implicit biases and to prepare them to interact productively with the district's diverse, and ever-shifting, student population. Finally, the district's curriculum and pedagogy must be culturally responsive and designed to maximize the educational opportunities of all the students.

External Lessons

Central to the Morris district story are three related external lessons. One is that law and litigation may be an important, or even necessary, component of a serious effort to advance the cause of true integration. The second is that a legal underpinning is strongest when buttressed by effective grassroots mobilization and support. The third lesson is that school integration should not be viewed in isolation from other major, structural reforms and these even extend beyond the education realm.

For example, policymakers could deal with housing segregation, one of the major causes of school segregation would be abated. If communities and neighborhoods were integrated, the schools would tend to follow. Of course, even the end of housing segregation would not assure that schools became truly integrated, but it would advance the objective in many states and communities throughout the nation and make the achievement of true integration a realistic prospect on a broad scale. However, as we have shown, even with housing segregation intact, the Princeton Plan with a creative geography-based student assignment plan can decouple neighborhood segregation from school segregation.

Even within the educational realm, integration should be seen in a broad context. If states gave meaningful priority to integration and real and equitable educational opportunity in their statutes and policies, the ways in which school districts are configured and education is funded—as well as schools, teachers, and students are evaluated—likely would be substantially different. Said another way, integration can be the opening wedge for major reforms in the way we have historically, and not very successfully, conceived of public education. By rationalizing and modernizing the education system to meet today's circumstances and needs, we might even improve results as we reduce costs. It is our hope that one day we can achieve what the New Jersey constitution, and a number of others, require—that the state provide an "efficient system of free public schools," as it affords all of its students a "thorough" education.

HOW SHOULD MSD APPLY WHAT WAS LEARNED?

The Lessons Learned concluding sections of Chapters 2–5 provide a more complete picture of what future efforts will be required of MSD to reach true integration of all its schools. The section that follows will provide an overview, highlighting the major challenges.

As this book has demonstrated, the Morris district has succeeded in maintaining impressive diversity at the district and individual school level. What is still a work in progress is the achievement of true integration within each of its schools. Strides are being made through efforts like Superintendent Pendergrast's Equity and Inclusion Plan, but the problem is deep-seated and may begin early in a student's education in MSD, and even before, given the research that shows opportunity gaps as early as kindergarten. New Jersey has a state law that early childhood education must be provided starting at age 3, but it is not implemented outside of the Abbott districts. To the extent some teachers have and manifest different attitudes toward students based on their race, ethnicity, or social class, that may compound the problem. Therefore, the district must build dramatically on the implicit bias training they have started to implement. It also must continue to recast the administration and teaching staff of the district to be more reflective of the student body and to be more responsive to its needs and aspirations.

Students who arrive at MSD from other countries at an older age, perhaps even in their teens, present other, more complicated challenges. Not only must the district find ways to overcome any SES-related educational gaps, since many Latinx students are from low-income backgrounds, but it also must deal with the possibility they have been traumatized in their home countries. Some newcomer students arrived in the United States as unaccompanied minors, and for most, English is not their native language (nor is Spanish if they grew up speaking a local dialect). Some Latinx students may have received little formal education in their home countries. Despite these challenges, we found during our study that district personnel have a remarkably can-do attitude and that, as we describe in Chapter 5, the district has taken impressive strides, and invested substantial resources, in trying to build on the students' strengths and meet the academic and social-emotional needs of ELL students. Work still remains to be done in integrating ELL students more effectively into the educational and social environments of MSD and exposing them to English-speaking peers.

One of the other problems the Morris district has been confronting is diversifying Honors and AP courses and other higher-level programs, or even considering a commitment to fully de-track the curriculum. Differential access of White and Asian students to high-track courses and programs, and disproportionate representation of Black and Latinx students being subjected to disciplinary action, seem to be unfortunate hallmarks of most diverse school districts that have fallen short of true integration. MSD is trying hard to become an exception, and that is a story still to be written. The district is giving increasing priority to that effort and has some positive results to show from it, but too many members of the Black and Latinx communities, and too many students of all races, including White students, still believe the district is not doing enough to truly integrate students at the classroom level.

Finally, the district needs to move forward with its implementation of the superintendent's Equity and Inclusion Plan, and even to consider moving beyond it when the "political" climate is more accepting of full-scale de-tracking of the curriculum and the incorporation of a comprehensive culturally responsive curriculum and pedagogy. These are steps essential to the full achievement of true integration, but they must be taken with care, skill, and sensitivity. Ultimately, culturally responsive school leadership needs buy-in and support from the school staff and parent community to be successful.

HOW CAN OTHER SCHOOL DISTRICTS
APPLY THE LESSONS LEARNED FROM MSD?

Taking what we have learned from MSD, we believe that New Jersey offers important lessons with regard to school integration, in part because its laws and public policies prioritize desegregation, which, in turn, should have an enabling effect on district, school, classroom, and community levels toward inclusivity and integration. If there finally is to be meaningful movement in the direction not just of school desegregation, but also school integration in the United States, New Jersey should be in the forefront of that movement for several important reasons.

First, New Jersey has the strongest body of state law in the nation that goes beyond barring segregation to affirmatively requiring racial balance in the schools "wherever feasible." Almost 50 years ago, the state's highest court derived that integration-oriented command from the education clause of the New Jersey constitution. Under that provision, New Jersey students have been deemed to have a fundamental constitutional right to a "thorough and efficient" education and, as indicated, "racial balance" has been found to be an integral aspect of that right. This provision supplements, and actually goes well beyond, New Jersey's unique state constitutional provision that explicitly bars segregation in the public schools. Even beyond that, the New Jersey courts have construed the state constitution to:

- bar de facto, as well as de jure, school segregation;[20]
- empower the state commissioner of education to merge school districts and take other strong action, including cross-district action, to ensure racial balance in the schools;[21]
- require the state and localities to assure that every region has affordable housing and, at the same time, to bar exclusionary zoning;[22] and
- require that all students, and especially those who are educationally at risk, receive the funding necessary to provide them with a meaningful opportunity to achieve a "thorough and efficient" education.[23]

Second, the demographic profile of New Jersey students is remarkably similar to the national profile, so perhaps what can be accomplished regarding school integration here can become a viable national model. In fact, New Jersey is second only to Illinois in its alignment with the national profile.[24] Of course, in a remarkable touch of irony, the four states that mirror most closely the U.S. demographic profile for students—Illinois, New Jersey, New York, and Maryland—are also regularly listed as having among the nation's most segregated public education systems where the White-Black and White-Latinx exposure indexes are very low.[25]

This paradox of having high levels of diversity accompanied by high levels of segregation dramatically demonstrates a core concept underlying this book—that diversity at the largest and most remote unit, in this case a state, hardly assures that smaller units within it—school districts, schools, and classrooms—will themselves be comparably diverse. Of course, this applies to states as well as to the national picture. Consequently, our analysis in this final chapter will focus on four tiers or concentric circles—the state, the school district, the schools within the district, and the classrooms within each school. Within those four units, there are policies, communities, organizations, and individuals that have to do the work of true integration. And, even then, "true integration" requires more—that the teaching staff, the curriculum, and the learning process have been imbued with meaningful culturally responsive and sustaining pedagogies and leadership.[26]

Third, despite New Jersey's disappointing record of school segregation on the ground, there are both some encouraging signs of serious efforts to force that reality to align better with its constitutional and statutory promise of meaningful integration, and a statutory and regulatory infrastructure that can be easily adapted to achieve that result.

In this chapter, we will describe the legal, policy, and educational context in which the movement to fully integrate New Jersey's schools should proceed. First, we will explain the statutory and constitutional requirements, unique in the nation, to ensure that schools provide a thorough and efficient education for all students in a racially balanced setting wherever feasible. We will detail how these provisions provide the authority for students to cross existing district lines and for changing existing district lines, which could become vehicles for achieving New Jersey's constitutional promise of a racially, ethnically, and socioeconomically balanced education for all its students. Finally, we will provide practical solutions to achieve true school integration in MSD and beyond—state and district policy (laws and regulations), community relationships, institutional practices, interpersonal skills, and individual attitudes.

Integration in New Jersey Schools: The Legal Context

Compared to other states, New Jersey has the nation's strongest state law requiring racial balance wherever feasible. The state prohibited school segregation in 1947, 7 years prior to *Brown,* giving the commissioner of education the legislative and constitutional authority to ensure that schools provide a thorough and efficient education for all students in a racially balanced setting wherever feasible. State supreme court decisions of the 1960s and early 1970s extended the integration commands of state law far beyond the emerging federal law. These forces combine to provide New Jersey with a special opportunity to move toward "true integration"—diversity not only at the district and school levels, but also at the classroom, program, and curricular level.

For more than 50 years, the New Jersey Supreme Court has repeatedly emphasized the scope of the commissioner's power and duty to provide students access to racially balanced schools and admonished the commissioner whenever he has failed to act on it. There are two constitutional sources of that power and duty—the thorough and efficient education clause, which the court has ruled is violated if students who could be educated in a racially balanced setting are not, and an explicit clause, unique in the nation, that bars segregation in the public schools.

Of the two, the education clause is far more common and vastly broader. Indeed, every state has its own education clause, and a significant number mirror New Jersey's core phrase of "a thorough and efficient system of free public schools" or have a close approximation. The education clause is the foundation for most of New Jersey's multiple volumes of state education legislation.

The antisegregation clause, which prohibits the segregation of any person "in the public schools because of religious principles, race, color, ancestry, or national origin," actually is unique in the nation. The Connecticut state constitution has an antisegregation clause, but it does not provide explicitly for the public schools.

New Jersey's education clause and antisegregation clause overlap as a result of the state supreme court's construction of the education clause as being violated if students who could be educated in a balanced and diverse setting are being denied that opportunity. The New Jersey courts also have construed both constitutional provisions as being violated by de facto segregation in the schools, not just by de jure segregation as the federal courts have done. In a second important aspect, the New Jersey courts, unlike the federal courts, have ruled that school district borders are not an impediment to remedies for segregation in the schools.

Thus, New Jersey has what is almost certainly the nation's strongest state constitutional law barring segregation in the public schools and requiring racially balanced education wherever feasible. Nonetheless, as the Tractenberg and Coughlan report and the LAN case's complaint point out in detail, New Jersey's record on the ground is far removed from its constitutional promise and commitment. Researchers have documented that New Jersey has the sixth or seventh most segregated public school systems in the country for Black and Latinx students, respectively, significantly more segregated than the systems of all the southern states.[27]

That remains true even as New Jersey's general and pupil populations have become increasingly diverse, closely mirroring the national demographic profile with 46% White, 15% Black, 27% Latinx, and 10% Asian. As we have previously indicated, almost 25% of the state's school districts and students have become quite diverse in comparison to the statewide profile, largely because of recent demographic shifts. At the same time, though, almost 25% of the state's students are isolated in school districts where more than 90% of the students are Black or Latinx, or, in a dwindling number of cases, more than 90% are White. The problem is compounded because a very high percentage of the students isolated in the predominantly Black and Latinx districts are low-income—and this problem actually is worsening.

Although a few of the state's urban districts are becoming somewhat more racially and socioeconomically diverse because of gentrification, that does not mean the same is true of the public schools in those districts. Newly arrived wealthier White and Asian residents with school-age children often eschew the public schools in favor of private schools, charter schools and selective programs or schools that tend to be disproportionately White, Asian and/or high-income students. In fact, the gentrification phenomenon has triggered integration lawsuits in districts such as Hoboken and Red Bank. Therefore, finding a way to provide an integrated educational experience for the very large number of low-income Black and Latinx students still isolated in those districts has to be a top priority. Clearly, to do something significant in the relatively near term will require moving large numbers of urban students across district lines to nearby predominantly White suburban districts, or vice versa, or altering district lines to create more diverse districts as Morristown and Morris Township did almost 50 years ago. In either case, finding the necessary political will to act boldly and comprehensively will be a major challenge in a state such as New Jersey, which has a strong affinity for home rule and local control of the schools. It is hard to imagine the kind of sea change required can occur without major prodding by the New Jersey courts, and the pending LAN case could provide just such an impetus.

Moving to a meaningfully integrated statewide public education system in New Jersey requires more than a court inspired or mandated restructuring of school districts and attendance patterns, however. It requires a transformation of not only organizational structure, but also of state and district policy, community relationships, organizational strategies, and individual attitudes. To have any chance of achieving this ambitious agenda, the state must have a comprehensive action plan that it is committed to implement strategically and thoroughly. Later in this concluding chapter, we will present some ideas about elements, which should be part of that plan, derived from our Morris study. We also have attached as Appendix B a highly relevant action plan developed for another project. Whatever the details of an eventual plan, they must build upon New Jersey's emerging educational reality by:

1. taking advantage of the increased diversity in 25% of the state's districts and among 25% of the state's students by extending diversity and cultivating integration at the school, classroom, and program levels, and then ensuring that the pedagogy, curricula, and educational materials are culturally responsive;
2. finding the admittedly elusive path to ending the extreme segregation of another 25% of New Jersey's students, most of whom are isolated in the larger urban districts; and
3. promoting increased diversity in the remaining districts, which cover the span between significant diversity and significant segregation.

As a way to build political support, the plan must make the case that restructuring the state's education system to accomplish integration goals will not only enhance the educational opportunities of all students, but also will produce significant cost savings and increased educational efficiency, an explicit element of the state constitutional mandate of a "thorough and efficient system of free public schools."

The core problem of achieving integration seems to lie more at the feet of the state's executive branch than its legislative or judicial branches, however. The state's education laws provide an adequate basis for the commissioner and state board of education to implement the constitutional promise. Certainly, the legislature could have been more explicit and directive in its insistence that every aspect of the state education laws should be implemented to advance racial, ethnic, and socioeconomic balance and diversity in the schools—and amendments to that effect are appropriate, if not necessary. Still, the legislature's failure to have done so consistently does not strip the commissioner and state board of education of their inherent power and duty to enforce the constitutional command. We know this definitively because the New Jersey courts consistently have said so for more than half a century, and the New Jersey Supreme Court, in particular, has described as one of its primary roles being the "designated last-resort guarantor" of students' constitutional rights,[28] including the right to be educated in an integrated, or "racially balanced," environment "wherever possible."[29]

Almost a century and a half ago, the legislature adopted a statute, still on the books (NJSA 18A:38-5.1), that prohibits exclusion of any child from public school "on account of his race, creed, color, national origin, or ancestry." Much more recently, the legislature incorporated into a number of statutes provisions explicitly addressing racial composition and the effect on racial balance. These include statutes involving termination of sending-receiving relationships (NJSA 18A:38-13, 20.1), and the creation and monitoring of charter schools (NJSA 18A:36A-8[e]); see also implementing regulations at NJAC 6A:11-2.1 (b) (4) (ii), (j). As another notable, but relatively isolated, example of executive branch recognition of the state's commitment to school integration NJAC 6A:7.1-7 (a)(2) imposes on school districts responsibility for "attaining within each school minority representation that approximates the district's overall minority representation."

In many other statutes, although the legislature did not explicitly address racial balance, it provided opportunities for the commissioner and state board to do so. For example, in the elaborate statutory provisions relating to the definition and implementation of a thorough and efficient system of free public schools, as well as those that vest unbridled supervisory and enforcement authority in the commissioner and state board, the legislature has not hedged in the power and duty of those executive officers to advance the constitutional command that racial balance should be provided New Jersey students wherever feasible. This is a point acknowledged and built upon by the state courts in numerous decisions that upheld the commissioner's and state board's power and duty to deal with racial imbalance and foster racial balance even though the statutes did not make that an explicit mandate. As indicated previously throughout this book, one of the most important examples is the *Jenkins* case, where the New Jersey Supreme Court ruled that the commissioner had the inherent authority to order a merger of two school districts for racial balance purposes.

In sum, the primary responsibility for moving toward school integration throughout New Jersey should rest with the executive branch and the commissioner and state board of education. Even under the current statutory framework, these stakeholders have ample basis for increasing the level of school integration. For example, there is a surprising, and little noted, degree of existing statutory authority, often buttressed by constitutional authority, for students to cross existing district lines and for the district lines themselves to be changed. Although this statutory authority often does not specify school integration as a goal, let alone mandate it, and it typically has not been used for that purpose, it also does not exclude that use. To leave no doubt, the legislature should enact amendments to those statutory provisions giving priority to school integration as a state objective.

STATUTORY AND CONSTITUTIONAL AUTHORITY FOR STUDENTS TO CROSS EXISTING DISTRICT LINES

The degree to which New Jersey students already attend, or are authorized to attend, schools outside of the district and municipality where they reside is often overlooked in legal and policy debates on school integration. This is important because, although the LAN lawsuit correctly identified as a core cause of school segregation the combination of residential segregation, school districts contiguous with the borders of segregated municipalities, and an attendance statute that mainly assigns students to the public schools of their districts of residence, state law already contemplates extensive cross-district movement of students for a wide variety of reasons, but not, with rare exceptions, school integration.

Because more than 315,000 New Jersey students live in districts whose schools are deeply segregated by race, ethnicity, and socioeconomic status,[30] their only hope of having an integrated educational experience, at least in the near term, is by having them, or their counterparts in other nearby districts, cross district lines, or by changing those lines. Students have the ability to cross district lines through sending-receiving relationships, through participating in the Interdistrict Choice Program, or through attending a charter school or a vocational-technical school. Overall, these statutory programs and other even more specialized ones, result in as many as 140,000 students, about 10% of New Jersey's total public school population, attending schools in districts other than the ones in which they live or that are operated by districts other than the one in which they reside.[31]

Curiously, despite the fact that one of the state's paramount educational obligations is to assure that students attend racially balanced schools wherever possible, most of those programs do not stipulate that obligation. They are neither constructed nor used to advance school integration. In some cases that may not even require legislative amendments since the commissioner of education's broad supervisory powers and duties may be sufficient. With minor adjustments, however, those programs could advance school integration. As Kuscera and Orfield stated, when school districts [and impliedly the state] "do not make integration a goal, it cannot happen."

Cross-District Education Statutes. An entire article of the state education code is entitled "Attendance at School Without District," (meaning outside of the student's district of residence)—NJSA Title 18A, Subtitle 6, Part 2, Ch. 38, Art. 2. The broadest statute, applicable to all school districts, provides that "any person not resident in a school district, if eligible except for residence, may be admitted to the schools of the district with the consent of the board of education upon such terms, and with or without the payment of tuition, as the board may prescribe" (NJSA 18A:38-3). This provision is rarely used and virtually never used to promote diversity in a district's schools. It can be readily adapted, however, to encourage or even require that result.

This provision was used, however, in one notable case involving school diversity in which the predominantly White, Asian, and high-income Englewood Cliffs school district sought to terminate a longstanding sending-receiving relationship with predominantly Black and low-income Englewood so that it could enter into a new one with Tenafly, which racially and socioeconomically mirrored Englewood Cliffs. Ironically, the provision was used to impede rather than advance diversity. While Englewood Cliffs' effort was pending, Tenafly adopted a private tuition program pursuant to NJSA 18A:38-3 under which it admitted to Tenafly High School more than 100 mostly White students from Englewood Cliffs and Englewood whose public high school otherwise would have been Dwight Morrow in Englewood. The court found that the selection process and parent-paid tuition amounts were akin to those of a private school. Both Englewood Cliffs' effort to terminate the sending-receiving relationship and Tenafly's effort to sustain its private tuition program failed because the New Jersey courts deemed them to be racially discriminatory.[32]

The education statutes also provide for enrollment in a district other than the district of residence where the latter's education program is defective or limited, that is, where the district of residence does not have "sufficient accommodations" (NJSA 18A:38-8), where the district of residence determines that it is "advisable" for its students to attend a school in another district to "secure better school facilities," "or for reasons of economy or other good cause" (NJSA 18A:38-10), where the high school in the district of residence does not provide a "particular high school course of study" that a student wishes to pursue (NJSA 18A:38-15), where the district of residence does not provide approved evening high school courses (NJSA 18A:38-16), or where the district of residence does not furnish instruction beyond 12th grade (NJSA 18A:38-17). A complete list of the statutory provisions permitting cross-district programs in the state education code is in Appendix A. Some of the most prominent programs, and the extent to which they are currently used by New Jersey students, will be discussed below.

Sending-Receiving Program. By far, the program which accounts for the greatest number of students attending schools outside of the districts of their residence is the sending-receiving program. Because about 40% of New Jersey's school districts are too small to permit the operation of full K–12 educational systems—and more than a dozen districts are too small to operate even a single school (the so-called "nonoperating districts")—under sending-receiving arrangements between boards of education, students who live in one district receive part or even all of their public education in the schools of another district with negotiated tuition dollars following those students.

According to our analysis of enrollment figures from each district's public User-Friendly Budget Summaries, 30,423 students were "received" at public schools in districts other than where they lived in 2017–18. An additional 6,607 students were "shared" with public schools in other districts for part of the school day because their home districts did not provide the curricular program or special education services they required. Although these students made up only a small portion of the state total, they came from 504 unique school districts, representing about 80% of all traditional public school districts across the state.

Yet, the structure of the widely used sending-receiving program does not fully comply with the constitutional mandate to achieve racial balance whenever feasible. This is the case because once an interdistrict agreement is adopted, its termination requires approval of the commissioner of education and an explicit criterion that the commissioner must apply is the termination's impact on the racial balance of the districts (NJSA 18A:38-13, 38-21.1[a][4]). Paradoxically, though, racial balance was not a criterion or goal at the front end when the sending-receiving agreement was created (NJSA 18A:38-11). With a minor statutory amendment it could be.

Other Cross-District Programs. Among the other major cross-district programs that could be used to advance school integration, but have not been, are:

- The Interdistrict Public School Choice program, which by definition and design, seeks to facilitate enrollment of students in districts other than their districts of residence (NJSA 18A:36B-14, 36B-16). In 2017–18, at least 5,500 students participated in the Interdistrict Choice Program, based on estimates of Choice Aid in the 2017–18 Revised State School Aid Budget.

- County vocational schools, which also, by definition, are open to students from any district in the county who apply and are admitted (NJSA 18A:54-20) and, under certain circumstances, can even admit students from other counties (NJSA 18A:54-23.5). Local school districts run vocational programs as well, which can enroll students from other districts (NJSA 18A:54-7). The total enrollment of all students at vocational schools in 2017–18, according to budget enrollment counts, was over 34,345 students. These counts do not distinguish between students living in or out of the districts in which their schools are located, however, so it is unclear exactly how many students are crossing district lines to attend vocational schools.
- Charter schools, which can enroll nonresident students if they have space available, but also can give preference to students who reside in the school district in which the charter school is located (NJSA 18A:36A-8); pursuant to state regulations, though, charter schools can choose to be formed on a regional, multidistrict basis (NJAC 6A:11-2.1[b][4], 2.1[l]) and, in that event, must "ensure the enrollment of a cross section of the school-age population of the region of residence, including racial and academic factors" (NJAC 6A:11-2.1[b][4][ii], 2.1[j]). According to Charter Aid Notices detailing the number of students in each charter school who live in each residential school district, 7,975, or 16% of all 48,622 charter school students in 2017–18, attended a charter school located outside of the district in which they lived.[33]
- Programs under which special education students may attend schools of a district other than the one in which they reside that has the "necessary facilities" (NJSA 18A:46-20). Over 14,070 special education students attended public schools in other districts for part or all of their day, and an additional 10,284 were sent to private schools in 2017–18, according to budget enrollment counts.

Although none of these provisions or statutes directly address the issue of segregation, a curious phenomenon in a state with such a clear and strong constitutional commitment to school integration, the New Jersey Supreme Court has stated that "schools with feasibly correctable racial imbalances might well currently be viewed as not affording suitable educational facilities within the meaning of the statutory language," and that this might even be a denial of the students' constitutional right to a "thorough and efficient system of free public schools."[34] In a 2000 decision, the court cited an even earlier integration precedent, *Booker v. Board of Education of Plainfield*, 45 N.J. 161 (1965), to the effect that: "In *Booker* we held that the Commissioner had the responsibility and power of correcting de facto segregation or imbalance which is frustrating our State constitutional goals."[35]

The *Booker* decision would mean the commissioner has a constitutional duty to make some of the provisions above mandatory upon districts, instead of merely discretionary. Likewise, if students in some districts are being denied their constitutional rights to a diverse or balanced education, and their own districts cannot cure the deficiency, then the commissioner has the power and duty to act by having students cross district lines pursuant to some of the statutory provisions cited above, or by changing district lines as the commissioner did in the MSD pursuant to *Jenkins*.

Statutory and Constitutional Authority for Changing Existing School District Lines

Another important mechanism for promoting school integration is changing district lines rather than having students cross them. As was true of students attending schools outside of their districts of residence, there is abundant legal authority for regionalization by local decision and state edict, but state authority has only been used once, almost 50 years ago, to advance the cause of school integration. The resulting MSD is, of course, the focus of this book.

Research has shown that the success of the Morris district is largely due to the merger remedy, and over time the importance of stable and committed leadership, strong community-school partnerships, buy-in from a diverse group of families, and a strong sense of pride, trust, and hope for a truly equitable school system. Regionalization for purposes other than school integration has been used only a few times during the past half century notwithstanding statutory authority, blue-ribbon commission recommendations, and longstanding educational and fiscal research that extoll the educational advantages, efficiency, and cost benefits of regionalization. The failure of state government to act upon these repeated recommendations is especially inexplicable because of the state constitutional education clause requiring the legislature to provide for the "maintenance and support of a thorough and efficient system of free public schools for the instruction of all the children in the State between the ages of five and eighteen years."[36]

PRACTICAL RECOMMENDATIONS

Throughout the book, we have chronicled one community's journey toward true integration. In this final section, we provide a list of practical recommendations inspired by the Morris case that center on reimagining education for equity and integration. These recommendations can be considered as possible elements of a statewide action plan to integrate New Jersey's or, for that matter, any other state's education system, but they also can be considered as freestanding reform proposals (see Appendix B for a comprehensive action plan for the state).

These reform proposals focus on the powerful role of *state and district policy*, or laws and regulations, which can advance—or impede—the efforts of districts to integrate, the meaningful effects of *community* relationships that can help shift districts toward more integrative practices both directly and indirectly, the *institutional* strategies that districts can deploy in order to create integrated schools, as well as the importance of challenging and transforming *individual* attitudes regarding diversity.[37]

We believe this list of promising practices can be achieved with top-down state and district policy changes, as well as bottom-up support from various school-level stakeholders. Indeed, it would be most effective if both could be brought to bear. The underlying theme running through each of these tactics is to center the needs and experiences of students and families of color, instead of catering to the advantaged (mostly White) families that historically hold the most privilege and power in educational spaces.

1. State and District Policy

- *Draw on statutory and constitutional authority for changing existing district lines.* State education officials should research the enrollment patterns and demographic shifts across districts. Then, they should consider district consolidation by one of two approaches, or perhaps both. The first would involve selectively and individually consolidating smaller underenrolled districts with adjacent districts that would in effect combine two segregated districts into a new integrated district. In that regard, the Morris School District's merger remedy could be treated as a model, and adapted to each set of districts' unique circumstances. The second would involve larger-scale or even statewide restructuring of school districts. One model in wide use in most of the southern tier of states is to use counties as the geographical basis for school districts. If that approach were adopted in New Jersey, the number of school districts would drop precipitously from 674 to 21. This idea has recently been raised by New Jersey Senate President Steve Sweeney in connection with the recommendations of a study commission he convened.[38] Some have even proposed that districts be consolidated on a different, and perhaps broader basis, including the housing regions generated by the *Mount Laurel* affordable housing case decided by the New Jersey Supreme Court.[39]

- *Mandate affordable and integrated housing policy within the boundaries of each school district, pursuant to guidelines set out in the* **Mount Laurel** *cases.* Most school-aged children attend their zoned school based on their home address. Thus, "exclusionary zoning policies (such as banning apartment buildings, townhouses, or houses on modest-sized lots) that discriminate based on income and exclude the nonrich from many neighborhoods—and thus from their associated schools" is a problem that needs to be addressed if the state is serious about school integration.[40] One idea comes from Charlotte, North Carolina, where Mayor Foxx improved neighborhoods to achieve integration in housing. He brought in businesses and jobs to the most segregated neighborhoods in the city, obtained capital improvement grants to install new sidewalks, created affordable housing, and improved the public transportation system.[41] Other urban neighborhoods that have revitalized include Washington Park in Cincinnati; in Denver, where the low-income housing is spread throughout the city instead of being clustered in certain areas; Minneapolis recently "became the first major city to enact the bold policy reform to eliminate single-family zoning to address the history of racist housing segregationist practices and alleviate the affordable housing crisis."[42] New Jersey's major urban centers could use these models, and others, to first diversify their neighborhoods, and then diversify their schools as well.

- *Utilize statutory and constitutional authority for students to cross existing district lines to receive part or all of their education outside of their districts of residence.* Diverse magnet school options, such as those in Hartford, Connecticut, could be implemented to allow students to rank and choose specific themed programs, but have diversity in admissions targets. This connects to the discussion above regarding the ways in which New Jersey students can and already do cross district lines. One idea comes from New York City's public school Diversity in Admissions program. The program allows individual schools to set aside a percentage of kindergarten seats for students in certain subgroups to offset rapid increases of White and/or advantaged students, which can create a temporary state of diversity, but can also turn into new segregation (e.g., school gentrification). Today, over 75 schools citywide are enrolled in the Diversity in Admissions program, setting aside a certain percentage of seats—anywhere from 10% to 100%—for students who are low-income (FRPL eligible), English Language Learners, involved in the child-welfare system, homeless, or with incarcerated parents.[43]

- *Ensure student assignment policies result in racially and SES-balanced schools within districts.* One idea comes from MSD, which uses a combination of the Princeton Plan and geography to achieve racial diversity in the primary (K–2) and intermediate (3–5) schools by designating the center of town as an open assignment area because it continues to be where many of the low-income Black and Latinx residents live. Students living in this area are bused to various schools across the district to desegregate those schools and to achieve racial and SES balance. Students in every other assignment area, which look like pie-shaped pieces radiating out from the center of town, attend their "neighborhood" school based on address. Because of this pie-shaped configuration, most students are bused and thus the burden is not entirely on students of color in the open assignment area. Another idea comes from Jefferson County, Kentucky, which includes Louisville and the surrounding suburban schools. As detailed in Rucker Johnson's book, the school superintendent used geography-based school choice, but provided economic incentives for neighborhoods to become more diverse by offering the following exemptions to the school integration plan: (1) to families already living in integrated neighborhoods; (2) to Black families who moved to White neighborhoods using public housing vouchers; and (3) to families living in neighborhoods that eventually evolved into integrated areas.

- *Establish a statewide School Integration Office in the state department of education under the supervision of the commissioner.* This will essentially resuscitate an office that functioned in the NJ department of education for many years until it was phased out in the 1980s. This new office also could administer a program of special state funding to help districts working toward integration bear extra costs for busing and other expenses. The director and staff of the new office would be responsible for working with school districts to complete equity audits, devise integration plans, provide resources and support for the implementation of the individualized plans, and for evaluating their progress each year. Without statewide support and resources, it would be difficult for districts with limited financial resources to successfully integrate their schools, even if they have diverse student populations. Equity audits would be completed by each district to report yearly on student, teacher, and administrator demographics, between- and within-school segregation levels, school choice policies and statistics, tracking and specialized programs by race and SES, PTA and district foundations fundraising amounts, and disciplinary rates broken down by race and SES.

2. Community Relationships

- *Change realtor perceptions about public school quality.* One idea comes from the Pasadena public schools, where they implemented a program called "Realtors Read Across Pasadena." The poor reputation of the Pasadena public schools was perpetuated by realtors who in most cases did not know what was going on in the schools—55% of families living in the city did not send their children to the schools.[44] However, the school district's reputation is slowly changing as district officials are attempting to bring families back in. As the superintendent explained, part of this larger initiative is to invite realtors into the schools to give them *facts and personal knowledge* of the schools that they can relay to prospective families:

> This is a way for realtors and their clients to see beyond a rating or report card, and to consider quality public schools—that are tuition free. It's a way to personally experience the great things happening at our schools: kids excited about learning, teachers actively engaging kids in advanced academics—all in facilities designed to ignite learning.

In Chapters 2 and 3, we describe how George Jenkins, as an individual Morristown realtor, has sought to inform his clients in more detail about the MSD schools, and how the district itself has sought to institutionalize George's efforts by inviting local realtors into the high school every year for a school tour and otherwise keeping them informed about the district. These efforts in MSD could be expanded to help combat negative and stereotypical attitudes about its racially diverse schools. Local efforts such as these also could be magnified at the state level by having the New Jersey Board of Realtors partner with the state board of education on training and incentive programs to encourage realtors to engage with their local school districts.

- **Hire community liaisons and diversity officers at the district and school levels.** Parent involvement and school-community relations are important factors that can enhance a district's and school's ability to meaningfully integrate students from historically marginalized backgrounds.

  » *Community liaisons* can help emergent bilingual students and their families, as identified in Chapter 5, feel more welcome in schooling spaces. Districts can benefit from hiring bilingual staff in each school to help increase and sustain parental involvement. In general, community liaisons help districts and schools work toward true integration both by helping teachers to better understand the context of the families they serve and by directly reaching out to parents themselves.[45] Most importantly, schools can strive to be present in the community in ways that encourage involvement through a history of positive interactions with the school. In Morris, the district created a unique position called a Community Outreach Teacher. The teacher, who advocated for the position and was a longtime high school Spanish teacher and Morristown alumna, spends half of her time doing community outreach to the growing Latinx population and the other half in the classroom.

» *Diversity officers* are often seen as the province of higher education, but, in a K–12 setting, they can help coordinate a systemic effort to make schooling spaces more inclusive. Diversity officers can take the educational mission of a given district and create programming to help actualize integration goals. They also can help to tailor professional development opportunities for teachers and staff to the needs of a given student body and assist districts in analyzing achievement data and other education indicators.[46]

3. Institutional Strategies

- ***Shift from tracking to de-tracking the curriculum.*** Tracking practices remain ubiquitous across most middle and high schools in the United States. Tracking has been criticized for being unfair and inequitable because it segregates students by race, class, and perceived ability; students in the low tracks do not receive access to high-quality teaching.[47] Low-track classes have predominantly teacher-directed, rote instruction and lower expectations for students. Research shows that students, as much as possible, should be equally represented by race, ethnicity, and SES in every course, elective, club, and extracurricular activity. De-tracking the curriculum, including the elimination of separate gifted programs,[48] is the most equitable practice because students are grouped heterogeneously. One idea comes from Rockville Centre Schools in Long Island, NY. When Principal Carol Burris de-tracked her high school mathematics curriculum and created heterogeneous, accelerated classes, the achievement gap narrowed significantly. From 1995 to 1997, the passing rate for Black and Latinx students on the state exams more than tripled from 23% to 75%, as the White and Asian student passing rate almost doubled from 54% to 98%.

- ***Shift from no-excuses discipline to nonpunitive discipline such as restorative justice practices.*** Punitive discipline policies disproportionately affect students of color because of teachers' and school leaders' implicit biases, and this can exacerbate the school-to-prison pipeline. As Welsh and Little contended, "the evidence suggests that remedies to discipline disparities should focus on the disposition and biases of teachers and school leaders' behavior management rather than student misbehavior."[49] This is the case because nonpunitive discipline programs alone have not been effective at reducing the *racial disparities in disciplinary outcomes*.

These programs must be combined with implicit bias training and culturally responsive practices, described in more detail below.

4. Interpersonal Skills

- ***Combine high-quality instruction with a culture of belongingness for Black and Latinx students who have been traditionally marginalized in schools.*** Latinx students are often triply segregated within schools because of their race, SES, and language. Leaders must change policies and programs that segregate English Learners into separate bilingual tracks for the entire day by incorporating them as much as possible into general education classrooms with their English-dominant peers.[50] Research has shown that students learn best in dual-language environments where their language is considered an asset, and not a deficit.[51] Black, Latinx, and low-income students are often relegated to lower ability groups and tracks because of their perceived ability, often measured by standardized tests. Standardized tests are highly correlated to a school's overall level of socioeconomic advantage or disadvantage, with students in schools that have mostly advantaged students performing four grade levels above schools with mostly low-income students.[52] Instead, schools should place less emphasis on outcome measures and institute culturally relevant practices that help build interpersonal skills for a diverse democracy. One way to do that is to

  > help students who are on the fringes of the classroom become the intellectual leaders of the class, build a learning community, legitimate students' real-life experiences as part of the curriculum, encourage students to engage in collective struggle against the status quo, and become aware of themselves as political beings.[53]

- ***Ensure that teachers, staff, and parents in school leadership positions are racially diverse.*** Research has shown that hiring teachers of color is vitally important for relationship-building with students of color, which, in turn, has short-term and long-term impacts on achievement, graduation, and college-going rates.[54] However, reflecting national trends, only 16% of New Jersey public school teachers are Black, Latinx, or Asian.[55] The percentage at MSD is only slightly higher, but the district is committed to increasing the number of teachers of color and of bilingual staff. The state department of education has taken small steps to address the issue by partnering with teacher educator programs at Rowan University and The College of New Jersey. These programs offer training, mentoring, and scholarships to preservice teachers for the purpose of increasing the number of men of color in the teaching field. Yet, the current programs also have long wait lists and should be expanded to further diversify the teaching staff in urban and suburban districts. The need for diversity extends also to the parents who fill leadership positions on PTA boards, educational foundations, and other school-related entities. When White parents dominate leadership positions, as they do generally, as well as in MSD, they have been found to influence policies and practices within the school through fundraising and other forms of parent involvement that benefit their children at the expense of others.[56]

5. Individual Attitudes

- ***Mandate implicit bias training in conjunction with nonpunitive discipline policies.*** Implicit bias training requires teachers and school leaders to interrogate their own implicit biases about race and class.[57] In conjunction with implicit bias training, restorative justice circles should be practiced with all students, not just students who misbehave. This work between teachers and students stems from the philosophy that when teachers and other school staff build student relationships that support the school's "underlying ethos that encompasses the values of respect, openness, empowerment, inclusion, tolerance, integrity. and congruence,"[58] the result is fewer behavioral incidents and more and better learning. Ultimately, social-emotional learning programs, including implicit bias training and student circle work, have been an effective way to decrease serious discipline incidents and referrals in racially diverse schools, and increase student achievement levels.[59]

- ***Offer professional development on culturally sustaining pedagogy.*** Related to uncovering teachers' implicit biases and developing relationships between teachers and students to reduce discipline disparities, culturally sustaining pedagogy (CSP) renounces deficit perspectives that blame the family for educational gaps, and seeks to humanize schooling spaces through an asset-based pedagogical stance.[60] This means recognizing the unique abilities and strengths that students of color bring to school, instead of framing them as problems. CSP also involves including the lives and experiences of students of color into the curriculum and teacher practices. Because schools often adopt colorblind and Euro-centric policies and practices, ample resources are needed for professional development for teachers, staff, students, and parents on restorative practices, implicit bias and antiracism trainings, interrupting micro-aggressions, socio-emotional learning, differentiation, classroom management, and de-tracking. Each of these practices has been found to improve the school climate. "If the school climate facilitates relationship building for the entire school community, it will (a) allow all students to be a part of the conversation, (b) invite teachers and school leaders into the lives of all students and not just students who engage in misbehavior, and (c) create a culture of connectivity."

- **Change parental attitudes about the value of integration for all students, particularly suburban White families who have historically been the loudest dissenters to desegregation plans.** One idea comes from New York City's District 15 middle school equity plan. The district hired an outside urban planning and design organization, called WXY Studio, to publish statistics about school segregation and school choice patterns; facilitate roundtable discussions for parents to voice their opinions, concerns, and questions about what to do to foster greater access and opportunities; and disseminate recommendations based on their findings. After a year-long process, the district voted to eliminate all admission screens to the middle schools, which will result in greater diversity by race, class, and academic ability.

CONCLUSION

Policymakers, school leaders, and New Jersey residents are seeking alternatives to the highly fragmented, segregated, and unequal landscape of educational access and opportunity. New Jersey's LAN school desegregation case is one example of this effort. New Jersey offers two lessons that are helpful to other states interested in true integration. One, it has a longstanding legal and political commitment to integration—this infrastructure, codified in the 1947 antisegregation constitutional clause and given broader force and relevance by decisions of the New Jersey Supreme Court for more than half a century, gives the commissioner of education power to consolidate districts and allow students to cross district lines for racial balance purposes. It gives individual districts the broad capacity to prioritize diversity and ensure desegregation as a base. Two, although the state still battles racial isolation in schools, New Jersey is also the site of persistent and independent efforts on the part of a few local districts and communities, like MSD, which have maintained an interest in creating diverse and integrated schooling spaces. Several of our policy recommendations are derived from those efforts in New Jersey and across the country. Ultimately, we believe the Morris School District chronicled in this book should be used as a model for its embrace of equity-oriented policies and practices that seek to build bridges instead of walls among diverse students and their families.

Statutory Provisions That Enable Students to Receive Education in Districts Other Than Their Districts of Residence

NJSA 18A: 13-34—formation of regional districts

NJSA 18A: 36A-8 and NJAC 6A: 11-2.1(b)(4) and 2.1 (j), (l)—charter schools, including regional or multidistrict charters

NJSA 18A: 36B-14, -16—Interdistrict Public School Choice program

NJSA 18A: 36C-8—Renaissance Schools can enroll students from outside their "attendance area," if space permits

NJSA 18A: 38-3—authority of all districts to accept nonresident students

NJSA 18A: 38-7.12—if student lives in a multidistrict federal enclave

NJSA 18A: 38-8—if district of residence does not have "suitable accommodations"

NJSA 18A: 38-9—if student lives far from the school in his district of residence

NJSA 18A: 38-10—if district of residence determines that it is "advisable" for its students to "secure better school facilities" in another district, "or for reasons of economy or other good cause"

NJSA 18A: 38-11 et seq.—if district of residence does not provide a full K–12 educational program (or any educational program), it must enter into a sending-receiving relationship with another district for the education of its students

NJSA 18A: 38-15—if high school in district of residence does not provide "particular high school course of study" sought by a resident student

NJSA 18A: 38-16—if district of residence does not provide approved evening high school courses

NJSA 18A: 38-17—if district of residence does not provide instruction beyond 12th grade

NJSA 18A: 38-24—with consent of district of residence and commissioner of education, student can attend a "demonstration school maintained in connection with any State college"

NJSA 18A: 46-20—special education students can attend schools in districts other than their districts of residence that have "necessary facilities"

NJSA 18A: 47-5—"[c]hildren who are dependent and delinquent, or who are habitually truant or incorrigible, or who shall be found by the court to require special instruction, and who reside in a school district in which there is no such special school of instruction" may be assigned to such a school in another district

NJSA 18A: 54-1 et seq.—county vocational districts

NJSA 18A: 54-7—districts with vocational programs can receive students from other districts

NJSA 18A: 54-20.1—districts of residence must pay tuition to county vocational school district for students who apply for and are accepted by a county vocational school

NJSA 18A: 54-23.5—county vocational schools can accept nonresident students (students from other counties)

NJSA 18A: 54c-6—the county vocational district Marine Academy can admit students from other counties

NJSA 18A: 54f-3—the At-Risk Youth Employment pilot program presumably can accept students from multiple districts

NJSA 18A: 61-3—any deaf resident of New Jersey under the age of 21 can attend the Marie H. Katzenbach School for the Deaf, space permitting

NJSA 18A: 61A-1—any New Jersey resident with the requisite skills can attend the New Jersey School of the Arts, governed by the commissioner of education and supervised and directed by the state board of education

NJSA 30:4C-26: a child placed in a foster [resource family] home, a group home or an institution is considered a resident of the municipality and county in which the home or institution is located, except that for school funding purposes the district of residence will be determined by the commissioner of education; NJSA 18A: 61B-1—placed the State School District for Institutions (formerly the Garden State School District) under the state department of education.

An Action Plan to Diversify New Jersey's Schools

1. A clear, definitive, and strong policy statement from the governor making it a state priority to:
   a. Actually achieve residential and educational diversity wherever feasible and as soon as possible;
   b. Define educational diversity in a manner that comports to the state's current demography and establish the state's diversity goals based on that definition;
   c. Develop and implement an operational plan for achieving diversity that recognizes the state's varied circumstances;
   d. In those definitions and that plan, emphasize that the required educational diversity does not stop at the district or even school level, but applies to classrooms, courses, and programs and the achievement of "true integration," thereby necessitating that educators throughout the state and at every level evaluate and improve all relevant policies and practices, including those that relate to tracking and ability grouping, student discipline, special education classification, curricular development, and pedagogy;
   e. Require all districts to develop and implement plans to diversify their teaching, administrative and support staffs with CJ PRIDE (Central Jersey Program for the Recruitment of Diverse Educators), a program being implemented by 17 school districts, as a possible model;
   f. Rationalize the structure of the education system (bringing it into harmony with the state constitutional mandate of an "efficient system of free public schools") and ensure that it gives priority to promoting diversity;
   g. Develop and fully fund a school financing law that assures adequate resources to every district, that is adjusted regularly to reflect changing enrollments and demographics, that provides

Source: Adapted from Tractenberg & Coughlan, 2018, pp. 73–76.

incentives for districts to maintain or increase their diversity, and
that reduces reliance on disparate local property tax ratables; and

h. Charge relevant state agencies and officials with responsibility
for: implementing the elements of this Action Plan; reviewing
all existing statutes, regulations, policies, and practices that
potentially impact housing and educational diversity, and
proposing changes that would enhance the prospect of their
promoting diversity; and proposing new statutes, regulations, and
policies for that purpose.

2. A new blue-ribbon commission, with a broad but specific mandate
and a relatively short timeline, to study and recommend the best
means of achieving and sustaining educational diversity over the long
term, including by studying linkages between educational diversity
and:

a. school district and municipal structures;

b. the state and local tax structure;

c. residential segregation;

d. the availability of jobs; and

e. real and perceived issues regarding community safety.

3. A re-established highly visible and well-staffed office in the state
department of education to monitor the status of educational
diversity and to require districts to take actions to promote
educational diversity, including to extend districtwide diversity to the
school and classroom, course, and program levels.

4. Support for districts that already are diverse by choice or by
demographic happenstance, or are seeking to reach that status, to
enable them to maintain or extend their diversity. This could include
financial support for student transportation necessary to diversify
all of the districts' schools, and financial support and technical
assistance for training district and school staff to deal effectively
with an increasingly diverse student population.

5. Increase the number of diverse school districts by:

a. Supporting judicial efforts under *Mount Laurel* to assure the
construction of more affordable housing units and promoting
other measures to integrate housing throughout the state;

b. Enforcing the 2007 statutory mandate of the CORE Act to
require all districts to move to K–12 status, but with a specific
requirement that this be done in a manner that increases
educational diversity to the maximum extent feasible;

c. Identifying clusters of districts whose consolidation can feasibly
enhance educational diversity and inducing them to consolidate
(or, if need be, requiring them to do so); and

d. Establishing pilot projects to test the effectiveness of countywide
or other regional school districts as a vehicle for increased

educational diversity, as well as greater efficiency and overall student achievement.

6. Promote diverse schools in districts not yet diverse by:
   a. Supporting and promoting residential integration efforts, including neighborhood integration efforts;
   b. Modifying the Interdistrict Public School Choice law to require that increasing student diversity be a priority purpose;
   c. Establishing interdistrict magnet schools modeled after the *Sheff* magnet schools in Connecticut or the longstanding magnet programs in Massachusetts; and
   d. Modifying the charter school law to encourage or require more multidistrict charter schools with a specific mandate to enhance diversity.

7. Encourage districts where day-to-day diversity is not a realistic prospect in the near term to develop other ways to provide their students with an exposure to diversity and its benefits through extra-curricular or co-curricular means, periodic cross-district programming with districts different in pupil population than theirs (as, for example, by using immersive educational technology and Holodeck classrooms).

8. Establish high-quality professional development programs for teachers and administrators to enhance their ability to effectively educate diverse student bodies.

9. Require that, as a condition of New Jersey school districts purchasing textbooks, other instructional materials, and educational technology, those items must be sensitive and responsive to the racial, ethnic, cultural, and economic diversity of the state's students.

10. Foster or support citizen coalitions to promote greater educational and residential diversity by all appropriate means including political action, legislative lobbying, policy development, and, if necessary, litigation.

Notes

Chapter 1

1. Carter & Welner, 2013; Linn & Welner, 2007; Mickelson, 2016; Wells, Holme, Revilla, & Atanda, 2009a.
2. Mickelson, 2016.
3 Enos, 2014.
4. Joint Rutgers-Eagleton/FDU Poll: Most New Jerseyans Perceive No School Segregation (Aug. 26, 2019).
5. Tractenberg & Coughlan, 2018.
6. 347 U.S. 483 (1954).
7. Rothstein, 2017.
8. Carter, 2012; powell, 2001; Tyson, 2011.
9. Mickelson, 2016, n.p.
10. Taken from ASID's position paper on integration in NYC schools:
static1.squarespace.com/static/5afd4002f7939252a8566b77/t/5b12afe1575d1fa70d2
320ca/1527951378397/%23theagendaFINALFINAL.pdf
11. *Latino Action Network et al. v. State of New Jersey et al.*, Docket No. MER-L-001076 (filed May 17, 2018).
12. *Jenkins et al. v. Township of Morris School District and Board of Education et al.*, 58 N.J. 483 (1971).
13. Civil Rights Act of 1964, sec. 407(a), codified as 42 USCA sec. 2000c-6(a); see also the so-called Anti-Busing Amendments of 1972, codified as 20 USCA secs. 1651–1656.
14. *Parents Involved in Community Schools v. Seattle School Dist. No. 1*, 551 U.S. 701 (2007).
15. Denton, 2010, p. 23.
16. University of Virginia, Curry School of Education Professor Joanna Williams' recent lecture: news.virginia.edu/content/understanding-benefits-school-diversity-majority-minority-age.
17. Ibid.
18. Coughlin, 2012, n.p.
19. In this book, we use the racial/ethnic labels that respondents in Morris School District used, and understand that some of these terms can be viewed as derogatory. For example, Black and African American, and Latinx and Hispanic, were used interchangeably to refer to the population in MSD
20. Couglin, 2012, n.p.
21. Ibid.
22. Ibid.
23. Ibid.
24. Ibid.
25. Ibid.

26. Kingdon, 1995.

27. my.aasa.org/AASA/Resources/SAMag/2017/Nov17/TOC_Nov17.aspx

28. nytimes.com/1973/10/21/archives/in-morris-a-painful-schools-merger-merger-in-morris-is-proving. html

29. New Jersey Department of Education (2019). 2018–2019 Enrollment Data. nj.gov/education/data/enr/enr19/

30. nytimes.com/2016/01/10/realestate/morristown-nj-historic-with-a-lively-downtown. html

31. New Jersey Department of Education (2019). Taxpayers' Guide to Education Spending: Morris School District. state.nj.us/education/guide/2019/district.html

32. New Jersey Department of Education (2019). New Jersey School Performance Reports: Morris School District. rc.doe.state.nj.us/SearchForSchool.aspx

33. NCES, 1987–2019.

34. We use Hispanic here and throughout the book when statistics from the school district or Census data are referenced. However, when referring to students and families from Central or South America in the MSD, we prefer to use the widely accepted, gender-neutral term, Latinx, instead.

35. New Jersey Department of Education (2019). 2018-2019 Enrollment Data.nj.gov/education/data/enr/enr19/

36. Potter, Quick & Davies, 2016 tcf.org/content/report/a-new-wave-of-school-integration/?agreed=1

37. U.S. Census Bureau (2018). American Community Survey 2017 (5-year Estimates).

38. Stroub & Richards, 2013; Reardon & Owens, 2014 civilrightsproject.ucla.edu/research/k-12-education/integration-and-diversity/brown-at-62-school-segregation-by-race-poverty-and-state/Brown-at-62-final-corrected-2.pdf

39. U.S. Government Accountability Office (GAO), 2016 gao.gov/products/GAO-16-345

40. Geiger, 2017 http://www.pewresearch.org/fact-tank/2017/10/25/many-minority-students-go-to-schools-where-at-least-half-of-their-peers-are-their-race-or-ethnicity/

41. Flaxman, Kucsera, Orfield, Ayscue, & Siegel-Hawley, 2013.

42. Ibid.

43. Bischoff, 2008, p. 2.

44. 45. Frankenberg & Orfield, 2012; Holme & Finnigan, 2013; Reardon & Owens, 2014.

45. New Jersey Department of Education (2019). 2018–2019 Enrollment Data. nj.gov/education/data/enr/enr19/report-final-110917.pdf

46. Hartman & Squires (Eds.), 2010; Pulido, 1996.

47. Derrick Bell, *Silent Covenants: Brown v. Board of Education and the Unfulfilled Hopes for Racial Reform* (Oxford: Oxford University Press, 2005); Daniel Monti, *A Semblance of Justice: St. Louis School Desegregation and Order in Urban America* (Columbia: University of Missouri Press, 1985); Scott Baker, *Paradoxes of Desegregation: African American Struggles for Educational Equity in Charleston, South Carolina, 1926–1972* (Columbia: University of South Carolina Press, 2003); David Cecelski, *Along Freedom Road: Hyde County, North Carolina, and the Fate of Black Schools in the South.* (North Carolina: University of North Carolina Press, 1994); Adam Fairclough, *A Class of Their Own: Black Teachers in the Segregated South.* (Cambridge: Harvard University Press, 2007); Vanessa Siddle Walker, *Their Highest Potential: An African American School Community in the Segregated South* (Chapel Hill: University of North Carolina, 1996).

48. Cashin, 2004, p. 54.

49. Paris, 2012, p. 93.

50. Lewis-McCoy's *Inequality in the Promised Land* (2014) tells the story of the unequal distribution of resources in one suburban school district, as does Lewis and Diamond's *Despite the Best Intentions.*

Chapter 2

1. "K–12 Education: Better Use of Information Could Help Agencies Identify Disparities and Address Racial Discrimination." U.S. Government accountability Office, 2016, gao. gov/products/GAO-16-345; Gary Orfield, J. Ee, E. Frankenberg, and G. Siegel-Hawley, "Brown at 62: School Segregation by Race, Poverty, and State," Civil Rights Project, 2016, civilrightsproject.ucla.edu/research/K–12-education/integration-and-diversity/brown-at-62-school-segregation-by-race-poverty-and-state/Brown-at-62-final-corrected-2.pdf. The latest decision of the U.S. Supreme Court in *Fisher v. University of Texas* may provide a ray of hope, however. By a 4–3 margin, the Court sustained the University's race-conscious admissions program and, by doing so, validated the educational benefits of diversity. Ironically, the higher education community has been much better at making that case than the K–12 community.

2. G. Flaxman, J. Kucsera, G. Orfield, J. Ayscue, and G. Siegel-Hawley, "A Status Quo of Segregation: Racial and Economic Imbalance in New Jersey Schools, 1989–2010," Civil Rights Project, 2013, ielp.rutgers.edu/docs/Norflet_NJ_Final_101013_POST.pdf.

3. Carter & Welner, 2013.

4. Holme, 2002.

5. *Parents Involved in Community Schools v. Seattle School Dist. No. 1* et al., 551 U.S. 701 (2007), in a 5–4 decision the Court struck down voluntary school desegregation plans adopted by two school districts, Seattle and Jefferson County (metropolitan Louisville, Kentucky).

6. *Keyes v. School Dist. No. 1, Denver, Colo.*, 413 U.S. 189 (1973), in separate opinions, Justice Douglas, 413 U.S. at 214, and Justice Powell, 43 U.S. at 217, argued the U.S. Supreme Court should make *Brown v. Board of Education* a nationwide decision by rejecting the distinction between de jure and de facto segregation; *San Antonio Independent School Dist. V. Rodriguez*, 411 U.S. 1, 44 (1973), federal courts should not impose a national remedy for school funding provided by states.

7. *Brown v. Board of Education*, 349 U.S. 294 (1955) ("Brown II"), in dealing with remedy for unconstitutional school segregation, the Court used the much-quoted and frequently criticized phrase "with all deliberate speed."

8. Marion Manola Wright, *The Education of Negroes in New Jersey* (Teachers College Record Press: New York, 1941), accessed 2016, babel.hathitrust.org/cgi/pt?id=mdp.39015035886715;view=1up;seq=137.

9. R.S. 18:142 (1881), which served as the source for the current statutory prohibition against exclusion from any public school because of race, creed, color, national origin, or ancestry, NJSA 18A: 385.1 (making it a misdemeanor for any board of education member to vote for such exclusion).

10. L. 1945, c. 169.

11. N.J. Const. Art. I, sec. 5.

12. 58 N.J. 483 (1971) (ironically, the same page number as the initial decision in *Brown v. Board of Education*).

13. One of the clearest examples of that is the effect of the U.S. Supreme Court's 5–4 decision in *San Antonio Independent School District v. Rodriguez*, 411 U.S. 1 (1973). In that decision, the Court refused to strike down Texas' admittedly unequal state education funding statute because the majority's deference to local educational control led it to conclude that Texas had satisfied the lenient "rational basis" approach to the Equal Protection Clause. Had the Court found either that education was a fundamental constitutional right or that the Texas statute's unequal treatment discriminated against a "suspect classification," such as race, the state would have been required to demonstrate a "compelling state interest," almost certainly not possible (see Ladd, Chalk & Hansen (Eds.), *Equity and Adequacy in Education Finance: Issues and Perspectives* (National Academy Press, 1999). The long-term consequence of this narrow decision has been that legal advocators have, almost without

exception, over the past four and a half decades brought their school funding cases to state, rather than federal, courts, where they have had a record of substantial success. New Jersey and its landmark case of *Abbott v. Burke* (119 N.J. 287 (1990) ("Abbott II") (for a list of all 22 New Jersey Supreme Court opinions and orders thus far in this case, see www. edlawcenter.org) represents a prominent example of how state courts have taken a different road than the federal courts. The downside of this approach has been the need to separately litigate school funding reform cases in almost every state.

14. The *Rodriguez* decision exemplifies this downside as well. The five Justice–majority expressed concern about dictating a single national solution to this complex problem and, therefore, opted for a decision elevating the value of local control of education (411 U.S. at 42, 44, 55).

15. Laws of New Jersey (1850) 63–64.

16. Laws of New Jersey (1881), R. S. 18:142 (1881); now codified as NJSA 18A:38-5.1.

17. Laws of New Jersey 1945, c. 169, sec. 11; now codified as NJSA 10:5-1 *et seq.*

18. N.J. CONST. Art. I, Section 5

19. Tractenberg & Coughlan, "The New Promise of School Integration and the Old Problem of Extreme Segregation: An Action Plan for New Jersey to Address Both" (Center for Diversity and Equality in Education, 2018); Orfield, Ee, & Coughlan, "New Jersey's Segregated Schools: Trends and Paths Forward" (UCLA Civil Rights Project, 2017); Tractenberg, Orfield & Flaxman, "New Jersey's Apartheid and Intensely Segregated Urban Schools: Powerful Evidence of an Inefficient and Unconstitutional State Education System" (Rutgers-Newark Institute on Education Law & Policy, 2013); Flaxman (with Kuscera, Orfield, Ayscue & Siegel-Hawley), "A Status Quo of Segregation: Racial and Economic Imbalance in New Jersey Schools, 1989-2010" (UCLA Civil Rights Project, 2013).

20. *Latino Action Network, et al., v. State of New Jersey et al.*, Docket No. MER-L-001076-18. New Jersey had a prior statewide school desegregation case filed in 1970 as a companion case to *Robinson v. Cahill,* the predecessor to *Abbott v. Burke*. In a sense that case, *Spencer v. Kugler*, 326 F.Supp. 1235 (D.NJ 1971), aff'd, 404 U.S. 1027 (1972), was a mirror image of *Robinson* (not surprising since it was filed by the same attorney); the primary claim in *Robinson* related to funding equity and the secondary claim related to racial discrimination; the primary claim in *Spencer* was racial segregation and the secondary claim had to do with funding (compensatory education funding for students who were denied the educational and social benefits of school integration). Although the district court found that New Jersey's educational system had long been segregated, it found no federal constitutional violation because the segregation was de facto. Interestingly, Justice William O. Douglas, alone of the U.S. Supreme Court justices, would have had the Court note probable jurisdiction and set the case for oral argument. He had two bases for his view—first, that school segregation such as New Jersey's was in fact state-imposed even though it was not a product of an explicit school segregation law, and, second, that New Jersey's combination of de facto racially separate schools (assuming it was de facto) and unequal funding disfavoring the predominantly Black schools violated some vestige of *Plessy v. Ferguson*, 163 U.S. 537 (1896), which at that time had not been formally overruled. 404 U.S. at 1031. Justice Douglas suggested that the remedy for states such as New Jersey was redistricting. 404 U.S. at 1028. He made no reference to *Jenkins*, which had been decided more than 6 months earlier.

21. New Jersey School Enrollment Data Reports (2015–16), nj.gov/education/data/.

22. Way, "Merger Unit Detail Stand" (Morris County's Daily Record, Dec. 21, 1967).

23. N.J.S.A. 18:21A-20 (L. 1966, c. 302, sec. 20); replaced in 2008 by P.L. 2008, c. 36, which eliminated the appeal to the State Board of Education and made the commissioner's decision the final agency determination appealable directly to the state courts.

24. As a result of this cross-petition, Wiley wound up working with Frank Harding to represent the petitioners, as well as on behalf of the Morristown board.

25. 58 N.J. 483 (1971).

26. *Jenkins et al. v. The Township of MSD and Board of Education and The Town of Morristown School District and Board of Education and The Borough of Morris Plains Board of Education*, 58 N.J. 1 (1971) (dissent by Francis, J.).

27. Ibid. at 3.

28. See *Justice Nathan L. Jacobs—Tributes from His Colleagues*, 28 RUTGERS L. REV. 209 (1975); Fowler, *Nathan Jacobs, 83, an Ex-Justice of the New Jersey Supreme Court* (NY Times Jan. 26, 1989 (nytimes.com/1989/01/26/obituaries/nathan-jacobs-83-an-ex-justice-of-the-new-jersey-supreme-court.html).

29. *Jenkins et al. v. The Township of MSD and Board of Education and The Town of Morristown School District and Board of Education and The Borough of Morris Plains Board of Education*, 58 N.J. 483, 485 (1971).

30. Ibid. at 488.

31. Ibid. at 489.

32. Ibid. at 490.

33. Ibid.

34. Ibid.

35. Ibid. Although the reader might react to some of the hearing examiner's findings as reflecting stereotypical attitudes, those findings were probably factually accurate in 1971—and may still be.

36. Ibid.

37. Ibid. at 490–91.

38. This point is reminiscent of Justice Jacobs' opinion in *Booker* where he stressed that, "In a society such as ours, it is not enough that the 3 R's are being taught properly for there are other vital considerations. The children must learn to respect and live with one another in multiracial and multicultural communities and the earlier they do so the better." *Booker v. Board of Education of City of Plainfield*, 45 N.J. 161 (1965).

39. Jenkins, 58 N.J. at 493.

40. Ibid. at 495.

41. Ibid.

42. 45 N.J. 161, 180 (1965).

43. Justice Jacobs did refer back to the *Booker* opinion's citation of "several lower federal court decisions which had taken the position that in the circumstances presented to them the continuance of de facto segregation in the local public schools would violate the federal constitution, 58 N.J. at 497 (citing to 45 N.J. at 169–70), but that promising development was squelched by the U.S. Supreme Court. For a relatively recent academic treatment of the complicated and cloudy federal court treatment of de facto segregation, see Frankenberg & Taylor, 2018.

44. 58 N.J. at 499. Justice Jacobs drew heavily on a 1969 decision of the Eighth Circuit Court of Appeals in *Haney v. County Board of Education of Sevier County, Ark.*, 410 F.2d 920 (8th Cir. 1969), vacated & remanded on other grounds, 429 F.2d 364 (8th Cir. 1970).

45. 377 U.S. 533 (1964).

46. 58 N.J. at 500.

47. 58 N.J. at 500–01.

48. 58 N.J. at 508.

49. See "In Morris, a Painful Schools Merger" (*New York Times*); nytimes.com/1973/10/21/archives/in-morris-a-painful-schools-merger-merger-in-morris-is-proving.html, last visited 07/17/19).

50. 58 N.J. at 501.

51. *Board of Education of the Borough of Englewood Cliffs v. Board of Education of the City of Englewood v. Board of Education of the Borough of Tenafly*, 257 N.J. Super. 413, 476 (App.Div.1992).

52. 257 N.J. Super. at 476-77.

53. N.J.S.A. 18A-38-1. That statutory provision itself and a number of other state statutes do contemplate ways in which students can attend schools elsewhere. These include

sending-receiving provisions of the kind employed by Morristown and Morris Township prior to their merger into a single K–12 district.

54. See, e.g., *Alcantra et al v. Hespe et al.*, OAL Docket No.:EDU 11069-2014 S (Agency Ref. No. 156-6/14) (Lakewood challenging the State's school funding statute on the ground that it does not take into account Lakewood's unique demographics that result in almost half the district's budget being expended on resident nonpublic school students); and Jersey City Board of Education and E.H., a minor, by his guardian ad litem, *Shanna C. Givens v. State of New Jersey et al.*, Docket No.: MER-L-914-19 (Superior Court of New Jersey Law Div.: Mercer County) (Jersey City claiming that the State's school funding law doesn't provide it with adequate resources to meet its students' educational needs and fundamental constitutional rights). It is true—and highly relevant—that the students in the Lakewood and Jersey City schools districts are overwhelmingly low-income students of color.

Chapter 3

1. Coughlin, 2015.
2. "About Morristown" available at townofmorristown.org.
3. According to Census data, Asian families, which compose 5% of Morris students, reported earning the highest income in Morristown and Morris Township.
4. U.S. Census Bureau (2015). American Community Survey 2015: 5-year estimates.
5. Posey-Maddox, Kimelberg, & Cucchiara, 2013.
6. Khalifa, Gooden & Davis, 2016.
7. Ibid, p. 1274.
8. Ibid, p. 1275.
9. Green, 2015; Scribner, 2013, p. 3; Leithwood, Harris, & Hopkins, 2008.
10. Khalifa, Gooden, & Davis, 2016, p. 1277.
11. Khalifa, 2012.
12. Jenlink (Ed.), 2009, p. 10.
13. Cooper, 2009; Evans, 2007; Lewis, Diamond, & Forman, 2015; Siegel-Hawley et al., 2017.
14. Holme et al., 2013; McGrath & Kuriloff, 1999; Wells & Serna, 1996; Useem, 1992.
15. Lewis & Diamond, 2015, pp. 173–174.
16. *New York Times* Archives, Oct 21, 1973.
17. Coughlin, 2015.
18. Governor's Select Commission on Civil Disorder, 1968, p. x.
19. Ibid. p. xi.
20. Ibid., p xii.
21. Ibid.
22. Wells et al., 2009.
23. Douglas, 1995; Garland, 2013; Irons, 2002; Orfield & Eaton (Eds.), 1996.
24. National Advisory Commission on Civil Disorders, June 27 1967.
25. Garland, 2013, p. 81.
26. Johnson, 2019.
27. *Jenkins v. Township of MSD and Board of Education*, 1971.
28. The Princeton Plan: Fifty Years Later, documentary, available at princetonhistory.org/events/princeton-plan-panel-discussion/
29. Ibid.
30. For the purposes of this analysis, the small proportion of students identifying as something other than Asian, Black, Hispanic, or White were excluded. As a result, the overall proportions of students do not perfectly match other parts of the book where the "Other" category of students was included.

31. Johnson, 2019.

32. Frankenberg & Orfield, 2012.

33. Boisjoly, Duncan, Kremer, Levy, & Eccles, 2006; Brown & Hewstone, 2005; Pettigrew & Tropp, 2000.

34. Johnson, 2019, p. 6.

35. Noguera, 2003; Tatum, 1997; Hancock & Warren, 2017.

36. Benson & Borman, 2010.

37. Ready & Silander, 2011..

38. Ryan, 2010.

39. Hannah-Jones, 2019.

40. Frankenberg & Orfield, 2012.

41. NJ Department of Education (2019). "2017-2018 School Performance Reports Database." rc.doe.state.nj.us/ReportsDatabase.aspx

42. Coughlin, 2014.

43. Roda, 2015; Roda & Kafka, 2019.

44. Lucas, 1999; Oakes, 2005.

45. Hallinan & Kubitschek, 1999; Rui, 2009.

46. Siegel-Hawley, 2013, p. 455.

47. Starr, 2019.

48. Ibid, n.p.

49. Blackparentsworkshop.org

50. Rui, 2009.

51. Equity and Inclusion Action Plan: resources.finalsite.net/images/v1562767240/morrisschooldistrictorg/ar5negkds6fbqeugf8yh/MSDEquityInclusionActionPlan_LifelongSuccess.pdf

52. Ryan, 2010.

Chapter 4

1. Carter, 2005.

2. Wells et al., 2016.

3. Morristown's acting police chief willing to stay on; would be department's first African American chief (June 15, 2019). *Morristown Green*, retrieved from morristowngreen.com/2019/05/29/morristowns-acting-police-chief-willing-to-stay-on-follows-turbulent-time-for-the-bureau/. We use the terms *Black* and *African American* interchangeably throughout this chapter to reflect how the participants used the terms. We acknowledge that there is considerable diversity within the Black racial category.

4. DiAngelo, 2018, p. 31.

5. U.S. Census Bureau (2018). American Community Survey 2017 (5-year estimates).

6. Berrey, 2005, p. 8.

7. Chang, 2016, p. 32.

8. Fall 2018 newsletter, https://www.morrisedfoundation.org/what-we-do/news.html.

9. Khalifa, Gooden, & Davis, 2016, p. 1297.

10. Guttiérez, R., 2009, p. 10.

11. Fall 2017 Newsletter, MEF website.

12. Rui, 2009

13. Oakes, 2005; Rui, 2009

14. Johnson, 2019, p. 3.

15. Gershenson et al., 2018.

16. Klopfenstein, 2005.

17. Dee, 2005; Egalite, Kisida, & Winters, 2015.

18. Noguera, 2003; Hancock & Warren, 2017.

19. Bristol & Goings, 2019; Bryan & Milton-Williams, 2017; El-Mekki, 2018; Milner, 2016; Pabon, 2016.

20. National Center for Education Statistics, 2015.

21. Bonilla-Silva, 2018.

22. Oakes, 2005; Roda, 2015.

23. Fletcher & Navarrete, 2011; Skiba et al., 2011.

24. Lindsay & Hart, 2017; Skiba et al., 2011.

25. Cooper, 2009, p. 719; see also Lopez et al., 2006; Shields & Sayani, 2005.

26. Michael, 2015; Yoon, 2016; DiAngelo, 2018.

27. Coughlin, 2017.

28. Spring 2018 MEF newsletter (www.morrisedfoundation.org/what-we-do/news.html).

29. Chang, 2016, p. 32.

Chapter 5

1. Ovando & Collier, 1985.

2. Ibid.

3. Ibid.

4. Ibid.

5. Gandara, 2012.

6. Spener, 1988.

7. Ibid.

8. Ibid.

9. Kaestle & Smith, 1982.

10. Hornberger, 2005.

11. Ovando, 1998.

12. Ibid.

13. Ibid.

14. ERIC Clearinghouse on Languages and Linguistics, Washington, DC., 1990.

15. Gandara & Hopkins, 2010.

16. Martinez-Wenzl, Perez, & Gandara, 2012.

17. Ovando, 1998.

18. Martinez-Wenzl, Perez, & Gandara, 2012.

19. U.S. Department of Education, 2015.

20. Ibid.

21. U.S. Department of Education, 2015, p. 3.

22. Bilingual Education, n.d.

23. The District uses ESL to describe its course offerings but refers to English Language Learners and has an office of ELL/Bilingual Education.

24. MSD, n.d.

25. Dodson, Formoso, & Scorsune, 2015.

26. Batalova & Lesser, 2017.

27. Batalova & Lesser, 2017.

28. Park, 2014.

29. "Trump warns against admitting unaccompanied migrant children," n.d.

30. Ibid.

31. "Wednesday's GOP debate" transcript, annotated—*The Washington Post*," September 16, 2015.

32. Banks in Gandara & Hopkins, 2010.

33. Orellana, 2001; Foley, 1997; Carhill-Poza, 2017; Moll, Amanti, Neff, & Gonzalez, 1992.

34. Ovando, 1998, p. 22.

35. Gandara, 2012.

36. Gandara, 2012; Gandara & Orfield, 2012; Perez & Holmes, 2010.

37. Echevarria, Short, & Powers, 2006.

38. Decapua & Marshall, 2010; DeCapua, 2007.

39. "Supporting immigrant and refugee children amid family separation and trauma" (n.d.).

40. Decapua & Marshall, 2010.

41. Paris, 2012; Paris & Alim, 2014, 2017; Ladson-Billings, 2009.

42. Brooks, Adams, & Morita-Mullaney, 2010.

43. Ibid.

44. Ibid.

45. Murray et al., 2014.

46. Epstein, 1987; Inoa, 2017.

47. Benner, Boyle, & Sadler, 2016.

48. Inoa, 2017.

49. Murray et al., 2014.

50. Inoa, 2017.

51. Murray et al., 2014.

52. Ibid.

53. Ibid.

54. Ibid.

55. See Morristown Neighborhood House—About, n.d.

Conclusion

1. Orfield & Lee, 2007; Clotfelter, 2004.

2. Orfield, 2001; Reardon & Owens, 2014.

3. See, e.g., Rothstein, Richard (2017). *The Color of Law: A Forgotten History of How Our Government Segregated America*. New York, NY: Liveright. Books such as Rothstein's raise serious questions about whether segregation, whether in housing or in schools, ever truly was de facto—a function of unintended circumstances.

4. Forty-four years before Rothstein's book, Justices Lewis Powell and William Douglas had joined ranks across a considerable ideological divide to express a similar view. In Douglas's words, "I think it is time to state that there is no constitutional difference between de jure and de facto segregation, for each is the product of state actions or policies." *Keyes v. School District No. 1, Denver, Colo.*, 413 U.S. 189, 215–216 (1973).

5. Johnson, 2019.

6. Like Carter and Welner and others, we use the term "opportunity gap" in lieu of "achievement gap" because the former places the onus on the system fixing the problem instead of on the student.

7. Johnson, 2019, p. 210.

8. Mickelson, 2016, n.p.

9. Carter & Welner, 2013.

10. Reardon & Owens, 2014.

11. Clotfelter, Ladd & Vigdor, 2005; Darling-Hammond, 2010; Gamoran, 1992.

12.civilrightsproject.ucla.edu/research/k-12-education/integration-and-diversity/new-jerseys-segregated-schools-trends-and-paths-forward/New-Jersey-report-final-110917.pdf

13. Stroub & Richards, 2013.

14. Tractenberg & Coughlan, 2018.

15. Wells et al., 2016.

16. Brooks et al., 2013; Lewis & Diamond, 2015; Mickelson, 2016; Oakes, 2005; Roda, 2015.

17. Skiba et al., 2011.

18. Cooper, 2009; Evans, 2007; Yoon, 2016.

19. Holme et al., 2013; Jenlink, 2009.

20. *Booker v. Board of Education of City of Plainfield*, 1965.

21. *Jenkins v. Township of MSD and Board of Education*, 1971.

22. *Mount Laurel I* (1975) and *Mount Laurel II* (1983)

23. *Abbott v. Burke*, 1981; all states have state education clauses and most states have had school funding reform litigation.

24. Tractenberg & Coughlan, 2018.

25. Flaxman et al., 2013.

26. Gay, 2010; Ladson-Billings, 1995; Paris, 2012; Khalifa et al., 2016.

27. Flaxman et al., 2013; Frankenberg et al., 2019.

28. *Robinson v. Cahill*, 69 N.J. 133, 154 (1975).

29. *Jenkins, et al. v. Morris Township School District and Board of Education, et al.*, 58 N.J. 483 (1971).

30. Tractenberg & Coughlan, 2018.

31. For example, although charter schools and county vocational schools are physically located within the borders of particular school districts, they are not operated by the local school district. In that sense, students who live in the district where the charter or county vocational school happens to be located are still attending, as an operational if not geographic matter, a school not in the district where they live.

32. *Board of Education of Borough of Englewood Cliffs v. Board of Education of City of Englewood v. Board of Education of Borough of Tenafly*, 170 N.J. 323 (2002).

33. Charter Aid Notices were obtained through an Open Public Records Act request by Dr. Julia Sass Rubin of the Bloustein School of Public Policy and Planning at Rutgers and generously shared with us aggregated to the district level. These data were compared to public geospatial data on each charter school's location and each residential district's boundaries to identify how many students attended a charter school located outside of the district in which they lived.

34. *Jenkins*, 58 N.J. at 507.

35. In Grant of Charter School Application of Englewood on the Palisades Charter School, 164 N.J. 316, 324 (2000).

36. NJ Const. Art. VIII, par. 4.

37. Taken from Urie Bronfenbrenner's Ecological Framework for Human Development.

38. See *Mount Laurel* decision.

39. Kahlenberg et al., 2019, n.p.

40. Johnson, 2019.

41. Ibid., pp. 257-258.

42. Ibid.

43. Miyake-Trapp, 2018.

44. Murray et al., 2014.

45. Healey, 2016.

46. Abu El-Haj & Rubin, 2009; Oakes, 2005; Oakes, Wells & Datnow, 1997.

47. Roda, 2015.

48. Welsh & Little, 2018, p. 773; see also Skiba et al., 2011.

49. Gandara, 2012; Gandara & Orfield, 2012.

50. Ovando, 1998.

51. Johnson, 2019.

52. Abu El-Haj & Rubin, 2009, p. 457.

53. Carver-Thomas, 2017.

54. O'Dea, 2019.

55. Cucchiara, 2013; Lewis, 2003; Posey-Maddox, 2014.

56. Doucet, 2017.

57. Hopkins, 2002, p. 144.

58. Welsh & Little, 2018; Gonzalez, 2012, 2015.

59. Paris, 2012.

60. Welsh & Little, 2018, p. 783.

References

Abu El-Haj, T. R., & Rubin, B. C. (2009). Realizing the equity-minded aspirations of detracking and inclusion: Toward a capacity-oriented framework for teacher education. *Curriculum Inquiry, 39*(3), 435–463.

Batalova, J., & Lesser, G. (April 7, 2017). *Central American immigrants in the United States.* Migration Policy Institute. Retrieved from www.migrationpolicy.org/article/central-american-immigrants-united-states-4

Benner, A. D., Boyle, A. E., & Sadler, S. (2016). Parental involvement and adolescents' educational success: The roles of prior achievement and socioeconomic status. *Journal of Youth and Adolescence, 45*(6), 1053–1064.

Bonilla-Silva, E. (2018). *Racism without racists: Color-blind racism and the persistence of racial inequality in the United States.* Lanham, MD: Rowman & Littlefield.

Bristol, T. J., & Goings, R. B. (2019). Exploring the boundary heightening experiences of Black male teachers: Lessons for teacher education. *Journal of Teacher Education, 70*(1), 51–64.

Bronfenbrenner, U. (1979). *The Ecology of Human Development: Experiments by Nature and Design.* Cambridge, MA: Harvard University Press.

Brooks, K., S. R. Adams, & T. Morita-Mullaney. (2010). Creating inclusive learning communities for ELL students: Transforming school principals' perspectives. *Theory Into Practice, 49*(2), 145–151. doi.org/10.1080/00405841003641501

Bryan, N., & Milton-Williams, T. M. (2017). We need more than just male bodies in classrooms: Recruiting and retaining culturally relevant Black male teachers in early childhood education. *Journal of Early Childhood Teacher Education, 38*(3), 209–222.

Carhill-Poza, A. (2017). "If you don't find a friend in here, it's gonna be hard for you": Structuring bilingual peer support for language learning in urban high schools. *Linguistics and Education, 37,* 63.

Carter, P. L. (2005). *Keepin' it real: School success beyond black and white.* New York, NY: Oxford University Press.

Carter, P. L. (2012). *Stubborn roots: Race, culture, and inequality in U.S. and South African schools.* New York, NY: Oxford University Press.

DeCapua, A. (2007). Schooling, interrupted. *Educational Leadership, 64*(6), 40–46.

DeCapua, A., & Marshall, H. W. (2010). Reaching ELLs at risk: Instruction for students with limited or interrupted formal education. *Preventing School Failure, 55*(1), 35–41. doi.org/10.1080/10459880903291680

Baker, S. (2003). *Paradoxes of desegregation: African American struggles for educational equity in Charleston, South Carolina, 1926–1972.* Columbia, SC: University of South Carolina Press.

Bell, D. (2005). *Silent covenants: Brown v. Board of Education and the unfulfilled hopes for racial reform.* New York: Oxford University Press.

Benson, J., & Borman, G. (2010). Family, neighborhood, and school settings across seasons: When do socioeconomic context and racial composition matter for the reading achievement growth of young children? *Teachers College Record, 112*(5), 1338–1390.

Berrey, E. (2005). *The enigma of diversity: The language of race and the limits of racial justice.*

Chicago, IL: The University of Chicago Press.

Bischoff, K. (2008). School district fragmentation and racial residential segregation: How do boundaries matter? *Urban Affairs Review, 44*(2), 182–217.

Boisjoly, J., Duncan, G., Kremer, M., Levy, D., & Eccles, J. (2006). Empathy or antipathy? The impact of diversity, *American Economic Review, 96*(5), 1890–1905.

Brooks, J., N. W. Arnold, & Brooks, M. C. (2013). Educational leadership and racism: A narrative inquiry into second-generation segregation. *Teachers College Record, 115*(1), 1–27.

Brown, R., & Hewstone, M. (2005). An integrative theory of intergroup contact. *Advances in Experimental Social Psychology, 37*, 255–343.

Carter, P. L., & Welner, K.. (2013). *Closing the opportunity gap: What America must do to give every child an even chance.* New York: Oxford University Press.

Carver-Thomas, D. (2017). *Diversifying the field: Barriers to recruiting and retaining teachers of color and how to overcome them.* San Antonio, TX, and Palo Alto, CA: Learning Policy Institute and Intercultural Development Research Organization.

Cashin, S. (2004). *The failures of integration.* Cambridge, MA: Public Affairs.

Cecelski, D. (1994). *Along freedom road: Hyde County, North Carolina, and the fate of Black schools in the South.* Chapel Hill: University of North Carolina Press.

Center for Disease Control. (February 5, 2019). The social-ecological model: A framework for prevention. Retrieved from cdc.gov/violenceprevention/publichealthissue/social-ecological-model.html

Chang, J. (2016). *We gon' be alright.* New York, NY: Picador.

Clotfelter, C. T. (2004). *After* Brown: *The rise and retreat of school desegregation.* Princeton: Princeton University Press.

Clotfelter, C. T., Ladd, H. F., & Vigdor, J. (2005). Who teaches whom? Race and the distribution of novice teachers. *Economics of Education Review, 24*(4), 377–392.

Cooper, C. W. (2009). Performing cultural work in demographically changing schools: Implications for expanding transformative leadership frameworks. *Educational Administration Quarterly 45*(5), 694–724.

Coughlin, K. (May 4, 2012). No clichés here: May 10 gala will salute living legend Steve Wiley . . . "Mr. Morristown." Retrieved from morristowngreen.com/2012/05/04/no-cliches-here-may-10-gala-will-salute-living-legend-steve-wiley-mr-morristown/.

Coughlin, K. (July 15, 2014). Morris school superintendent calling it a career. Retrieved from morristowngreen.com/2014/07/15/morris-schools-superintendent-thomas-ficarra-calling-it-a-career/

Coughlin, K. (October 12, 2015). Remembering Steve Wiley, Morristown's man for all seasons. Retrieved from morristowngreen.com/2015/10/12/remembering-steve-wiley-morristowns-man-for-all-seasons/.

Cucchiara, M. B. (2013). *Marketing schools, marketing cities: who wins and who loses when schools become urban amenities.* Chicago, IL: The University of Chicago Press.

Darling-Hammond, L. (2010). *The flat world and education: How America's commitment to equity will determine our future.* New York, NY: Teachers College Press.

Dee, T. S. 2005. A teacher like me: Does race, ethnicity, or gender matter? *American Economic Review, 95*(2), 158–165.

Denton, N. (2010). From segregation to integration: How do we get there? *The Integration Debate.* New York, NY: Routledge.

DiAngelo, R. (2018). *White fragility: Why it's so hard for white people to talk about racism.* Boston, MA: Beacon Press.

Dodson, S., Formoso, A., & Scorsune, M. (2015). *Morris School District, Heritage 1, 2, 3 Curriculum, Grades 9 through 12.*

Doucet, F. (2017). What does a culturally sustaining learning climate look like? *Theory Into Practice, 56*(3), 195–204.

Douglas, D. M. (1995). *Reading, writing and race: The desegregation of the Charlotte schools.* Chapel Hill: University of North Carolina Press.

Echevarria, J., Short, D., & Powers, K. (2006). School reform and standards-based education: An instructional model for English language learners. *Journal of Educational Research, 99*(4), 195–211.

Egalite, A. J., Kisida, B., & Winters, M. A. (2015). Representation in the classroom: The effect of own-race teachers on student achievement. *Economics of Education Review, 45*, 44–52.

El-Mekki, S. (2018). Learning from black male teachers who thrive. *Educational Leadership, 75*(8), 65–70.

Enos, R. D. (2014). Causal effect of intergroup contact on exclusionary attitudes. PubMed.gov. Retrieved from ncbi.nlm.nih.gov/pubmed/24567394.

Epstein, J. L. (1987). Toward a theory of family-school connections: Teacher practices and parent involvement. In K. Hurrelmann, F.-X. Kaufmann, & F. Lösel (Eds.), *Prevention and intervention in childhood and adolescence, 1. Social intervention: Potential and constraints* (p. 121–136). Berlin, Germany: Walter De Gruyter.

Evans, A. E. (2007). Changing faces: Suburban school response to demographic change. *Education and Urban Society, 39*(3), 315–348.

Fairclough, A. (2007). *A class of their own: Black teachers in the segregated South.* Cambridge, MA: Harvard University Press.

Flaxman, G., Kucsera, J., Orfield, G., Ayscue, J., & Siegel-Hawley, G. (2013). *A status quo of segregation: Racial and economic imbalance in New Jersey schools, 1989–2010.* Los Angeles, CA: Civil Rights Project. Retrieved from ielp.rutgers.edu/docs/Norflet_NJ_Final_101013_POST.pdf

Fletcher, T. V., & Navarrete, L. A. (2011). Learning disabilities or difference: A critical look at issues associated with the misidentification and placement of Hispanic students in special education programs. *Rural Special Education Quarterly, 22*(4), 37–46.

Foley, D. (1997). Deficit thinking models based on culture: The anthropological protest. In R. Valencia (Ed.), *The Evolution of Deficit Thinking: Educational Thought and Practice* (pp. 113–131). London: Falmer Press/Taylor and Francis.

Fowler, G. (1989, January 26). *Nathan Jacobs, 83, an ex-justice of the New Jersey supreme court.* Retrieved from nytimes.com/1989/01/26/obituaries/nathan-jacobs-83-an-ex-justice-of-the-new-jersey-supreme-court.html).

Frankenberg, E., Ee, J., Ayscue, J. B., & Orfield, G. (2019). *Harming our common future: America's segregated schools 65 years after Brown.* Los Angeles: Civil Rights Project. Retrieved from civilrightsproject.ucla.edu/research/k-12-education/integration-and-diversity/harming-our-common-future-americas-segregated-schools-65-years-after-brown/Brown-65-050919v4-final.pdf

Frankenberg, E., & Orfield, G. (2012). *The resegregation of suburban schools: A hidden crisis in American education.* Cambridge, MA: Harvard University Press.

Frankenberg, E., & Taylor, K. De facto segregation: Tracing a legal basis for contemporary inequality, *Journal of Law and Education, 47*(2).

Gamoran, A. (1992). The variable effects of high school tracking. *Sociology of Education, 57*(4), 812–828.

Gandara, P. (2012). Overcoming triple segregation. *Educational Leadership, 68*(3), 60–64.

Gandara, P., & Hopkins, M. (2010). *Forbidden language: English learners and restrictive language policies.* New York, NY: Teachers College Press.

Gandara, P., & Orfield, G.. (2012). Segregating Arizona's English Learners: A return to the "Mexican Room"? *Teachers College Record, 114*(9), 1–27.

Garland, S. (2013). *Divided we fail: The story of an African American community that ended the era of school desegregation.* Boston, MA: Beacon Press.

Gay, G. (2010). *Culturally responsive teaching: Theory, research, and practice* (2nd ed.). New York, NY: Teachers College Press.

Geiger, A. W. (2017). Many minority students go to schools where at least half of their peers are their race or ethnicity. *Pew Research Center.* Retrieved from pewresearch.org/fact-tank/2017/10/25/many-minority-students-go-to-schools-where-at-least-half-of-their-peers-are-their-race-or-ethnicity/

Gershenson, S., Hart, C. M. D., Hyman, J., Lindsay, C., & Papageorge, N. W. (2018). *The long-run impacts of same-race teachers*. NBER Working Paper No. 25254. Retrieved from ftp.iza.org/dp10630.pdf

González, T. (2012). Keeping kids in schools: Restorative justice, punitive discipline, and the school to prison pipeline. *Journal of Law & Education, 41*(2), 281–335. Retrieved from www.restorativejustice.org/articlesdb/articles/10643

González, T. (2015). Socializing schools: Addressing racial disparities in discipline through restorative justice. In Daniel J. Losen (Ed.), *Closing the school discipline gap: Equitable remedies for excessive exclusion* (pp. 151–165). New York, NY: Teachers College Press.

Governor's Select Commission on Civil Disorder. (1968). *"Report for action," State of New Jersey, February, 1968*. Retrieved from www.ncjrs.gov/pdffiles1/Digitization/69748NC-JRS.pdf

Green, T. L. (2015). Leading for urban school reform and community development. *Educational Administration Quarterly, 51*(5), 679–711.

Gutiérrez, R. (2009). Embracing the inherent tensions in teaching mathematics from an equity stance. *Democracy and Education, 18*(3), 9–16.

Hallinan, M.T., & Kubitschek, W.N. (1999). Curriculum differentiation and high school achievement. *Social Psychology of Education, 3*, 41–62.

Hancock, S., & Warren, C. A. (2017). *White women's work: Examining the intersectionality of teaching, identity, and race*. New York, NY: Information Age Publishing.

Hannah-Jones, N. (July 12, 2019). It was never about busing, *The New York Times*. Retrieved from www.nytimes.com/2019/07/12/opinion/sunday/it-was-never-about-busing.html

Hartman, C., & Squires, G. D. (Eds.). *The integration debate: Competing futures for American cities*. New York, NY: Routledge

Healey, L. (November 21, 2016). *K–12 school districts work to improve inclusion through teacher training*. INSIGHT into Diversity. Retrieved from insightintodiversity.com/k-12-school-districts-work-to-improve-inclusion-through-teacher-training/

Holme, J. J. (2002). Buying homes, buying schools: School choice and the social construction of school quality. *Harvard Educational Review, 72*, 177–206.

Holme, J. J., Diem, S., & Welton, A. (2013). Suburban school districts and demographic change: The technical, normative, and political dimensions of response. *Educational Administration Quarterly, 50*(1), 34–66.

Holme, J. J., & Finnigan, K. (2013). School diversity, school district fragmentation and metropolitan policy. *Teachers College Record, 115*, 1–29.

Hopkins, B. (2002). Restorative justice in schools. *Support for Learning, 17*, 144–149.

Hornberger, N. H. (2005). Heritage/Community language education: U.S. and Australian perspectives. *International Journal of Bilingual Education and Bilingualism, 8*(2),101–108.

Inoa, R. (2017). Parental involvement among middle-income Latino parents living in a middle-class community. *Hispanic Journal of Behavioral Sciences, 39*(3), 316–335.

Irons, P. (2002). *Jim Crow's children: The broken promise of the Brown decision*. New York, NY: Penguin Books

Jenlink, P. (Ed.). (2009). *Equity issues for today's educational leaders: Meeting the challenge of creating equitable schools for all*. Lanham, MD: R&L Education.

Johnson, R. C. (2019). *Children of the dream: Why school integration works*. New York, NY: Basic Books.

Kaestle, C., & Smith, M. (1982). The federal role in elementary and secondary education, 1940–1980. *Harvard Educational Review 52*(4), 384–408. doi.org/10.17763/haer.52.4.021g4v7641j98xg2

Kahlenberg, R., Potter, H., & Quick, K. (2019). A bold agenda for school integration. *The Century Foundation*. Retrieved from tcf.org/content/report/bold-agenda-school-integration/

Khalifa, M. (2012). A "re"-new-"ed" paradigm in successful urban school leadership: Principal as community leader. *Educational Administration Quarterly, 48*(3), 424–467.

Khalifa, M., M. A. Gooden, and J. E. Davis. (2016). Culturally responsive school leadership: A synthesis of the literature. *Review of Educational Research, 86*(4), 1272–1311.

Kingdon, J. (1995). *Agendas, alternatives, and public policies.* New York, NY: Harper Collins College Press.

Klopfenstein, K. (2005). Beyond test scores: The impact of Black teacher role models on rigorous math taking. *Contemporary Economic Policy, 23*(3), 416–428.

Ladd, H. F., Chalk, R. & Hansen, J. S. (Eds.). (1999). *Equity and adequacy in education finance: Issues and perspectives* Washington, DC: National Academy Press.

Ladson-Billings, G. (1995). But that's just good teaching! The case for culturally relevant pedagogy. *American Educational Research Journal, 32,* 159–165.

Ladson-Billings, G. (2009). *The dreamkeepers: Successful teachers of African American children* (2nd ed.). San Francisco, CA: Jossey-Bass.

Leithwood, K., A. Harris, and D. Hopkins. (2008). Seven strong claims about successful school leadership. *School Leadership & Management, 28*(1), 27–42.

Lewis, A. E. (2003). Race in the schoolyard: Negotiating the color line in classrooms and communities. New Brunswick, NJ: Rutgers University Press.

Lewis, A. E., & J. B. Diamond. (2015). *Despite the best intentions: How racial inequality thrives in good schools.* New York, NY: Oxford University Press.

Lewis, A. E., Diamond, J. B., & Forman, T. A. (2015). Conundrums of integration and desegregation in the context of racialized hierarchy. *Sociology of Race and Ethnicity, 1*(1), 22–36.

Lewis-McCoy, R. L. (2014). *Inequality in the promised land.* Stanford, CA: Stanford University Press.

Lindsay, C. A., & Hart, C. M. D. (2017). Exposure to same-race teachers and student disciplinary outcomes for Black students in North Carolina. *Educational Evaluation and Policy Analysis, 39*(3), 485–510.

Linn, R. L., & Welner, K. (Eds.). (2007). *Race-conscious policies for assigning students to schools: Social science research and the Supreme Court cases.* Washington, DC: National Academy of Education.

Lopez, G. R., Gonzalez, M. L., & Fierro, E. (2006). Educational leadership along the U.S.¬Mexico border: Crossing borders/embracing hybridity/building bridges. In C. Marshall & M. Oliva (Eds.), *Leadership for social justice: Making revolutions in education* (pp. 64¬84). Boston: Pearson Education.

Lucas, S. R. (1999). Tracking inequality: Stratification and mobility in American high schools. New York, NY: Teachers College Press.

Martinez-Wenzl, M., Perez, K., & Gandara, P. (2012). *Is Arizona's approach to educating its ELs superior to other forms of instruction?* The Civil Rights Project, UCLA. Retrieved from escholarship.org/uc/item/7d36h5m8

McGrath, D. J., & Kuriloff, P. J. (1999). "They're going to tear the doors off this place": Upper-middle-class parent school involvement and the educational opportunities of other people's children. *Educational Policy, 13*(5), 603–629.

Michael, A. (2015). *Raising race questions: Whiteness and inquiry in education.* New York, NY: Teachers College Press

Mickelson, R. A. (2016). *Twenty-first century social science research on school diversity and educational outcomes, Brief No. 5.* Washington, DC: National Coalition on School Diversity. Retrieved from schooldiversity.org/pdf/DiversityResearchBriefNo5.pdf

Milner, H. R. (2016). A Black male teacher's culturally responsive practices. *The Journal of Negro Education, 85*(4), 417–432.

Miyake-Trapp, J. (2018). Changing the perception of Pasadena Unified School District through an innovative realtor outreach program. *Poverty and Race Research Action Council.* Retrieved from school-diversity.org/pdf/PasadenaRealtorFieldReport.pdf

Moll, L. C., C. Amanti, D. Neff, & N. Gonzalez. (1992). Funds of knowledge for teaching: Using a qualitative approach to connect homes and classrooms. *Theory Into Practice, (2),* 132.

Monti, D. (1985). *A semblance of justice: St. Louis school desegregation and order in urban America.* Columbia, MO : University of Missouri Press.

Murray, K. W., N. Finigan-Carr, V. Jones, N. Copeland-Linder, D. L. Haynie, and T. L. Cheng. (2014). Barriers and facilitators to school-based parent involvement for parents of urban public middle school students. *SAGE Open*, 4(4). Retrieved from ncbi.nlm.nih.gov/pmc/articles/PMC4833392/

N.J.A.C. 6A:15, Bilingual Education.

National Advisory Commission on Civil Disorders (June 27, 1967). The Report of the National Advisory Commission on Civil Disorders. Retrieved from ncjrs.gov/pdffiles1/Digitization/8073NCJRS.pdf.

New York Times (archives). (October 21, 1973). In Morris, a painful schools merger. Retrieved from nytimes.com/1973/10/21/archives/in-morris-a-painful-schools-merger-merger-in-morris-is-proving.html

Noguera, P. (2003). How racial identity affects school performance. *Harvard Educational Letter*, March/April, 19(2).

NYC ASID (2019). Critical terms. Retrieved From www.nycasid.com/critical-terms

Oakes, J. (2005). *Keeping track: How schools structure inequality.* (2nd ed.) New Haven, CT: Yale University Press.

O'Dea, C. (2019). Lawmakers look to increase diversity among NJ public school teachers. *NJ Spotlight.* Retrieved from njspotlight.com/stories/19/02/07/lawmakers-look-to-increase-diversity-among-njs-public-school-teachers/

Orellana, M. (2001). The work kids do: Mexican and Central American immigrant children's contributions to households and schools in California. *Harvard Educational Review*, 71(3), 366–388.

Orfield G. (2001). *Schools more separate: Consequences of a decade of resegregation.* Civil Rights Project. Cambridge, MA: Harvard University.

Orfield, G., & S. Eaton. (eds.). (1996). *Dismantling desegregation: The quiet reversal of* Brown v. Board of Education. New York, NY: New Press.

Orfield, G., Ee, J., Frankenberg, E., & Siegel-Hawley, G. (2016). Brown *at 62: School segregation by race, poverty, and state.* Retrieved from civilrightsproject.ucla.edu/research/K–12-education/integration-and-diversity/brown-at-62-school-segregation-by-race-poverty-and-state/Brown-at-62-final-corrected-2.pdf.

Ovando, C. J., & Collier, V. (1985). *Bilingual and ESL classrooms: Teaching in multicultural contexts.* New York, NY: McGraw-Hill.

Ovando, C. J. (1998). *Bilingual and ESL classrooms: Teaching in multicultural contexts* (2nd ed.). Boston, MA: McGraw-Hill.

Orfield, G., & Lee, C. M. (2007). *Historic reversals, accelerating resegregation, and the need for new integration strategies.* Civil Rights Project. Cambridge, MA: Harvard University.

Pabon, A. (2016). Waiting for black superman: A look at a problematic assumption. *Urban Education*, 51(8), 915–939.

Paris, D. (2012). Culturally sustaining pedagogy: A needed change in stance, terminology, and practice. *Educational Researcher*, 41(3), 93–97. doi.org/10.3102/0013189X12441244.

Paris, D., & Alim, H. S. (2014). What are we seeking to sustain through culturally sustaining pedagogy? A loving critique forward. *Harvard Educational Review*, 84(1), 85–100. doi.org/10.17763/haer.84.1.982l873k2ht16m77.

Paris, D., & Alim, H. S. (2017). *Culturally sustaining pedagogies: Teaching and learning for justice in a changing world.* New York, NY: Teachers College Press.

Park, H. (2014). Children at the border. *The New York Times.* Retrieved from www.nytimes.com/interactive/2014/07/15/us/questions-about-the-border-kids.html

Pettigrew, T. F., & Tropp, L. R. (2000). Does intergroup contact reduce prejudice: Recent meta-analytic findings. In *Reducing Prejudice and Discrimination*, ed. Stuart Oskamp, 93–114. Mahwah, NJ: Lawrence Erlbaum Associates.

Perez, D., & Holmes, M.. (2010). Ensuring academic literacy for ELL students. *American Secondary Education*, 38(2), 32–43.

Posey-Maddox, L. (2014). *When middle-class parents choose urban schools: Class, race & the challenge of equity in public education.* Chicago: The University of Chicago Press.

Posey-Maddox, L., Kimelberg, S., & Cucchiara, M. (2014). Middle-class parents and urban public schools: Current research and future directions. *Sociology Compass*, 8, 446–456.

Potter, H., Quick, K., & Davies., E. (2016). A new wave of school integration. *The Century Foundation*. Retrieved from tcf.org/content/report/a-new-wave-of-school-integration/?agreed=1

powell, j. (2001). *An "integrated" theory of integrated education*. Paper Presented at the Conference on Resegregation of Southern Schools, Chapel Hill, NC.

Pulido, L. (1996). *Environmentalism and economic justice: Two Chicano struggles in the Southwest*. Tucson: The University of Arizona Press.

Ready, D., & Silander, M. (2011). School racial and ethnic composition: Isolating family, neighborhood, and school influences. In E. Frankenberg and E. DeBray (Eds.), *Integrating schools in a changing society*. Chapel Hill: The University of North Carolina Press.

Reardon, S.F., & Owens, A. (2014). Sixty years after *Brown*: Trends and consequences of school segregation. *Annual Review of Sociology*, 40, 199–218.

Roda, A. (2015). *Inequality in gifted and talented programs: Parental choices about status, school opportunity, and second-generation segregation*. New York, NY: Palgrave Macmillan.

Roda, A., & Kafka, J. (August 28, 2019). How G&T programs hurt NYC: They create a climate of scarcity and drive segregation inside the system. *Daily News*. Retrieved from www.nydailynews.com/opinion/ny-oped-sayonara-g-and-t-programs-20190828-2yh-6q2cgq5dkzgat6lfbsqxtly-story.html

Rothstein, R. (2017). *The color of law : A forgotten history of how our government segregated America*. New York, NY: Liveright

Rui, N. (2009). Four decades of research on the effects of detracking reform: Where do we stand?—A systematic review of the evidence. *Journal of Evidence Based Medicine, 2*(3), 164–183.

Rutgers Eagleton Center for Public Interest Polling (August 26, 2019). Joint Rutgers-Eagleton/FDU poll: Most New Jerseyans perceive no school segregation. Retrieved from eagletonpoll.rutgers.edu/rutgers-eagleton-fdu-race-schools-segregation-august-2019/

Ryan, J. E. (2010). *Five miles away, a world apart: One city, two schools, and the story of educational opportunity in modern America*. New York, NY: Oxford University Press.

Scribner, S. M. P. (2013). Beyond bridging and buffering: Cases of leadership perspective and practice at the nexus of school-community relations. *Journal of Cases in Educational Leadership*, 16(3), 3–6.

Shields, C. M., & Sayani, A. (2005). Leading in the midst of diversity: The challenge of our times. In F. W. English (Ed.), *The Sage handbook of educational leadership: Advances in theory, research, and practice* (pp. 380–406). Thousand Oaks, CA: Sage.

Siddle-Walker, V. (1996). *Their highest potential: An African American school community in the segregated South*. Chapel Hill: University of North Carolina Press.

Siegel-Hawley, G. (2013). City lines, county lines, color lines: The relationship between school and housing segregation in four southern metro areas. *Teachers College Record, 113*, 1–45.

Siegel-Hawley, G., Thachik, S., & Bridges, K. (2017). Reform with reinvestment: Values and tensions in gentrifying urban schools. *Education and Urban Society, 49*(4), 403–433.

Skiba, R. J., Horner, R. H., Chung, C., Rausch, M. K., May, S. L., & Tobin, T. (2011). Race is not neutral: A national investigation of African American and Latino disproportionality in school discipline. *School Psychology Review, 40*(1), 85–107.

Spener, D. (1988). Transitional bilingual education and the socialization of immigrants. *Harvard Educational Review, 58*(2), 133–154. doi.org/10.17763/haer.58.2.x7543241r7w14446

Starr, J. (Sept. 17, 2019). What NYC can learn from my experience ending tracking—and running into the politics of "keeping white people happy." Retrieved from chalkbeat.org/posts/ny/2019/09/17/what-nyc-can-learn-from-my-experience-ending-tracking-and-running-into-the-politics-of-keeping-white-people-happy/

State of NJ Department of Education (2005). *Statement of Gordon MacInnes, Assistant Commissioner for Abbott Implementation New Jersey Senate Education Committee February 3, 2005: Student achievement in the Abbott Districts*. Retrieved from state.nj.us/education/archive/abbotts/info/statement.html

Stroub, K. J., & Richards, M. P. (2013). From resegregation to reintegration: Trends in the racial/ethnic segregation of Metropolitan Public Schools, 1993–2009. *American Educational Research Journal, 50*(3), 497–531.

Tatum, B. D. (1997). *Why are all the Black kids sitting together in the cafeteria? And other conversations about race.* New York, NY: Basic Books.

Tractenberg, P., & Coughlan, R. (2018). The new promise of school integration and the old problem of extreme segregation: An action plan for New Jersey to address both. *Center for Diversity and Equality in Education.* Retrieved from buildingoneamerica.org/sites/default/files/attachments/2018_the_new_promise_of_school_integration_and_the_old_problem_of_extreme_segregation_full_report_1.pdf

Tractenberg, P., Orfield, G., & Flaxman, G. (2013). New Jersey's apartheid and intensely segregated urban schools: Powerful evidence of an inefficient and unconstitutional state education system. Retrieved from clime.newark.rutgers.edu/sites/CLiME/files/IELP%20final%20report%20on%20apartheid%20schools%20020101013.pdf

Tyson, K. (2011). *Integration interrupted: Tracking, black students, and acting white after Brown.* New York, NY: Oxford University Press.

U.S. Department of Education (U. S. D. of J.). (2015). *Ensuring English Learner students can participate meaningfully and equally in educational programs.* Retrieved from www2.ed.gov/about/offices/list/ocr/ellresources.html

U.S. Government Accountability Office (GAO). (2016). K–12 education: Better use of information could help agencies identify disparities and address racial discrimination. Retrieved from gao.gov/products/GAO-16-345

Useem, E. L. (1992). Middle schools and math groups: Parents' involvement in chil- dren's placement. *Sociology of Education, 65*, 263–279.

Washington Post Staff (September 16, 2015). Wednesday's Republican presidential GOP debate transcript, annotated. *The Washington Post.* Retrieved from washingtonpost.com/news/the-fix/wp/2015/09/16/annotated-transcript-september-16-gop-debate/?utm_term=.841c7d6bb950

Way, R. (1967, December 22). Merger unit detail Stand[s]. *Daily Record.*

Wells, A. S., Baldridge, B., Duran, J. Grzesikowski, C., Lofton, R. Roda, A., Warner, M., & White, T. (2009). *Boundary crossing for diversity, equity and achievement: Interdistrict school desegregation and educational opportunity.* Cambridge: The Charles Hamilton Houston Institute for Race & Justice. Retrieved from school- diversity.org/pdf/Wells_BoundaryCrossing.pdf

Wells, A. S., Fox, L., & Cordovo-Cobo, D. (2016). *How racially diverse schools and classrooms can benefit all students.* New York: The Century Foundation. Retrieved from tcf.org/content/report/how-racially-diverse-schools-and-classrooms-can-benefit-all-students/

Wells, A. S., Holme, J. J., Revilla, A. T., & Atanda, A. K. (2009). *Both sides now: The story of school desegregation's graduates.* Berkeley, CA: University of California Press.

Wells, A. S., & Serna, I. (1996). The politics of culture: Understanding local political resistance to detracking in racially mixed schools. *Harvard Educational Review 66*, 93–118.

Welsh, R. O., & Little, S. (2018). The school discipline dilemma: A comprehensive review of disparities and alternative approaches. *Review of Educational Research, 88*(5), 752–794.

Yonezawa, S., Wells, A. S., & Serna, I. (2002). *Choosing tracks: "Freedom of choice" in detracking schools. American Educational Research Journal 39*(1), 37–67.

Yoon, I. H. (2016). Trading stories: Middle-class White women teachers and the creation of collective narratives about students and families in a diverse elementary school. *Teachers College Record, 118*(2), 1–54.

Index

NAMES

Abramovitz, Jill, 93
Abu El-Haj, T.R., 83,
  179n46, 180n52
Adams, S. R., 136nn42–44
Alim, H. S., 136n41
Amanti, C., 134n33
Arnold, N. W., 158n16
Atanda, A.K., 1n1
Ayscue, J. B., 16nn41–42,
  29n2, 33n19n, 167n27

Baker, Scott, 20n47
Baldridge, B., 60–61n22
Barry, Michael J., 38
Batalova, J., 134nn26–27
Bell, Derrick, 20n47
Benner, A. D., 144n47
Benson, J., 67n36
Berrey, E., 97n6
Bischoff, K., 16–17n43
Boisjoly, J., 66n33
Bonilla-Silva, E., 112n21
Borman, G., 67n36
Boyle, A. E., 144n47
Bristol, T. J., 112n19
Bronfenbrenner, Urie,
  175n37
Brooks, J., 158n16
Brooks, K., 136nn42–44
Brooks, M. C., 158n16
Brown, R., 66n33
Bryan, N., 112n19
Burris, Carol C., 179

Cahill, William, 45
Candela, Sabrina, 152–153
Carhill-Poza, A., 134n33
Carter, Prudence L., 1n1,
  3n8, 29n3, 90, 156n6,
  157n9
Carver-Thomas, D., 180n53
Cashin, Sheryll, 21
Cecelski, David, 20n47

Chalk, R., 31n13
Chang, J., 97n7, 127n29
Cheng, T. L., 143n45,
  144n49, 144nn51–54,
  177n44
Chironma, John, 68
Chung, M. K., 112n24,
  158n17, 179n48
Clotfelter, C. T., 156n1,
  157n11
Collier, V., 130nn1–4, 134
Cooper, C. W., 56n13,
  118n25, 158n18
Copeland-Linder, N.,
  143n45, 144n49,
  144nn51–54, 177n44
Cordovo-Cobo, D., 91–
  92n2, 158n15
Coughlan, R., 2n5, 33n19,
  158n14, 165n24, 167,
  170n30
Coughlin, K., 8n18,
  9–10nn20–25, 52n1,
  59n17, 76n42, 124n27
Cucchiara, M. B., 54n5,
  180n55
Cunningham, John, 8

Daniels, Joe, 93
Darling-Hammond, L.,
  157n11
Datnow, 179n46
Davies, E., 15n36
Davis, J. E., 55–56, 106n9,
  110, 118, 165n26
DeCapua, A., 135n38,
  135n40
Dee, T. S., 112n17
Denise (Black parent),
  98–99, 109–110, 111,
  113–114, 120–123
Denton, Nancy, 4n15
Diamond, John B., 21n50,

  56–57, 112–113,
  158n16
Diana (real estate
  professional), 73
DiAngelo, Robin, 94,
  120n26
Diem, S., 56n14
Dodson, S., 132n25
Doucet, F., 181n56
Douglas, D. M., 61n23
Douglas, William O., 31n6,
  33n20, 156n4
Duncan, G., 66n33
Duran, J., 60–61n22

Eaton, S., 61n23
Eccles, J., 66n33
Echavarria, J., 135n37
Ee, J. B., 29n1, 33n19,
  167n27
Egalite, A. J., 112n17
El-Mekki, S., 112n19
Enos, R. D., 2n3
Epstein, J. L., 144n46
Evans, E. A., 56n13, 158n18

Fairclough, Adam, 20n47
Ficarra, Thomas, 70–73,
  76–77, 80, 110, 122,
  160
Finigan-Carr, N., 143n45,
  144n49, 144nn51–54,
  177n44
Finnigan, Kara, 17n44, 60
Flaxman, G., 16nn41–42,
  29n2, 33n19n, 165n25,
  167n27
Fletcher, T. V., 112n23
Foley, D., 134n33
Forman, T. A., 56–57,
  56n13
Formoso, A., 132n25
Fowler, G., 40n28

206

SUBJECTS

About the Authors

Paul L. Tractenberg is professor emeritus at Rutgers Law School in Newark, where he was Board of Governors Distinguished Service Professor and Alfred C. Clapp, Jr., Distinguished Public Service Professor of Law. Since he began his career at Rutgers in 1970, his primary research and advocacy work has involved using education law and policy to improve the education of all children, but especially those who have been the most marginalized by the education system. School funding reform, primarily through New Jersey's landmark case of *Abbott v. Burke*, and school integration have been at the center of his efforts. Professor Tractenberg established and was the first director of the Education Law Center, and he established the Institute on Education Law and Policy at Rutgers-Newark. In 2016, upon his retirement, he founded the Center on Diversity and Equality in Education, which is the locus of his ongoing work. Professor Tractenberg is the author or editor of six books. He also has written about 100 book chapters, articles, book reviews, reports, and papers.

Allison Roda is assistant professor of education in Molloy College's Educational Leadership for Diverse Learning Communities, Ed.D. program. Dr. Roda's research and teaching interests focus on urban education policy, educational stratification, families and schools, school integration, and qualitative research methods. She is the author of *Inequality in Gifted and Talented Programs: Parental Choices About Status, School Opportunity, and Second-Generation Segregation* (Palgrave Macmillan, 2015). Roda's work has appeared in the *Review of Research in Education, American Journal of Education, Peabody Journal of Education, Teachers College Record, Educational Policy,* and the *Journal of Education Policy.* Her works have also been published by The Century Foundation and the Hechinger Report.

Ryan Coughlan is assistant professor of education in Molloy College's Educational Leadership for Diverse Learning Communities, Ed.D. program. Dr. Coughlan's research uses geospatial statistical methods to study school zoning practices, patterns of school segregation, educational outcomes, and social bonds between neighborhoods and schools. His research has been published in numerous academic journals. Along with his work on the social context of schooling, Dr. Coughlan has edited and authored books on the history of progressive education, the social foundations of education, and the sociology of education. His research has been featured in *The New York Times, The Philadelphia Inquirer,* Chalkbeat, and on NPR's "All Things Considered."

Deirdre Dougherty is assistant professor of educational studies at Knox College. Dr. Dougherty is interested in the historical origins of contemporary educational inequalities and has studied school desegregation from both ethnographic and historical perspectives. She regularly presents at the American Educational Research Association and at the History of Education Society annual conferences. Her work has been published in *Educational Studies*, *The Journal of Urban History*, and *Media History*.